CW01394816

WERNER HERZOG

WERNER HERZOG
ECSTATIC TRUTH AND OTHER USELESS CONQUESTS

KRISTOFFER HEGNSVAD

Translated from Danish by C. Claire Thomson

REAKTION BOOKS

Published by
REAKTION BOOKS LTD
Unit 32, Waterside
44–48 Wharf Road
London N1 7UX, UK
www.reaktionbooks.co.uk

First published in English 2021
English translation by C. Claire Thomson
English translation copyright © Reaktion Books 2021

First published in Danish as *Werner Herzog – Ekstatisk sandhed
og andre ubrugelige erobringer*
Copyright © Kristoffer Hegnsvad og Jensen & Dalgaard, 2017

The publishers gratefully acknowledge the financial assistance
of the Danish Arts Foundation

K:
Danish Arts
Foundation

All rights reserved

No part of this publication may be reproduced, stored in a retrieval
system or transmitted, in any form or by any means, electronic,
mechanical, photocopying, recording or otherwise, without the
prior permission of the publishers

Printed and bound in India by Replika Press Pvt. Ltd

A catalogue record for this book is available from the British Library

ISBN 978 1 78914 410 9

CONTENTS

ONE
NEW IMAGES:
AN INTRODUCTION
TO WERNER HERZOG

On walking with Herzog: The Rogue Film School

'I am Werner Herzog. Thank you for coming.'

It is March. Munich, 2016. Outside, the sun is shining, but I'm standing in a dark, drab hotel lobby with around forty other men and women, gathered in a semicircle around Werner Herzog. We are all enrolled in the German film director's provisional film school – the Rogue Film School – which he sets up at irregular intervals, then promptly disbands again.

'We are here in total secrecy, and with time to concentrate. I hope you will help me to keep it that way over the next few days. No telephones, no computers, no dictaphones, cameras or other recording equipment. Thank you for keeping the coordinates of our rendezvous a secret. The press has been persistent, of course, but I managed to lead them astray. Right now, any journalists who followed the directions I gave them will be standing in the elephant house in Munich Zoo.'

When Werner Herzog has the opportunity to define himself, he rarely uses the word 'director'. More often, he describes himself as a chronicler, or compares himself to a storyteller in a Marrakesh marketplace: the guys who are in competition with the shouting stallholders and snake charmers and yet still succeed in gathering a crowd of people around them and captivating them with a good yarn. In a dull hotel lobby, surrounded by filmmakers who have travelled from as far afield as India, Australia and Mexico with the sole purpose of listening to him, Herzog naturally commands his audience's attention. But I'm convinced that he would have beaten any competition from dancing snakes and twirling acrobats in the average Moroccan souk. Werner Herzog has a special aura that draws his listeners towards him.

The first thing you notice is his enormous presence. His self-confidence sends shockwaves through a room every time he opens his mouth or makes eye contact; he adopts a stance of exalted calm, as though he has achieved some kind of mastery – not just over his own mind, but over the capriciousness of the world. As he wrote in his poetic diary-novel *Vom Gehen im Eis* in 1974 (*Of Walking in Ice*, 1980): 'My steps are firm. And now the earth trembles. When I move, a buffalo moves. When I rest, a mountain reposes.'[1]

Right now, Herzog is at rest. He is in gentle control of the room, but the legend of his daredevilry haunts every sentence. The flesh-and-blood man in front of us fuses with his artistic persona: fuses with the man who, in Guadeloupe in 1976, picked up a camera and hiked up the volcano La Soufrière, in the full knowledge that experts had predicted an imminent eruption with the power of five atomic bombs. He fuses with the man who spent four years filming in the Amazon and, in the face of illness, not to mention a plane crash and attacks by indigenous tribes, wrested the film *Fitzcarraldo* 'from the claws of the Devil', as he likes to say.

What plays most clearly in my mind's eye, standing there in the hotel lobby, is a television interview from 2006. This was a short while after Herzog made his mainstream comeback with the film *Grizzly Man*. The BBC's Mark Kermode is interviewing him on a hillside near the famous Lookout Mountain in Hollywood, where Herzog has lived since 1996. The interview has scarcely begun when a bang is heard, and Herzog's body jerks involuntarily. He's been shot. Hit in the stomach. Right in the middle of a sentence in which he'd been bemoaning the lack of appreciation for his films in Germany. The lack of respect in his homeland is clearly a serious matter. It worries him. Being shot, on the other hand, is something he can deal with.

'Someone's shooting at us. We should go,' he says calmly, and reassures the terrified television crew that the bullet is not 'of significant calibre'.[2]

It's almost as though Herzog is more comfortable after he's been shot. He actually looked a bit out of sorts while he was standing there, prattling like a director in a celebrity interview. Now he's *functioning*. The author Bruce Chatwin noticed something similar. In a short passage in his essay anthology *What Am I Doing Here?*, he describes Herzog as a 'compendium of contradictions': 'Immensely tough yet vulnerable, affectionate and remote, austere and sensual, not particularly well-adjusted to the strains of everyday life but functioning efficiently under extreme conditions.'[3]

In the television footage from 2006, we see Herzog effectively take charge of the BBC journalists, who meekly follow his lead. Really, it seems the rational choice in the circumstances: to follow the guy who has made films on every continent, including Antarctica – not to mention handling the actor Klaus Kinski's legendary temperament while shooting in the Amazon jungle and in Africa. When Herzog has led everyone to safety, well away from the scene of the crime, he insists on finishing the interview.

'But you're bleeding!' says Kermode.

'It's only a flesh wound,' answers Herzog, who later insisted that the incident shouldn't be treated as a serious attempt at murder, but rather as an extremely vivid example of the fabled spirit of Los Angeles, at whose expansive madness we should always remember to smile a little.

Anyone who has heard Werner Herzog's voice, even just once, will never forget it. The clear diction. The thick German accent when he speaks English. 'It's not a significant *bull-it*,' he says in the television clip. He sounds like a parody of a German scientist in a Hollywood film. Strict, serious and with a past reverberating with megalomania, and bombs. When he speaks, he does so with a sense of necessity, which makes people listen. And at the Rogue Film School, everyone is listening. Over the next few days he will emphasize that risk-taking is not a virtue in its own right. The point is never the surge of adrenaline or the ego-boosting tall tales, but to wrestle a film – and a little glimpse of truth – out of the world.

The only thing Herzog does on the first day is make the rounds and bid everyone welcome. It's obvious that he has watched our films. He goes up to people and asks their names, and then immediately starts referring to scenes, images or themes he liked – or didn't like. For example, there's an Italian director who is lavished with praise for his visuals, but is told that a particular yoga scene gives the film very disturbing New Age undertones: 'I think there should be a holy war against yoga classes. It turns us away from real thinking.' He's blunt, yet interested all the same.

I'm trying to hover in the background. I sent my documentary *Looking for Exits – Conversations with a Wingsuit Artist* to Herzog. I wrote (decorously summarized here) that I have a degree in philosophy, have filmed in Africa and would love to go for a walk with him. It worked. But my double life as a filmmaker and a newspaper journalist makes me nervous about how he'll respond to me in person.

I've interviewed Herzog before. On one of those occasions, in 2015, he'd heard that I was writing a book about him. So his eyes had a worried look. He was wary. I was careful to specify that it was

In 2005 Herzog experienced an international comeback with the documentary *Grizzly Man* (top) about the lovable eccentric Timothy Treadwell, who was eaten by his ursine friends in the wilderness with the camera mic switched on. Until then Herzog was best known for the films he made with Klaus Kinski. The two of them swore they would kill each other on more than one occasion. The lower image shows them on the set of *Cobra Verde*, their final collaboration.

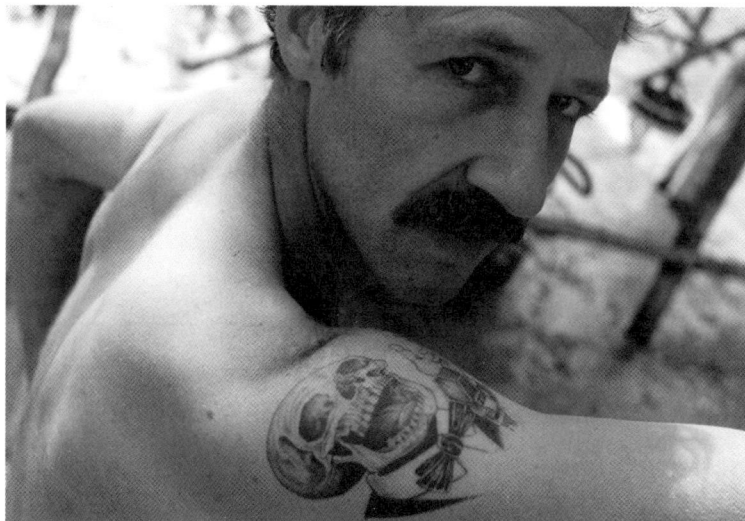

There is often an encounter between a poet, a fool and death in Herzog's works – the most famous instance is probably *Grizzly Man*, with Timothy Treadwell. Treadwell was eccentric, but he was also a filmmaker who uncompromisingly went in search of images and made himself a laughing stock in the process. As a colleague, Herzog felt a sense of responsibility towards Treadwell. A director is an illusionist and a poet, but also a jester in the marketplace. And often the jester must bear public humiliation. During the struggle to shoot *Fitzcarraldo*, Herzog had the contradictions of the filmmaker's life tattooed on his shoulder: a deviant Death figure, a skeleton roaring with laughter, clad in a tuxedo and bow tie, his arm raised as if acting in *Hamlet*. But Death is not reciting 'To be, or not to be'. He has a rakish grasp on a 1950s microphone and is crooning like a latter-day Frank Sinatra. This is a cruel and ridiculous Death, a Death who is simultaneously taunting his prey and laughing at himself – and feeling only scorn for both parties. This is *Weltschmerz* and pop combined in a macabre torch song duet.

a monograph I was working on (that is, an introduction to, and analysis of, his oeuvre; not a biographical study).

'I'm not interested in how many times you've been married,' I said (the answer is three), 'or how many children you have' (the answer is three), 'or what you dream about at night' (the answer is that Herzog claims he never dreams). 'I'm interested in the dreams you've made a reality: your works. I'm interested in your poetry: your quest for new images.'

I should add to this a more profound reason for my interest: Werner Herzog is one of the strongest voices of the European New Waves that revolutionized cinema in the post-war period – and his is the voice that has continued to develop its language and make itself relevant, again and again. He debuted in 1962 with the short film *Herakles*, and his breakthrough came with his first feature, *Lebenszeichen* (*Signs of Life*), which was awarded the Silver Bear in Berlin in 1968. He followed this with the ambitious films *Jeder für sich und Gott gegen alle* (*The Enigma of Kaspar Hauser*, 1974) and *Fitzcarraldo* (1982), both of which won prizes at Cannes.

This record alone would place Herzog among the great directors of his generation. His talent was lauded at the time by Fritz Lang (who saw in him a new hope for German cinema) and by François Truffaut (who called him the most important director of the era). But Herzog's productivity has persisted, and in recent times it has been primarily his pioneering work in documentary that has garnered attention. With films such as *Lektionen in Finsternis* (*Lessons of Darkness*, 1992), *Grizzly Man* (2005) and *Encounters at the End of the World* (2007), he has been instrumental in paving the way for a more artistically daring, and more widely appreciated, documentary film art.

'Speaking personally, I've always wanted to read a book about film that contains everything I love at once,' I continued during that interview in 2015. Herzog just sat there looking at me expectantly. 'Film enthusiasm as well as film analysis. The joy, the craft, the philosophy. A book that belongs to the director, the journalist and the academic.'

That mollified him a bit, but not much. Not surprising, when you think about how scrupulously Herzog has tried to control the interpretation of his films and his persona. The interview book *Herzog on Herzog* and the film *Werner Herzog – Filmemacher* (*Portrait Werner Herzog*) are wonderful biographical (and perhaps fictional) works in their own right. He has been so strict, in fact, that the film scholar Eric Ames was able to trace an impressively stringent consistency in his interviews since the 1970s, right up to the present day. The many stagings of Herzog's persona, as well as the myths associated with his works, must be understood as bolt-on equipment or collaborative retro-fittings in Herzog's artistic laboratory. Who can watch, for example, *Herz aus Glas* (*Heart of Glass*) without an awareness that all the actors were performing under hypnosis? And it's hard to watch any of the films featuring Kinski without remembering that Herzog threatened to shoot him during the production of *Aguirre*, when the blond madman indulged in one tantrum too many.

So in 2015, when Herzog heard about my book project, he said: 'I'll give you two and a half minutes.'

I wasn't deterred. First, because my study of Herzog's oeuvre was not dependent on him talking to me. Second, I recognized this strategy. As it happens, Herzog often specifies an extreme time frame for interviews. This could be a means of constructing a kind of cat flap that he can sidle out of should the conversation become too boring; or a way of controlling the situation, much as a firm handshake and a steady gaze can do. The very first time I spoke with him, in 2010, the time frame was five minutes. Those five minutes expanded to 45. This time, I haggled the two and a half minutes upwards, minute by minute, to six, as if we were bartering in a Marrakesh marketplace – not because I believed this would bear any relation to the actual interview time, but because I sensed that a bit of resistance would go down well. We ended up talking for almost two hours. Despite the inevitable power struggle over the parameters of the conversation, with Herzog, the keyword is still *conversation*. He hates simple questions regurgitated from a notebook, and he claims he has never done a journalistic interview. What interests him is a living conversation, with give and take, and where every reply prompts a change of direction.

In Munich, after Herzog has conversed with 35 other filmmakers, it's my turn. He's wearing a fleece, and trousers that would be good for walking in. Over the years, his face has evolved from the moustachioed young German to an older gent with a craggy physiognomy, but the serious eyes have remained the same. His spectacles are hanging from a cord around his neck and are the unpretentious type that can be folded at the ridge and quickly placed on the nose. He is a practical man, always ready to throw himself at a problem – and solve it. But under the surface lurks a warm Bavarian sense of humour. He looks at me intently, without asking my name. 'I'm sorry. I'm bad at putting names to faces,' he says. 'I always have been. Don't take it personally . . . It all started with my mother. I never could recognize her either.'

As if in a voiceover from one of his documentaries, where he never clearly indicates what is meant as a joke and what is serious, he quickly continues, 'I have watched your film.'

'It's the premiere quite soon,' I answer enthusiastically; I sound far too conceited. And then I bite my tongue, realizing that I've just shut down the possible criticism I would actually like to hear.

'You probably have no need for me, then,' he says, holding my gaze.

Yes I do, I think, but I say nothing.

'A word of advice. Don't imagine it ever gets any easier,' he says – and then he smiles: 'Welcome.'

Previously unseen images

The next morning, at breakfast, a British director asks me which film I think is Herzog's best. At first I avoid the question, but the American director beside me holds me to it: so name his *five* best films, she suggests. I wriggle out of it again, but regret it later when I'm sitting alone at the desk in my hotel room. I love reading other people's film lists, favourite scenes and that sort of thing, but I hate making such lists myself. Luckily, the filmmaker Wong Kar-wai, who feels the same way, comes to my rescue, saying that you should always refuse to answer when it comes to the one film, but, having negotiated, you may agree to listing your top five films, with the caveat that this list always includes at least ten films, and that they should always be regarded as a postcard mailed home from the state of mind you're in at the moment of writing. So, sitting there alone at my desk, I come up with a Top Five.

1. *Encounters at the End of the World*
2. *Grizzly Man*
3. *Auch Zwerge haben klein angefangen* (*Even Dwarfs Started Small*)
4. *Lebenszeichen* (*Signs of Life*)
5. *Die große Ekstase des Bildschnitzers Steiner* (*The Great Ecstasy of Woodcarver Steiner*)
6. *Lektionen in Finsternis* (*Lessons of Darkness*)
7. *Into the Abyss: A Tale of Death, a Tale of Life*
8. *Gasherbrum – Der leuchtende Berg* (*The Dark Glow of the Mountains*)
9. *Little Dieter Needs to Fly*
10. *Stroszek*

But actually, for me it's not about this film or that film, or about the ranking. Most great auteurs direct films that span a range of quality, with clear differences between masterpieces and duds. But

Werner Herzog and the photographer Peter Zeitlinger in classic Rückenfigur composition, their backs turned, during the shooting in the Antarctic of *Encounters at the End of the World*, 2007.

as the Pulitzer Prize-winning American film critic Roger Ebert said of Herzog, 'even his failures are spectacular.'[4]

The director Jonathan Demme (of *The Silence of the Lambs* fame) said something in 2008 that describes precisely why Herzog's work is so important, and why, over time, he has become a role model for so many young filmmakers – a director's director. Demme was speaking at a film symposium in New York, and remarked that he knew that his great idol, Werner Herzog, was not the type to go around with a stack of business cards in his pocket. But if he should happen to get some printed, what it would say under Herzog's name was not director, producer or author. The card would say: 'Previously unseen images, previously unheard sounds and thoughts.'[5]

It is these previously unseen images that characterize Herzog's work. Not all his films are well-wrought narratives. Far from all are masterpieces in that respect, and only a few have had popular success. Some are pretentious intellectual productions, others are demanding visual experiments, and still others humorous documentaries that don't take themselves too seriously. But when I watch any of them, what they all have in common is that they offer an artistic experience: a moment when I feel I am witnessing something new; an insight into a new dimension of the world, or a new dimension of the human; a new realization, or a new feeling of understanding and belonging. The feeling sometimes arises from the concept underlying the film as a whole, and sometimes from a smaller element in it: a sequence or a frame. Such images propagate through cinema culture. A shot born of a delirious dream of a boat on a river, under a hail of arrows from an unseen jungle enemy (*Aguirre*), or an image of thousands of crabs migrating (*Invincible*), will later turn up in films such as *Apocalypse Now* and *Pirates of the Caribbean*.

Throughout his life as a director, Herzog has been on the lookout for these previously unseen images, sounds and thoughts, and has quite literally travelled to find them. I'm in Munich not just as a film director, but to round off an investigation into Herzog's new images, a project that has obsessed me for years. With me I've brought three rucksacks. One of them is full of the set texts that Herzog has asked participants to read before their arrival. The second is full of Herzog's films and books – his collected works. And the third is full of academic tomes, and several years' worth of my own film analyses and notes on Herzog.[6] Later they will be revised into the sentences you're reading now.

The motto on that imaginary business card was not something that Jonathan Demme conjured up out of nowhere. It encompasses both Herzog's films and the broader project of the German New Wave (Der Neue Deutsche Film). The movement was officially launched on 28 February 1962 at the Oberhausen Short Film Festival, where 24 young directors led by the filmmaker and philosopher Alexander Kluge called a press conference announcing an uprising against the German film industry, or, as they called it, *Papas Kino*: Dad's cinema. Their manifesto declared: 'Conventional film is dead. We believe in the new film.'[7] This new cinema, they thought, should liberate itself from post-war film culture. Suffocating under American dominance, the German film industry was failing to engage critically with the past or the present, churning out nice, safe fare full of Alpine beauties frolicking in cornfields.

In contrast, the new cinema should offer new stories and new styles, and be produced without commercial involvement. It would be funded in part by state support for young filmmakers, Kuratorium junger deutscher Film, and underpinned by West Germany's first film school, Institut für Filmgestaltung. Kluge was instrumental in establishing this framework, and many filmmakers of note, Herzog included, benefited from the economic and moral support it provided.

Later Herzog tended to distance himself from the German New Wave (and indeed from any other film movement). This was not disingenuous; although he did attend the festival in question,

Nosferatu the Vampyre, 1979.

Herzog brought along 10,000 rats to the shoot of *Nosferatu* in Delft (the Netherlands). They were healthy white laboratory rats, so they all had to be dipped in grey paint before filming started. It's Herzog's own feet that can be glimpsed in the film, since no one else dared to direct the great mass of rats. The local town council created so many problems for the production that he threw a stink bomb into the council chamber the day the shoot wrapped. 'It was important to take a kind of harmless revenge,' he explained at the Rogue Film School.

he chose not to sign the Oberhausen Manifesto. At the tender age of nineteen, he already had his own film company, Werner Herzog Filmproduktion, and was making films in his own right. Nonetheless, it is hard to dissociate him from the New German Cinema, either historically (film historians date the end of the New Wave to 1979) or in terms of his collaboration with other key names in German cinema such as Wim Wenders, Rainer Werner Fassbinder, Edgar Reitz and Volker Schlöndorff, with all of whom Herzog has either worked or expressed an affinity. Most striking in this regard is the influence on Herzog of Kluge and of his favoured German philosophers: Walter Benjamin and Theodor W. Adorno.

The German New Wave should be seen less as a coherent artistic and ideological movement, and more as a showdown with its own time. Herzog has often maintained that this generation of filmmakers was 'fatherless'. This was also true for many young Germans whose formative years were shaped by their confrontation with the actions of their parents' generation during the Second World War, opening up an intergenerational abyss of incomprehension. More concretely, many had been brought up fatherless by war widows. But the concept was particularly resonant for filmmakers, who were working in a medium that had lost all legitimacy in the wake of the Nazis' misuse of film in the service of propaganda.

Herzog's filmmaking practice was born out of this context; his worldview was formed by it too, as he himself has said. He was born in Munich on 5 September 1942. (His birth name was Werner Stipetić, but he later jettisoned his mother's family name for his absent father's surname, largely because 'Herzog means "duke" in German and I thought there should be someone like Count Basie or Duke Ellington making films.'[8])

A few days after Herzog was born, the building his family lived in was bombed, and shards of glass from the shattered window-panes filled his cradle. His mother, Elisabeth, dug the infant out from under the shrapnel and fled with her two sons to Sachrang, an isolated village in the Kaisergebirge mountains on the border with Austria. There, Werner Herzog grew up in poverty, without running water or a telephone line. He has claimed that his earliest memory is of his mother waking him and his older brother to show them the town of Rosenheim, Hermann Göring's hometown in flames after the Americans had bombed its infrastructure with 431 tonnes of ordinance. That raid took place on 18 April 1945, less than two weeks before Adolf Hitler killed himself in his Berlin bunker. It's clear that the horrors of the Second World War are deeply imprinted on Herzog's brain.

Herzog is never directly political, and only rarely does Nazism feature explicitly in his films. But Germany's past is the source of a question that is fundamental to his work. 'The Germans were a dignified people, the greatest philosophers, composers, writers and mathematicians. And, in the space of only ten years, they created a barbarism more terrible than had ever been seen before,' he says.[9] In a range of interviews he has explained that as a young man, he felt the need to visit the Congo, in the period after independence, when the country descended into a kind of barbarism. He wanted to understand why Germany, in such a short space of time, had fallen into a barbaric culture. He wanted to understand what unleashed it; how it was possible. How stable is our civilization?

Herzog's experiences as a young man in parts of Africa hit by civil war, and his intense engagement with the colonial interventions in South America, were journeys into the darkest regions of the human heart. He undertook them in order to witness and comprehend the breakdown of other civilizations, and they inspired one of his best-known comments: 'civilization is like a thin layer of ice upon a deep ocean of chaos and darkness.'[10]

Both for Herzog and for the New German Cinema project more generally, it was important to re-establish the legitimacy of German cinema by building a historical bridge to 1933. 'After the war there were two jobs of reconstruction,' he explains. 'The cities had to be rebuilt physically, but just as important was the necessity of rebuilding Germany's legitimacy as a civilized nation again. This is still a struggle. Half a century on and Germany is still not completely there.'[11] The young Herzog contributed to that battle by adopting the film historian Lotte Eisner as his mentor. She was Jewish – a declared opponent of Nazism and therefore not morally compromised – and in her Parisian exile she had written a great, weighty work on German Expressionism, *L'Écran démoniaque* (The Haunted Screen). Herzog persuaded Eisner to record the voiceover to his poetic documentary *Fata Morgana* (1971) – a voiceover that was translated into English and recorded by another Jewish film historian, the American Amos Vogel, who had fled Vienna before the Holocaust. Eisner and Vogel lent moral legitimacy to Herzog's film project; they were also visionary film scholars, who fought for cinema as art. Both became good friends of Herzog's, encouraging and supporting him when he occasionally lost faith in his mission. With Alexander Kluge, they were a trio of academic and private mentors on whom Herzog depended during the first part of his career.

These influences became more apparent to the outside world when Herzog directed his version of *Nosferatu* in 1979. The film was a tribute to F. W. Murnau's 1922 masterpiece of the same name:

> What I really sought to do was connect my *Nosferatu* with our true German cultural heritage, the silent films of the Weimar era . . . In many ways, for me, this film was the final chapter of the vital process of 're-legitimization' of German culture that had been going on for some years.[12]

Herzog took another very concrete step in 1984, shifting his focus from this re-legitimization project to reunification of the divided German nation. Provoked by a political process that at the time was in abeyance, he decided to undertake a symbolic walk around the border of the German states. This was the only way he could contribute to healing the divided nation, thought Herzog. He was stopped by a knee injury halfway round the route, but the Wall fell anyway, five years later.

It's one thing to want to re-legitimize German film culture and grasp the fragility of civilization. But it's quite another thing that I'm looking to understand: what does Herzog want with his films? He has never clearly formulated an answer to this. We have to delve into the interviews and appearances where he hints at an answer. Wim Wenders has included interviews with Herzog in two of his films: *Chambre 666* (1982) and *Tokyo-Ga* (1985). In the latter, Herzog says: 'We desperately need images that correspond to our civilization and ourselves.'

Werner Herzog's friend Les Blank made a short film, *Werner Herzog Eats His Shoe* (1980), about a happening in UC Theatre, California. Herzog ate his shoe before the premiere of *Gates of Heaven* by Errol Morris. Herzog had sworn that he would do so if Morris ever finished a real project. In the film we follow Herzog before, during and after the happening as he gives advice and statements on film and filmmaking.

Herzog had said something similar a few years earlier. In the short film *Werner Herzog Eats His Shoe* (1980; directed by Les Blank, who, like Wenders, has made two films featuring Herzog), he declared 'Holy War' on a global culture that was depleting the power of the image. Herzog promised to do what he could to create new visual resources that would challenge what we are bombarded with daily in television series, talk shows and advertisements:

> Our civilization lacks adequate images, and I believe that a
> civilization is doomed or is gonna die out like dinosaurs that
> does not develop an adequate language of images. I see it
> as a very, very dramatic situation. For example we've found
> out that there are serious problems facing our civilization,

like energy problems, environment problems, nuclear power and over-population of the world. But generally it is not understood yet that a problem of the same magnitude is that we do not have adequate images. And that is what I am working on – a new grammar of images.

In *Tokyo-Ga*, Herzog says that he is ready to travel to 'any place whatever' to find these new images; he will scale the highest mountain, travel into space or 'go right into a war zone', if the circumstances demand it.

Gangster priests

At the Rogue Film School, the most important thing is an attitude to life and to film practice: preparing yourself to travel to any place whatever, if the circumstances demand it. Our homework includes some hefty literature: a mixture of classics such as Virgil's *Georgics*, the Icelandic *Edda* and short stories by Hemingway, but also oddities such as J. A. Baker's *The Peregrine*, Bernal Díaz's historical work *The Conquests of New Spain*, and *The Warren Commission Report (Complete and Unabridged)* on the assassination of JFK. Herzog recommends this report as a fantastic piece of crime fiction that no one reads, but everyone ought to – and if they did, they would give the Oliver Stone-style conspiracy theories a rest.

Barring a thorough workshop on *The Peregrine* (which I'll come back to later), we don't devote a lot of time to the preparatory texts. Herzog tosses the reading list to one side and starts teaching us how to pick locks – so that doors, gates and handcuffs will never be a hindrance. And as he's explaining how to use compasses and bolt cutters, we start to feel like Edward Furlong in *Terminator 2*, being lectured by a sensible mother trying to prepare us for a post-apocalyptic world. Listening to Herzog is like being trapped in an endless Chuck Norris Fact – those memes that make fun of Norris's unrivalled masculinity and bravery ('When the zombie apocalypse comes, it won't be Chuck Norris who's struggling to survive, it'll be the zombies'; 'When Chuck Norris does press-ups, he's not pushing himself up, he's pushing the planet down', and so on). The only difference is that while all the stories make Herzog sound superhuman, he actually has footage to document most of it. He really has travelled to any place whatever to find his new images: scaling the world's highest mountains (*Scream of Stone*), filming under the Antarctic ice (*Encounters at the End of the World*) and experiencing jail in the Congo (during the shooting of *Fata Morgana*). When Herzog demonstrates how to fake a filming permit, because capturing the footage is far more important than any bureaucratic or physical limitation, we believe him. And we believe him when he says there is no film school in the world like this one.

The first time Werner Herzog set up a temporary film school was in 1990, when he erected a circus tent at the Viennale film festival in Vienna and lectured in 'wild fantasies and an agitation of mind over seemingly odd questions'.[13] But I think it all began earlier, in 1975, albeit in a less organized way. That was when the young American journalist Alan Greenberg arrived in Munich to interview Herzog, who had been awarded the Jury Prize at Cannes the year before (for *The Enigma of Kaspar Hauser*), and had started to attract a degree of international attention.

In his memoir *Every Night the Trees Disappear*, Greenberg writes that the Herzog he encountered was friendly. Yet the filmmaker was unimpressed that Greenberg was wasting his time interviewing him, when he could be making a contribution to changing the world, just a little, while he still could. Herzog was moved, however, as Greenberg was the first journalist to travel across the world to meet him, and invited him to his home, where, instead of conducting an interview, they talked as equals. After an evening of poetry, music and tall tales, Greenberg was no longer a journalist but a burgeoning author and filmmaker – and he'd been persuaded to stay in Europe to help Herzog revolutionize cinema.

Today Herzog is both doyen and active pioneer. In recent years he has attracted the attention of a new generation, and at the Rogue Film School he tries to keep up with the demand for advice from younger filmmakers. Herzog himself selects attendees from among the applications, and is in charge of everything during the long teaching days. In this image, he appears in *Incident at Loch Ness* (2004), Zak Penn's mockumentary, in which Herzog makes fun of how his own public persona has been idolized – the crazy, daredevil director and the powerful, even violent, mode of expression in his films. At the Rogue Film School, Herzog discusses this mode of expression as something inherently Bavarian. He sums up the distinction between German and Bavarian culture in terms of the Prussian ability to form an army and wage war versus the Bavarian ability to build crazy castles in the mountains and stage great opera.

'There is work to be done, and we'll do it well,' said Herzog to Greenberg. 'On the outside, we'll look like gangsters, while on the inside we'll wear the gowns of priests.'[14]

Over time other people joined in, people who don't necessarily look like film crew, but who have a striking *and* in their CV – the kind of *and* that seems important to Herzog. People like Henry Kaiser, film composer *and* deep-sea diver; Peter Zeitlinger, cinematographer *and* elite ice-hockey player; Ulrich Bergfelder, set designer *and* scholar of troubadour literature; Claude Chiarini, photographer *and* psychiatrist *and* foreign legionnaire; and Herb Golder, who has been assistant director on several of Herzog's films *and* is a black belt in karate *and* has a day job as a professor of classical studies. More famous friends can also be added to this list: the philosopher, private detective *and* film director Errol Morris; the art auctioneer *and* author Bruce Chatwin. Each in their own way is a member of Herzog's artistic guerrilla band of gangster priests, or Rogues, as he calls them. They set to work without waiting for permission, and they are willing to go to 'any place whatever' to find images. That's the spirit of the Rogue Film School – or 'Die Filmschule für Schurken' (the Gangster Film School), as a German director in the classroom translates it.

The School of Life

Werner Herzog stole his first film camera from the Munich Film School – he sneaked in under cover of darkness and 'took what was his by natural law'. Then he set about making a film with some money he'd earned from working as a welder. As a young man, he wrote film reviews and studied history and literature at the University of Munich. Along the way he was an exchange student in Pittsburgh, but he soon dropped out and travelled around the United States and Mexico, where he worked for a short time at a rodeo. His stage name was El-Alamein, a biting little reference to the Nazis' defeat in the desert war of 1942. 'It suited the stupidity of the situation, that I was in Mexico doing something I was really bad at,' he comments. But he never attended a traditional film school. 'In that kind of place you get learning but no life experience,' he says. 'You create art with no connection to the world.'

And so here, at the sixth iteration of the Rogue Film School,[15] Herzog's most important advice to aspiring filmmakers bears all the traces of his experience at the School of Life: 'Head out to where the real world is. Roll up your sleeves and work as a bouncer in a sex club or a warden in a lunatic asylum or a machine operator in a slaughterhouse. Travel on foot, learn languages, train yourself in a profession or a craft that has nothing to do with film. Life experience should be the basis of filmmaking.'

None of this has anything to do with a political stance on the sex industry or factory farming, for better or worse. It's about being present in the world that we are a part of. It's about whether we dare to look the world in the eye, see it as it is, and do the work that's needed.

'The system is against you,' Herzog says in Munich:

> That is not a paranoid line from a bad film. Hollywood *is* against you; the television companies *are* against you. The distributors *are* against you. The film festivals are against you, too. Even though you probably believe otherwise, they have their own agenda. And don't bother dreaming about indie film. I hate that word. Nothing is independent. It's just another system, and it's against you too. My point is that you have to recognize all this and keep on going. Don't give in to the constant whining that the film industry likes so much. All the victims, the complaints, the taking offence. Just make your films. You are the only one that you can rely on to make your films. Learn how to be lonely. Get comfortable with standing completely alone. If no one will help you, drive a taxi for a year to earn the money to self-finance your film. Lie at the meetings with producers and distributors and say that your film has a three-act structure, just how the system likes it. Study law and read the contracts carefully, but don't let them slow you down once you've got started. Fake the filming permits. Hack the system. Attack it with guerrilla tactics. Never ask permission; only ever ask forgiveness. Work all the time. Send all your dogs out into the world; maybe one of them will return with prey.

Fitzcarraldo, 1982. Brian Sweeney Fitzgerald is so obsessed with his project of bringing opera to the jungle that he winches his ship over a mountain in the Amazon. Herzog's obsession with the film matched Fitzcarraldo's obsession. On a sign at the entrance to the spartan film camp in the jungle, he wrote: 'pelicula o muerte' – film or death.

TWO
LESSONS OF DARKNESS: AN INTRODUCTION TO HERZOG'S CONCEPTS

Standing alone

Herzog's advice about learning to stand alone is crucial to him as a person, and to many of the characters in his films with whom his persona seems to overlap. It is at this juncture that our focus begins to shift away from my meeting with Herzog at the Rogue Film School in Munich, and towards his works. Our first encounter is with the famous adventurer Fitzcarraldo, who, in the shape of Klaus Kinski, fantasizes about bringing opera to the jungle. 'As true as I'm standing here,' says Kinski in a crucial scene early on in *Fitzcarraldo*, in which he addresses the assembled upper class of South American rubber barons and tries to persuade them to invest in his dream project: a great opera house in the middle of the Amazon.

Fitzcarraldo feels that he stands alone against the whole world. The avaricious rubber barons regard him with scepticism. They will not help him. But he holds on to his dream. He fetches a gramophone and plays opera to them in an attempt to win them over, but to no avail. The magnate Don Araujo has his servants throw Fitzcarraldo out, and taunts him because he aspires to something apparently impossible and useless – at least according to capitalist, instrumentalist logic. But Fitzcarraldo will not give in: 'As true as I'm standing here, one day I shall bring grand opera to the jungle,' he declares. His speech oozes determination and excitement, as well as the barely suppressed rage for which Kinski is remembered. He is a volcano of a man, whose inner being bubbles viscerally up to the surface. His gaze is wild; he stares as though his eyes were fighting to leave their sockets. His hair sticks up in all directions. His body cannot contain the power he exudes. He is explosive. He is *ecstatic*. Even completely alone – in the most extreme minority – he exceeds himself. 'I will outnumber you!' he yells. 'I will outbillion you! I am the spectacle in the forest!'

How does one learn to embrace loneliness as a friend, as a free space? First and foremost, Herzog's advice is to 'read, read, read'. He repeats this mantra at the Rogue Film School. Another piece of advice is to walk alone, quite literally: to put great distances behind you by 'travelling on foot', as he says.

Around the same time as Alan Greenberg was initiated into Herzog's gangster priesthood, Herzog was contacted by a young Viennese woman, Regina Krejci, who dreamed of becoming part of his filmmaking team. Herzog set her a challenge: 'Walk from Vienna to Munich. That will tell me how much you want the job.'[1] Eleven days later Krejci was standing in Munich with blister plasters on her feet, and was hired as a scriptwriter. In principle, says Herzog, every initiation into the film industry ought to start with that sort of challenge: a test that has nothing to do with the normal film-school application forms; it's more like a pilgrimage. Along the way the film pilgrim can do a lot of thinking. 'After covering 5,000 km [3,000 mi.], for example, they could submit their journal as part of the application process.'

Loneliness can be overwhelming. It can seem as though it will crush you; when you are in the most extreme minority, walking in your own company, 'the brain rages.' So writes Herzog in *Of Walking in Ice*, his diary from a journey on foot in 1974 when he walked from Munich to Paris to reach the deathbed of his own great mentor, Lotte Eisner.[2]

In the solitude of walking, and in the lonely space of writing, there is a resistance to the pressure of the world. In these situations there is an ecstasy of the mind. This offers a fragile opportunity to find the strength to abandon the familiar and think beyond the conventional, thinking instead in terms of possible realities. Here, in the ecstasy of the mind, one is free, just like Fitzcarraldo, to feel that one can 'outbillion' everyone else. In what has not yet been realized, even the most extreme minority of one can become the majority of the future and be the spectacle in the forest.

In *Fitzcarraldo*, the great event of the narrative was also the great event of the shoot: hauling a 320-tonne steamship over the mountain that separates the rivers Urubamba and Camisea. Fitzcarraldo undertakes this to reach an otherwise inaccessible and therefore undiscovered rubber plantation, which he wants to exploit in order to fulfil his dream of building an opera house – to realize his ambition of transforming the world into music, into art and emotions.

Herzog could have achieved this sequence with special effects in a studio, but his vision for the film was precisely this fundamental metaphor of human obsession and drive; the magic would have been depleted had he resorted to creating it in post-production. Part of the power of the metaphor resides in our knowledge that Herzog insisted on doing it for real. The dream impinges on reality and reality impinges on the filmic image. For a moment, the boundary between the two is blown apart, illuminating the visionary obsession and drive of not one but two men.

'There was never any doubt in my mind,' Herzog says at the Rogue Film School. 'All those bad special effects we know from Hollywood and on television have made the audience lose faith in what they see. With *Fitzcarraldo*, their faith is restored. When

Klaus Kinski in *Fitzcarraldo,* with the now iconic gramophone that brings opera to the jungle.

In a key scene in *Fitzcarraldo*, Klaus Kinski, in the title role, tries to raise money for an opera house in the jungle. The rich rubber barons, among them Don Araujo, taunt him. Fitzcarraldo raises a glass and swears that he will fulfil his ambition:

Don Araujo: 'My servants will escort you to the kitchen. My dogs' cook will prepare you a meal. Thank you very much, sir, you were superb.'

Fitzcarraldo: 'To your dogs' cook. To Verdi. To Rossini. To Caruso.'

Don Araujo: 'To Fitzcarraldo, the Conquistador of the Useless!'

Fitzcarraldo: 'As true as I am standing here, one day I shall bring grand opera to the jungle. I will outnumber you! I will outbillion you! I am the spectacle in the forest!'

they see the ship moving over the mountain, at first they're on the lookout for tricks, but there are no tricks. And when they instinctively notice that, it builds courage. Courage to believe in the image, and courage to believe their own dreams.'

Herzog was the only one who believed that the project was feasible, just as Fitzcarraldo is in the film. In his diary from the shoot, he wrote: 'For a moment, the feeling crept over me that my work, my vision, is going to destroy me.'[3]

Everyone had shaken their heads at the idea of dragging the ship over the mountain in reality, when it could be reconstructed in a film studio. When Herzog insisted anyway, it was as though he had been cursed. Everything that could go wrong did go wrong. A territorial war broke out in the region. The film crew were involved in plane crashes, not once but twice. An extra was shot in the neck with an arrow by a member of an indigenous tribe. One of the local extras drowned when he borrowed a canoe for a night-time excursion. A forester who helped clear the mountainside had to amputate his own foot with a chainsaw when he was bitten by a venomous snake. There was one delay after another. Jason Robards, who was originally to play the lead role, became sick and delirious in the jungle and had to withdraw completely. Mick Jagger, who had a supporting role, could wait no longer and had to go on tour with the Rolling Stones.

Meanwhile, the production had become a media event. Misguided leftists travelled to the region to show the local people images from Auschwitz, so that they could see what kind of nightmare the allegedly fascist German director was really dreaming of, and a group of indigenous people set fire to the production

Herzog on the set of *Fitzcarraldo* with the famous boat that nobody besides himself believed could be pulled over the mountain.

headquarters in protest against the presence of white men. Back in Germany, a media scandal erupted amid claims that Herzog was guilty of an assault on the local tribes and on the rainforest. This reached such a pitch that a tribunal was held in Germany (while Herzog was in the Amazon), and Amnesty International had to intervene and absolve him of all charges.

Throughout all of this, Herzog was alone. Totally alone. The engineer who had been hired to supervise the transportation of the ship over the mountain on weights and pulleys gave up. He said, just like all the others, that the project was impossible: a 40-degree incline in the rainforest was too much; it was not just unfeasible, it was dangerous even to attempt it. When Herzog eventually persuaded Kinski to take on the role instead of Robards, the film – already half finished – had to be shot from the beginning again. 'The question everyone wanted answered was whether I would have the nerve and the strength to start the whole process from scratch,' wrote Herzog in his diary from the shoot. 'I said yes: otherwise I would be someone who had no dream left, and without dreams I would not want to live.'[4]

Herzog the chronicler

Ten years after *Fitzcarraldo*, Werner Herzog's dreams got him into trouble again. This time, he dared to screen his documentary *Lektionen in Finsternis* (*Lessons of Darkness*) at the Berlinale in February 1991. Once again he stood completely alone, and once again he held firm.

A few months before, he had again shown his willingness to travel to 'any place whatever' to find new, adequate images, this time among the burning oil wells of Kuwait after the First Gulf War. He hoped to craft visual alternatives to the images CNN had been serving up 24 hours a day during the war. The yellow-green images of rocket launches and points of light had burned them-selves into the collective consciousness of the West as the reality of modern warfare. Herzog's images in *Lessons of Darkness* were totally different. They did not look like CNN's 'official' documentary images of the war, but neither did they subscribe to the countercultural guerrilla aesthetic that has dominated since the advent of war photography, which has tended to use raw realism to expose the falsity of established truth. Herzog allowed himself a thoroughly aestheticized, visually beautiful narrative of fire and war, and set it to great opera. An audience of 1,500 in Berlin reacted with an anger rarely seen at a film festival. They booed and spat, but Herzog bravely stood up, walked through the auditorium, took the microphone and stood his ground: 'Idiots! You're all wrong. Dante did the same in *Inferno*, and so did Goya, and Hieronymus Bosch.'

This time it wasn't an obsession with a real ship in a fiction film that had sparked the furore, but fictional elements in a documentary. And it wasn't Kinski swearing 'as true as I'm standing here!' and reeling off his operatic heroes Verdi, Rossini, Caruso. It was the director himself listing his patron saints. Notably, they were not the saints of documentary history.

Just as *Fitzcarraldo* breaches the conventions of fiction film with its unusual central metaphor, *Lessons of Darkness* eschews documentary norms. Or at least, it eschews the norms of the kind of documentary that has shaped our understanding of the genre since the 1950s: films that are journalistic, factually orientated or purely observational. Since the earliest days of cinema, there have been staged and poetic documentaries, but those were so rare by 1992 that Herzog declined even to call his new film a documentary.

'The word documentary should be handled with care because we seem to have a very precise definition of what the word means,' says Herzog.[5] Provocatively, he claims that if using the standard definition of the genre, he would rate his most ambitious fiction film, *Fitzcarraldo*, as his best documentary. This is because *Fitzcarraldo*, more than any other film he has made, documents an event down to the tiniest details: a real ship that is really dragged over a real mountain. In contrast, he thinks it makes no sense to apply the term documentary to his film *Echos aus einem düsteren Reich* (*Echoes from a Sombre Empire*) of 1990. This film follows a journalist investigating conditions during the bloody regime of the dictator Jean-Bédel Bokassa in the Central African Republic. This is traditional documentary film material, but to categorize the film that way would be, according to Herzog, the equivalent of reducing Andy Warhol's paintings of Campbell's tins to a witness statement about tomato soup. In the same way, with his film, Herzog wants to say something greater and more universally human.

'I am not a journalist, I am a poet,' he said to the inmates on death row in Texas, whom he interviewed in *Into the Abyss: A Tale of Death, a Tale of Life* (and the television follow-up *On Death Row*).[6] His starting point was not a predefined agenda; it was not about revealing the truth behind the crimes of those sentenced to death. He was in search of something bigger, something undefined – a truth about what life means to people who are on the brink of death. A truth about the right of the state to kill, told by those who kill and will themselves be killed, without focusing on law or the facts of the actual cases. 'I know that by making a clear distinction between "fact" and "truth" in my films, I am able to penetrate into a deeper stratum of truth [that] most films do not even notice. The deep inner truth inherent in cinema can be discovered only by not being bureaucratically, politically and mathematically correct . . . Through invention, through imagination, through fabrication, I become more truthful than the little bureaucrats,' commented Herzog in 2002 to the film critic Paul Cronin, who compiled the interview book *Herzog on Herzog*.[7] It was this same approach that Herzog wanted to take to the war in Iraq and the burning oilfields in Kuwait.

Werner Herzog is not the first artist to try to shed the labels that limit him, but with him this is more than an affectation. He is often referred to as an *auteur* – a concept launched by the French New Wave to describe a director whose unmistakeable mark on his films transcends the restrictions of the studio apparatus, in much the same way as the stamp of a literary author can be discerned in every word of a book. If Herzog doesn't meet the auteur criteria, nobody does. But just as he declines to call his documentary films 'documentaries', he refuses to use the term 'auteur' to describe himself. This is consistent with his rejection of the word 'genius' and similar concepts that imply the idea of a single chosen one. He refers to himself as a storyteller in a marketplace, or as a chronicler. The latter term in particular has often been used by Herzog to explain the meaning of his films: 'Film does not have so much to do with reality as it does with our collective dreams. It chronicles our state of mind. The purpose is to record and guide, as chroniclers did in past centuries.'[8]

It is no coincidence that Herzog talks about films as chronicles of our shared histories and describes himself as a chronicler instead of an auteur. This is a gateway to understanding what he hoped to achieve with *Lessons of Darkness*, which is a much more interesting question than whether it can be called a documentary. *Lessons of Darkness* intervenes in a wider discussion about the documentation of war, and, more generally, about the writing of history. In this respect, Herzog is clearly influenced by the German-Jewish philosopher Walter Benjamin. In the last essay he wrote before his death in 1940, 'Über den Begriff der Geschichte' (Theses on the Philosophy of History), Benjamin decries the conventional and linear historiography that 'contents itself with establishing a causal connection between various moments in history'.[9] In his many discussions concerning *Lessons of Darkness*, this kind of history writing is what Herzog has called 'the truth of accountants'. An accountant's practice is additive. So too is the practice of a journalist or documentarist who merely orders the facts into a logical chain of events, which is then presented as an explanation of how things happened.

A now famous line in Benjamin's 'Theses on the Philosophy of History' goes like this: 'There is no document of civilization

Lessons of Darkness, 1992.

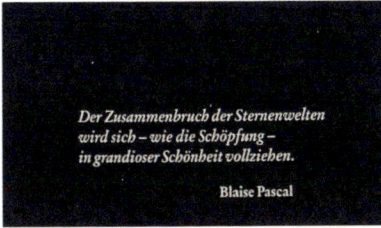

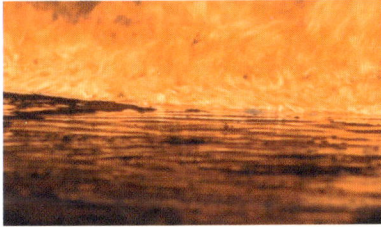

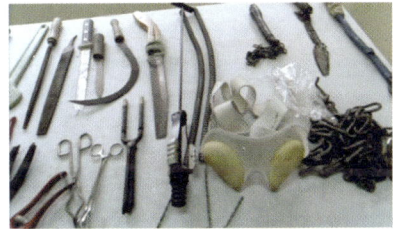

Framegrabs from *Lessons of Darkness* (arranged in thematic rather than chronological order, from top left). The falsified quotation from Pascal: 'The collapse of the stellar universe will occur – like creation – in grandiose splendour.' Then the greenish-yellow images we know so well from the media coverage of the war. Then Herzog's close-ups of fire and oil; his magnificent helicopter shots; the confrontation with instruments of torture; and finally the victims: the nameless, silent voices, trodden into the dust of history.

which is not at the same time a document of barbarism.'[10] By this he means that history is always written from the contemporary perspective of the victors, and that in any act of historiography, something always gets trodden underfoot. Benjamin was looking for a *storyteller* historian,[11] who could, like a *chronicler*, expand our concept of history and draw attention to the nameless contemporaries left in the dust by the victorious; a chronicler who was not marching in the triumphal procession of the victors, but who saw his task as to 'brush history against the grain', and thus to burst through the continuum of time.[12]

Werner Herzog is that kind of chronicler. His instinct is not to dredge the depths of history for an originative cause that can explain everything, or to bundle everything up into a belief that progress or contemporary power structures are necessarily good. Rather than making everything cohere, in the spirit of Benjamin he tries to write history through the filter of a unique, indisputable image of the present. Such an image is one from which we cannot escape; an image that hits like a bolt of lightning and is itself thrown into sharp relief, wrenched free of all historical context or filmic process; an image that is so incontrovertible that it transcends the differences between our individual or collective horizons of understanding and cannot be explained away with theory or ideology. Something that is so concretely confrontational that it stimulates thought. A dead baby. A civilian war casualty. A birth.

Real thinking entails not only forward movement but a moment of stasis in which matters can be rethought. This cannot be achieved by a mere representation of facts or of a chain of events (influenced by the victors' present-day perspective); instead, a constructive approach to historiography is needed, one that forces the audience off the train of thought to which they have become accustomed. Herzog has a term for this kind of rethinking: *ecstatic truth*. The concept applies to both the method and the results of constructive historiography (and storytelling). This is an ecstasy that blows a particular epoch, individual or thought out of history, so that it does not get written into Benjaminian 'homogeneous, empty time' but stands out as a singular event.[13] According to Benjamin, this is where 'a revolutionary chance in the fight for the oppressed past' is to be found.[14]

But how does Herzog create this kind of image? In the fiction film *Fitzcarraldo*, he constructed a space for rethinking via an element of the real: the ship that, on its way over the mountain, makes the audience gasp and gape and see, just for a second, not the truth in the sense of a fact, but really *see* the film's central metaphor and concept. Whether the film is good or bad, whether it coheres dramaturgically, whether the acting is consistently convincing – none of this is actually relevant here. What is relevant is the creation of a new image, a moment of ecstatic truth. In the documentary film *Lessons of Darkness* Herzog does the same thing using fictive elements, by being a chronicler who challenges the dominant media narratives about the First Gulf War.

Lessons of Darkness challenged the tired images we saw on television and attempted to create new ones, images that lived up to Benjamin's wish to 'retain that image of the past which unexpectedly appears to man singled out by history at a moment of danger'.[15] That is, to practise a historiography that takes into account the traces of the oppressed, and to create images that render visible the nameless and the invisible.

We will come back to the nameless and the invisible, but let us first take a look at the surface layer of the film that so provoked the audience at the Berlinale.

In their coverage of the war, the news media, led by CNN, endeavoured to maintain a realist aesthetic that Herzog, from the very beginning of *Lessons of Darkness*, turns on its head. He does not counteract CNN's alleged aesthetic of authenticity with a guerrilla aesthetic that signals authenticity in even more extreme terms. (That kind of approach would be no less beholden to explanations based on causality.) Instead, he adopts a grandiose, opulent aesthetic: beautiful images rather than grainy media realism, and, rather than synchronous sound, the opera of Wagner.

As if that were not enough, the news narrative of the Gulf War is replaced with a science-fiction narrative, with a godlike voiceover ruminating on a planet whose denizens love fire and war. This narrative frame is a move reminiscent of the divine perspective of chroniclers of the Middle Ages, a voice that invites us to see ourselves from the outside. The voiceover is Herzog's impression of the news-media commentators, and who are they? In his voiceover and in his treatment of images, Herzog blatantly misinforms the viewer: small ash heaps are presented as mountains, and firemen are described as pyromaniacs – which they do resemble when the images are seen out of context and from unfamiliar angles. *The same images can tell different stories.* This conclusion is also drawn in the film's epigraph, which is another lie, this time in the form of a 'quotation' from Blaise Pascal that Herzog actually concocted himself (and which he has provocatively claimed Pascal could not have phrased better): 'The collapse of the stellar universe will occur – like creation – in grandiose splendour.'

The German critics were merciless. Distracted by the gorgeous images and the obvious lies, they saw *Lessons of Darkness* as a shameless approach to war, and as a betrayal of the documentary genre. At the Berlin premiere they rose to the bait, so to speak, and let themselves be provoked by the revelation that the established truth is a constructed truth.

The essence of the critics' argument was that documentary film ought not to stage or aestheticize current political matters (the film premiered only three months after the last Kuwaiti oil-well fire was extinguished), but should strive to portray the war as factually as possible. There was also a degree of dissatisfaction that no one emerges as a hero in the film – not even the firemen.

Over time, Herzog has shrugged off countless accusations of fascism and manipulation. After *Fitzcarraldo* it became so bad that he was attacked on the street, but he never chose to debate with his critics directly. He stuck to discussing aesthetics. With *Lessons of Darkness*, however, something was smouldering; eight years after the premiere, he still felt the need to formulate a riposte. On 30 April 1999 he was interviewed on stage by the critic Roger Ebert at the Walker Art Center in Minneapolis, Minnesota. The event was billed as a public conversation as part of the Walker's retrospective of Herzog's work. But after he was introduced, Herzog stood up and addressed the three-hundred-strong crowd:

> Ladies and gentlemen, before we start this dialogue,
> I would like to make a statement. It is something that I
> have reflected upon for many years in the frustration of
> seeing so many documentary films. When you look at tele-
> vision, you probably have experienced a similar frustration.
> There's something ultimately and deeply wrong about the
> concept of what constitutes fact and what constitutes truth
> in documentaries in particular. And very recently, traveling
> around a lot, I was jetlagged, woke up a couple of times
> during the night, tried to switch on television, and it was
> all bad. Between 3:00 and 3:15 in the morning in Sicily,
> I wrote down quickly a manifesto, which I would like
> to read to you.[16]

After these introductory words, Herzog read the twelve points of the manifesto *Truth and Fact in Documentary Cinema 'Lessons of Darkness'*. There were echoes of both Klaus Kinski's confrontation with the rubber barons in *Fitzcarraldo* and Herzog's encounter with the angry audience in Berlin in 1991, but this time the room was friendlier. The audience cheered and laughed, and when Herzog had read the last point aloud, he made a direct appeal for their allegiance: 'Ladies and gentlemen. I've never had a majority on my side throughout my life. I wish you to adopt this as *The Minnesota Declaration* by acclamation.'

The auditorium validated the declaration with a round of applause, and the manifesto has enjoyed an impressive afterlife. In a perverse way, it initiated Herzog into the pantheon of documentary. He had made documentaries throughout his career, but until 1999 he was ignored in books about documentary, being just too difficult to use as an example. These days he's cited as an example of a critical voice, on the basis of *Lessons of Darkness* and *The Minnesota Declaration*. His work is treated as representative of the artistically staged and poetic-existential tendency in documentary, in contrast to the more journalistic, factual and observational documentary tradition. That was indeed the thinking behind the *Declaration*, but for Herzog it was also an opportunity to splice his ideas about documentary with his cinematic mission more broadly: his quest to find 'new images' and to create 'adequate images', rejecting the 'inadequate'. The manifesto collates and presents extant elements of his poetics (and his concepts, including the truth of accountants and ecstatic truth) in a digestible way.

In terms of their form, the twelve points of the manifesto play with religious commandments, or with other political or artistic manifestos of the twentieth century. Language-wise, the *Declaration* is a chimera combining philosophical aphorisms, political discourse and workaday pop culture. In one commandment Herzog talks about enlightenment and truth, in another about sin and death, and in another about glaciers farting.

Moreover, Herzog has flippantly recounted how at 4 a.m., an hour after writing the manifesto (after hours of bad documentaries on television), he switched channels again and landed on a hardcore porn movie, which struck him as real by comparison. What porn has in common with other genre films, such as musicals or kung fu, is that none of them pretends to tell the truth, and yet now and again they accidentally uncover little moments of it, like side effects – when the bodies are smacking against each other.

The first six points of *The Minnesota Declaration* are concerned with how the world is documented on film – what kinds of visual witnessing are delivered. With *Lessons of Darkness*, Herzog thought he was trying to say something true about human destructiveness and the horrors of war. He tried to demonstrate that CNN's facts constituted a flood of news – or a current-affairs soap opera – creating a spectacular tabloid image of the catastrophe, but communicating nothing about how it must be to experience the war at first hand as one of its victims, nor how it felt to live in a place mutilated by the conflict. In *The Minnesota Declaration*, Herzog's whipping boy is the documentary tradition of *cinéma vérité*, or Direct Cinema in North America, whose cinematic language informed CNN's coverage. Herzog pays little heed to the possible caveat that this tradition encompasses many different filmmakers, many of whom (especially among the self-reflective European version) would actually agree with his critique. He takes aim at CNN's caricature of the *cinéma vérité* methodology, and the resulting implication that their massive media coverage represented reality on a scale of 1:1. Provided CNN's journalists were present as 'flies on the wall' 24 hours a day, they could, or so it was suggested, re-mediate the truth as it *really* was. Thus the ideals of American documentary that had held sway since the advent of the handheld camera became welded – methodologically and stylistically – to television news to craft a set of autocratic truth claims.

The first point in *The Minnesota Declaration* goes like this: 'By dint of declaration the so-called Cinema Verité is devoid of verité. It reaches a merely superficial truth, the truth of accountants.' The criticism continues in the second point; here Herzog observes ironically that representatives of the movement claim that 'truth can be easily found by taking a camera and trying to be honest.' The third point claims that 'Cinema Verité confounds fact and

THE MINNESOTA DECLARATION

Truth and Fact in Documentary Cinema
'Lessons of Darkness'

1. By dint of declaration the so-called Cinema Verité is devoid of verité. It reaches a merely superficial truth, the truth of accountants.

2. One well-known representative of Cinema Verité declared publicly that truth can be easily found by taking a camera and trying to be honest. He resembles the night watchman at the Supreme Court who resents the amount of written law and legal procedures. 'For me,' he says, 'there should be only one single law; the bad guys should go to jail.' Unfortunately, he is part right, for most of the many, much of the time.

3. Cinema Verité confounds fact and truth, and thus plows only stones. And yet, facts sometimes have a strange and bizarre power that makes their inherent truth seem unbelievable.

4. Fact creates norms, and truth illumination.

5. There are deeper strata of truth in cinema, and there is such a thing as poetic, ecstatic truth. It is mysterious and elusive, and can be reached only through fabrication and imagination and stylization.

6. Filmmakers of Cinema Verité resemble tourists who take pictures of ancient ruins of facts.

7. Tourism is sin, and travel on foot virtue.

8. Each year at springtime scores of people on snowmobiles crash through the melting ice on the lakes of Minnesota and drown. Pressure is mounting on the new governor to pass a protective law. He, the former wrestler and bodyguard, has the only sage answer to this: 'You can't legislate stupidity.'

9. The gauntlet is hereby thrown down.

10. The moon is dull. Mother Nature doesn't call, doesn't speak to you, although a glacier eventually farts. And don't you listen to the Song of Life.

11. We ought to be grateful that the Universe out there knows no smile.

12. Life in the oceans must be sheer hell. A vast, merciless hell of permanent and immediate danger. So much of hell that during evolution some species – including man – crawled, fled onto some small continents of solid land, where the Lessons of Darkness continue.[17]

2017 ADDENDUM TO THE MINNESOTA DECLARATION

I. With the arrival of the new term 'alternative facts' in the political arena, the question of facts and the question of truth have acquired an unexpected urgency.

II. Facts cannot be underestimated as they have normative power. But they do not give us insight into the truth, or the illumination of poetry. Yes, accepted, the phone directory of Manhattan contains four million entries, all of them factually verifiable. But do we know why Jonathan Smith, correctly listed, cries into his pillow every night?

III. The argument of rearranging facts constituting a lie points only to shallow thinking and the fetish of self-reference.

IV. Patron Saints of the Minnesota Declaration:

William Shakespeare: 'The most truthful poetry is the most feigning.'

V. André Gide: 'I modify facts in such a way that they resemble truth more than reality.'

VI. Michelangelo: taking a good look at his statue of the Pietà, we notice that Jesus taken from the cross is a man of 33, but his mother is only 17.

Does Michelangelo lie to us? Does he mislead us? Does he defraud us?

He just shows us the innermost truth about the Man of Sorrows, and his mother, the Virgin.[18]

truth, and thus plows only stones,' because, as the fourth point says: 'Fact creates norms, and truth illumination.'

The fifth point gives us a glimpse of Herzog's own poetics. This is the aspect of the manifesto that most clearly emerges from his lifelong quest for 'new images' that are 'more adequate', and this is also the point that has featured in every analysis of Herzog's films since: 'There are deeper strata of truth in cinema, and there is such a thing as *poetic, ecstatic truth. It is mysterious and elusive, and can be reached only through fabrication and imagination and stylization*' (emphasis added).

In the sixth point, judgement is handed down: 'Filmmakers of Cinema Verité resemble tourists who take pictures of ancient ruins of facts.' These are dead images that do not carry the truth with them, but only enumerate facts or refer to established symbols (ruins of facts), and as such they are merely running errands for the established order. Herzog wants to do anything other than run errands for the established order, and sees it as his task to brush history against the grain. As he has repeatedly explained regarding the first six points, the filmmaker has to insist that he is a storyteller, that he gives form to things: 'We are not collectors of facts, like the telephone book. We should not be like a *fly on a wall*. No, we should be like the *hornet that stings.*'

That's what Herzog was trying to do with *Lessons of Darkness*: to sting the audience and force them to *see anew* the horrors of war by ripping the First Gulf War out of the hyperreal historical narrative produced by the Western news media. However idealistic the intentions behind its non-stop real-time reportage, CNN succeeded only in contributing to media representations of a clean war, a war that was seemingly transparent: complete with remote-controlled missiles with cameras on the warheads, articulated in strategically communicative ways and executed efficiently from the air to minimize the number of victims, at least on the winning side. But this mediation, according to Herzog,

In *Ballade vom kleinen Soldaten* (*Ballad of the Little Soldier*, 1984), Herzog investigates the local Moskito tribe's struggle against their former allies, the Sandinistas, who fought against Anastasio Somoza Debayle in Nicaragua. Herzog drew criticism from the European left wing, because the Sandinistas were still regarded as revolutionaries. Herzog has always insisted that the film was concerned with the use of child soldiers and attacks on local civilians. However, he has never believed in an unbiased camera: 'The only impartial camera is the camera you find in your bank. This camera and other cameras for decades have waited hoping for the bank robber but the bank robber never materializes. It is a very sad form of filmmaking.'[19]

does not represent war, only a landscape mutilated by signs – inadequate signs.

When Herzog talks about inadequate signs and images, and claims that accountants plough only stones, it's because he thinks the unreflective historiographer (the accountant from CNN) is trying to describe the war as it really was: as a logically ordered chain of events, based on the assumption that history is a continuum, something that has happened and can be recorded in homogeneous, empty time. The accountant ensures that the past is always written under the gaze of the present, an optics that always belongs to the victor. Herzog's project is not to impose control and order, but to try to evoke the event *qua* event – 'as it flashes up at a moment of danger', as Walter Benjamin writes.[20] Or, in Herzog's reformulation of this, every substance under pressure will reveal glimpses of truth about its nature, before the politically correct matrix of history bears down.[21] In this way, we pay attention to all the possibilities that could unfold from the event, but which have been crushed into dust, like the dirt on the road upon which the victors are parading.

In order to evoke the terror of war in an adequate way – war as a sensory experience for the people who actually lived there – Herzog entered the sea of flames from burning oil wells roaring at a thousand degrees Celsius. He made it out again with a roll of film that did not aspire to realism, but which would fuel the already superheated semiotic furnace, roiling the media circus in all its vacuousness and empty spectacle.

Paraphrasing the painter Francis Bacon, we might say that Herzog wanted to film the *scream* instead of the *horror*. The scream is undifferentiated power. Conversely, the horror would be bound to Operation Desert Storm, and thus its representative potential would be predicated on predetermined categories: a morally justified Western identity against a clearly identified villain, Saddam Hussein. Herzog does not position himself on one side or the other, nor does he adopt the role of a countercultural moralist blithely pointing his finger at the war or the politicians. Filming the scream is not really *about* Operation Desert Storm and the oilfields of Kuwait, nor is it about the two identities on either side of the divide; it is about *the nature of all wars*. To direct attention to the scream (and the scream is always uttered in defiance of pain), he had to elevate the images out of any predetermined historiography. He had to direct them away from the game of charades in which the media was engaged, with all its reliance on established gestures and forms.

And right there, amid some of the most beautiful images in the history of cinema and a voiceover intoned by the world's stupidest god, Herzog suddenly plummets to Earth. The pompous helicopter's-eye view gives way to footage shot with feet firmly planted on the ground, and there he meets two unnamed victims, both rendered speechless by the trauma of war. Through the poetry of form, through the artistry of lies and staging, the event is evoked – the event as it unfolded for the nameless subject at that moment of danger. Instead of simply registering ruins of facts, Herzog's ecstatic truth bursts through the continuum of history and lets the event flash up, screaming itself forth in all its singularity. And so we *see*. We see, and we listen to a semblance of what the silenced voices have to say.

Herzog is rarely openly political in his art and it is even rarer that he touches on the Second World War, but in *Invincible* (2001) we follow a Jewish strongman, Zishe, in Berlin in the 1930s and his employer, Hanussen (Tim Roth), who dreams of establishing a Ministry of the Occult as part of Hitler's regime. Hanussen is a real historic character said to have instructed Hitler in performance and the achievement of dramatic effect.

THREE
THE TRUTH
OF ACCOUNTANTS

The useless ones and the useless conquests

After a couple of days at the Rogue Film School, all of us had taken up smoking. In the classroom, we were analysing sequences from Werner Herzog's then brand-new documentary about the advent of the Internet, *Lo and Behold – Reveries of the Connected World*, and his volcano film *Into the Inferno*, which was in post-production. It transpired that Herzog had a habit of scrounging cigarettes during the breaks, so if you had a pack of fags up your sleeve, you could barter one for a few anecdotes or tips. For example, advice on the best balance-perfecting exercises for ski jumpers. And filmmakers.

When Herzog was a young boy, his dream was to become the world's best ski jumper. He trained his sense of balance by standing on one leg on top of a glass of water, bending down to pick up a lit cigarette from the floor with his mouth, and straightening up again. I don't know if this is true (or if he managed to perfect the exercise himself). But the story features in Harmony Korine's

Julien Donkey-Boy (1999), in which Herzog plays a father training one of his sons to be a wrestler, and in one scene pushes him to complete the same exercise. The son tries his best, and manages to bend over and pick up the cigarette between his teeth, ~~but then~~ he falls. Herzog is not happy. The son is going to have to work harder. He has to learn how to pick up the cigarette without falling, straighten up again, and then coolly smoke it, still standing on the glass. 'But I don't smoke,' says the son. 'You'll learn,' answers the uncompromising Herzog.

Korine, who famously wrote the screenplay for *Kids*, has called Werner Herzog his cinematic idol. In the films Korine himself has directed (*Gummo*, 1997; *Mister Lonely*, 2007; *Spring Breakers*, 2012), he has aspired to live up to Herzog's ideas and to strive for ecstatic truth. In 1999 the apprentice invited his master to play the role of the father in *Julien Donkey-Boy*, and Herzog accepted.

The film is full of Herzogian moments: a card player with no arms, an albino and a variety-show artiste whose star turn is eating smouldering cigarettes. Such moments ecstatically puncture the fiction film with reality effects that force us to look more closely. Particularly interesting is Herzog's own presence in this role, for which he draws on stories from his own life, not least his dream of becoming world champion ski jumper.

'My register as an actor is very limited,' says Herzog, without false modesty. 'I'm best at playing unpleasant characters. This character is completely dysfunctional and hostile. It was a wonderful experience.' He clearly enjoyed developing and playing a role corresponding to his worst nightmare: a domineering, know-it-all patriarch, something of a sadist, who makes all his decisions on the basis of warped ideals.

The father in *Julien Donkey-Boy* is a German immigrant, but he is completely infatuated with the American culture he knows from cinema; he wants his sons to be more like Dirty Harry. One of the sons suffers from schizophrenia, and the father finds this hard to handle: 'You look utterly and completely and irrevocably

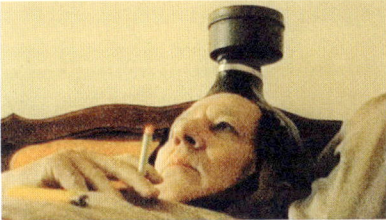

Herzog as the tough German father in *Julien Donkey-Boy* (1999). The film was a Dogme 95 project, shot with a washed-out video aesthetic by the cinematographer Anthony Dod Mantle. Of all Herzog's film roles, this is the one that has garnered most praise. His best-known role is probably as a villain in *Jack Reacher* (2012), playing opposite Tom Cruise, or as the mysterious Client in the *Star Wars* television show *The Mandalorian* (2019–).

stupid. You look so stupid. If I were so stupid, I would slap my own face!' In an English marked with his thick German accent, Herzog insists that the schizophrenic son slap himself: 'You might even become more intelligent.'

The father has totally lost any sense of decency, and he tries to maintain a semblance of order by pushing his children in the direction of his ideals of manliness and winner culture. They have no choice but to comply, unless they want to be verbally humiliated or drenched with cold water from the garden hose.

Ever since *The Minnesota Declaration*, the concept of 'the truth of accountants' tends to be applied to everything Herzog was against. But what does it mean exactly? His errant patriarch can be seen as a microcosm of the truth of accountants, if we isolate the concept from the narrow discussion about truth and staging in documentary, and ponder for a moment the conception of society that informs Herzog's art more generally – ponder what it is that he's working towards.

Throughout his career, Herzog has kept a careful eye on all forms of regimentation. He has been consistently suspicious of theorems that are lauded as truth, and suspicious of teachers who are lauded as having special access to truth. This applies not only to his focus on the most extreme manifestations of regimentation, such as his study of the emergence of Nazism in *Invincible* (2001), or African despots' bloody oppression of their own people in *Echoes from a Sombre Empire* (1990), or the exploitation of child soldiers in leftist revolutionary camps in Central America (*Ballad of the Little Soldier*). Oppression and segregation are ever-present risks – in Western democracies, too, as in the case of the treatment of disabled people in post-war West Germany, as tackled in *Behinderte Zukunft* (*Handicapped Future*, 1971).

The French philosopher and visual theorist Jacques Rancière has polemically claimed that Western democracies have developed in an undemocratic direction because the contemporary political sphere is dominated by *consensus*. We are, by and large, in agreement on the most essential values in our society: various high-minded ideas about democracy, freedom of speech and equality before the law. But we no longer think about or reconsider these values. We take the values of the majority for granted, to such a degree that they are no longer up for discussion, and so critical voices, dissenters and those who think differently – any kind of what Rancière calls *dissensus,* or disagreement – are suppressed and even segregated.[1]

Herzog's role as the father in *Julien Donkey-Boy* can thus be seen as a microcosm of broader mechanisms in society. We set ourselves up on a pedestal from where we patronisingly preach the truth in the form of ideals and explanatory models that simply *have to be* adhered to by anyone who is sufficiently rational and enlightened – or sufficiently manly and competitive. Anyone who refuses to fall into line gets a soaking with the garden hose, or is told they are stupid, like the sons in *Julien Donkey-Boy*. This striving for consensus is, according to Rancière, actually an expression of *hatred for democracy*, for the true basis of democracy ought to be an openness to difference. The cornerstone of democracy is *dissensus*; it is dissent or disagreement that challenges our thinking and expands our shared horizon of understanding.

It might seem overkill to single out one Herzog cameo and use it to shed light on his own filmmaking and his concepts of ecstatic truth and the truth of accountants – but this is what he himself does with his acting. Really, Herzog has appeared in so many films that we could say he's had a second career as a supporting actor, most recently almost propelled to acting stardom with his villain in the *Star Wars* television series *The Mandalorian*.

But most of his performances for other directors are also hidden references to his own films and theories. In the 1980s he had roles in the stylized documentaries of Wim Wenders (*Room 666* and *Tokyo-Ga*) and Les Blank (*Werner Herzog Eats His Shoe* and *Burden of Dreams*); in these films, he developed a persona as an artist-prophet proclaiming his aesthetic vision in lines about

Werner Herzog in the uniform of the Empire in the first season of *The Mandalorian* (2019–), Jon Favreau's *Star Wars* television series. Favreau was very aware of Herzog's public persona and used it for the villain, the Client, who is willing to do anything to succeed. Herzog used the paycheck to fully self-finance his film *Family Romance, LLC*, which is based on an idea from former Rogue Film School student Roc Morin, who produced it. It premiered at Cannes in 2019, the first time in many years he was back at the festival he had triumphed at earlier in his career with *Fitzcarraldo*, *Woyzeck* and *The Enigma of Kaspar Hauser*.

'new images', 'adequate images' and 'a new grammar of images'. In his more recent supporting roles in American fiction films, it might seem to the uninitiated filmgoer that he's simply good at playing unpleasant types, but for Herzog there's more at stake. He himself contributes to shaping the characters, all of whom are uncompromising loners pursuing a goal, for better or for worse. To take four examples:

a. *Jack Reacher* (2012; dir. Christopher McQuarrie), in which Herzog plays a one-time Gulag prisoner who once had to bite off his own fingers to survive frostbite in the Siberian cold. Now he is a gangster boss in the United States, and if his henchmen make a mistake, he demands the same self-mutilation of them: are they willing to do what he had to do to survive?

b. *The Grand* (2007; dir. Zak Penn), in which Herzog's role is a German poker player who brings cages of small animals with him to matches; he needs something to kill if he is to maintain his killer instinct at the poker table. He, too, will do anything to win.

c. *The Mandalorian* (2019; dir. Jon Favreau), in which Herzog plays the role of the Client – an officer loyal to the (evil) Empire in *Star Wars*. The Client puts a bounty on a small child, later named Grogu, that resembles Yoda from *Star Wars* (in media coverage, it was referred to as Baby Yoda). He wants to extract the magical powers the Child possesses at any cost: there is even talk of him eating the Child if necessary.

d. *Mister Lonely* (2007; dir. Harmony Korine). In this film, Herzog plays a Christian missionary who (just as Herzog himself has often done) flies in a small plane to the most remote parts of the continent to spread the good word. As he aviates over this poverty-stricken part of the world, his proselytizing strategy is to throw food out of the plane, along with some nuns making the ultimate sacrifice; it looks so pretty when they're falling from the sky.

All four roles exemplify what most people automatically associate with Herzog: the great madmen, fantasists driven by obsession, who feature in his early fiction films – the most famous of whom is of course Klaus Kinski in *Fitzcarraldo*, who bets everything to build an opera house in the jungle. The kind of character who throws himself into a crazy project that the rest of the world considers incomprehensible or pointless. Such people don't comply with the truth of accountants. But the fantasist doesn't care if others think he's mad; he is larger than life, and simply gets on with his *conquest of the useless* – an expression adopted as the English title of Herzog's fictionalized diary *Eroberung des Nutzlosen*, which he wrote during the *Fitzcarraldo* shoot.[2]

In his minor roles in other people's films, Herzog seems merely to play an evil pastiche of his own persona, a figure who has become conflated in the popular imagination with Kinski's parts as Aguirre and Fitzcarraldo. This book will not discuss Herzog's play with supporting roles any further, except to say that it is worth noting that the villains die, the poker player loses and the priest goes down with his plane en route to Rome, where he was to be honoured by the Pope. If any of these four had been central characters, as Herzog suggests, we would see that the fantasist never convinces the world of the worth of his project and never achieves it in a way that results in widespread recognition or a fundamental reorganization of society. Fitzcarraldo never managed to build his opera house, but whereas Herzog lets the evil conquerors go mad and perish, his more endearing fantasists, such as Fitzcarraldo, are permitted to attain some kind of insight and joy by pursuing their unbowed lust for life – and that personal journey was the point all along. When Fitzcarraldo returns home from his *conquest of the useless*, his magnificent fiasco, he toasts happily with those who scorn him, and tells a story that is pregnant with meaning:

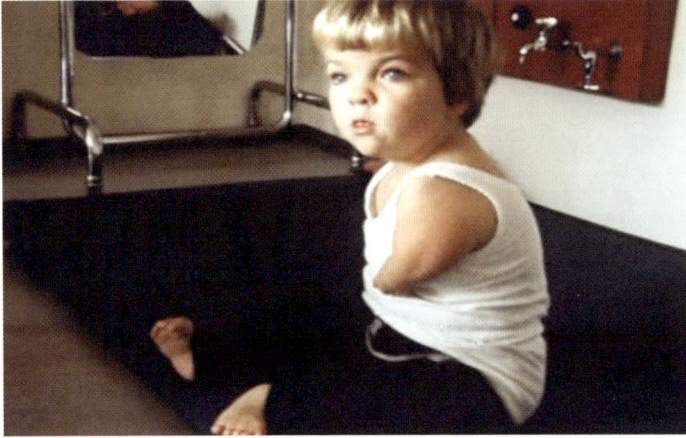

One of the disabled children in the documentary film *Handicapped Future* (1971), which is about the treatment of the disabled in post-war Germany.

> At the time when North America was hardly explored, one of those early French trappers went westward from Montreal, and he was the first white man to set eyes on Niagara Falls. When he returned, he told of waterfalls that were more vast and immense than people had ever dreamed of. But no one believed him. They thought he was a mad-man or a liar. They asked him, 'What's your proof?' And he answered, 'My proof is that I have seen them.'

To afford this kind of privilege to personal insight, to the life force of the curious, path-breaking genius, is not an argument for casting all our scientific theories onto the bonfire or overthrowing state and society in an anarchistic conflagration. Herzog is just trying to remind us that our theories should never be allowed to crystallize into orthodox explanatory models or the narrow-minded truth of accountants. If they are mistaken for absolute truths, we run the risk of suffocating reality and overshadowing the *conquests of the useless*. This is not another way to say 'anything goes', but an opening up to *dissensus*, an opening up to a different way of living,

A photograph taken during the preparations for *Signs of Life*, in which Herzog actively inserts the cradle of civilization, antiquity, into modern life by incorporating ancient sculptures into the modern soldier's defensive wall. 'With a bit of knowledge of antique sculpture you can easily work out that I constructed the wall,' says Herzog. 'Statues don't have foot soles, because normally they stand on pedestals.'

a possible new way of thinking – and that is the fundament of a living democracy.

Jack Reacher, The Grand, The Mandalorian and *Mister Lonely* gesture to Herzog's fantasists, the conquerors of the useless, but *Julien Donkey-Boy* is quite distinctive: with Herzog's oppression of the schizophrenic son, this film also embraces another personality type that is common in Herzog's films. That type is the apparently *useless ones*: the humiliated soldier in *Woyzeck* (1979); the psychologically disturbed Bruno S. in *Stroszek* (1977); the disabled children hidden away in *Behinderte Zukunft* (*Handicapped Future*); the blind, deaf-mute Fini Straubinger in *Land des Schweigens und der Dunkelheit* (*Land of Silence and Darkness*, 1971). All these characters are reminiscent of the sons in *Julien Donkey-Boy*. (It is significant in this respect that Korine originally planned to play one of the sons, so that the film father Herzog would be oppressing his film son.)

The truth of accountants is, then, for Herzog, more than just a critical term for a lazy approach to documentary. It is a more fundamental critique of the act of elevating one's own truth to the status of the only truth, and imposing it on the world so that this theory of truth appears to be reality. This limits both the free vitality of the individual and a shared understanding of the world, something that dates right back to the cradle of civilization. That Herzog thinks of this tendency as ancient can be seen, for example, in his debut feature film *Lebenszeichen* (*Signs of Life*, 1968), in which a group of Nazi soldiers is defending an old Greek castle. The ramparts are constructed from fragments of sculptures dating from antiquity, so that the foundations of civilization literally stick out through cracks in the walls. This is a discreet reminder that we have, since Plato, divided up the state into workers and thinkers, and throughout history have created further social classes: the nobility, peasants, capitalists, the proletariat and so on, as if they were determined by some natural order. The truth of accountants maintains that the predicates imposed on things are natural and unalterable, that the cells on the spreadsheet are rigid and clearly defined: one is a worker, an artist, a philosopher or a soldier, but not several things at once. Or, with more modern terminology, one is in full-time employment or a benefit claimant, a Brit or an immigrant, and so on. When Herzog talks about the truth of accountants, he means a distorting fiction. This fiction is not confined to a documentary style that makes truth claims. He is talking about a broader philosophical fiction that overshadows reality and segregates whomever and whatever falls outside the 'useful' categories in the social order: those regarded as *useless*, or the fantasists, the *conquerors of the useless*. The ones who want to do something totally different: to be both a rubber baron *and* an opera lover, or disabled *and* a university professor, or who in some other way want that all-important *and* that always characterizes Herzog's film crew – psychiatrist *and* photographer, set designer *and* scholar of troubadour literature.

It's not necessarily the case that the *useless ones* and *the conquerors of the useless* are physically oppressed. It's more that their voices don't get heard; they are classified as noise, nonsense or silence. The patronizing father played by Herzog does not see two sensitive sons who would rather be writing what he calls 'artsy-fartsy' poetry; he stubbornly tries to turn them into Dirty Harry. The words he uses to that end might be ugly, but in principle the point is the same as the one Rancière makes about how Socrates, in Plato's famous dialogue *Menon*, helps an enslaved boy to understand and articulate a truth that Socrates says was already inside him. He just needed a bit of help along the way. Socrates leads him towards a particular conclusion: Socrates' truth. The aim is not to emancipate the slave boy, but to enroll him in society's hierarchical division of power. In that power structure, the enslaved stand on the lowest rung and, with the gracious assistance of Socrates, can potentially move up through the system – but always within the predetermined order. The Marxists adopted a similar line of thought with their theories about the liberation of the working class; if the workers did not subscribe to those theories in real life, they were classified as living in false consciousness. This is the order of the truth of accountants: there is no point in objecting that you're not 'stupid like that' or suggesting ways of living other than Dirty Harry's, when that's the lifestyle the accountant has decided is the ideal one.

Every man for himself and God against all

Herzog was thinking about the social order long before Jacques Rancière published his philosophy and visual theory, and before Herzog himself started playing supporting roles in American films. In *Julien Donkey-Boy*, Herzog's performance, and the child-rearing methods adopted by his character, are particularly reminiscent of his great Cannes success of 1974, *Jeder für sich und Gott gegen alle* (*The Enigma of Kaspar Hauser: Every Man for Himself and God Against All*) – the story of Europe's best-known foundling, Kaspar Hauser, the *useless one* par excellence.

The film opens with an epigraph from the German author and dramaturge Georg Büchner (1813–1837), whose most important works, *Woyzeck* and *Lenz*, are considered by Herzog to be two of the greatest masterpieces in the German language. The epigraph to the film is a garbled quotation from Lenz, which later emerged as central to Herzog's concept of the truth of accountants: 'Don't you hear the terrible screams around you, the screams that men usually call silence.'[3] This quotation has traditionally been interpreted as referring to the scream of nature in the face of humanity's destructive acts of mastery, and the hope of returning to nature. But the film's epigraph actually points to the cries of civilization that go unheard by the society of accountants, because the excluded are granted no place in the extant order; their voices are regarded as incomprehensible noise, or as silence – an interpretation more in the spirit of Büchner.

Kaspar Hauser (1812–1833) arrived – out of the blue – in Nuremberg on 26 May 1828. It is thought that he had been taken from his

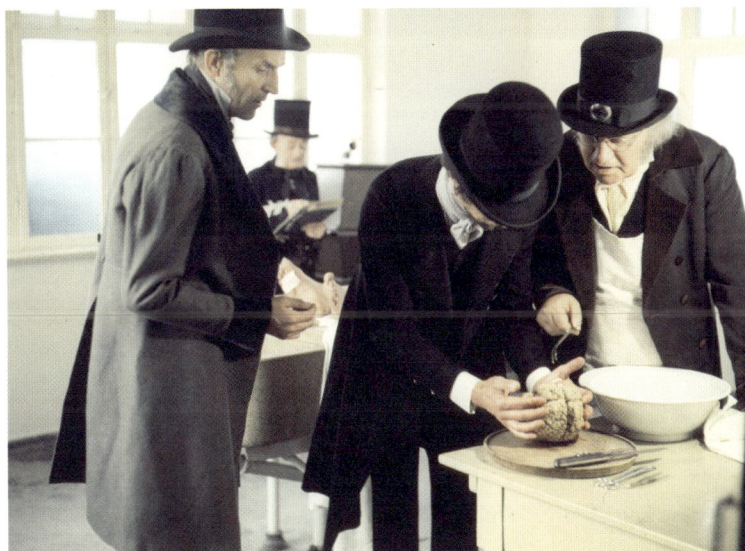

The mentally ill street musician Bruno S. plays Kaspar Hauser in *The Enigma of Kaspar Hauser*. Here we see three key scenes: Hauser, after growing up alone in a cave, lands in civilization in 1828, only to be murdered five years later; after which his body is autopsied. Bruno S. later played the title role in *Stroszek*. He died in 2010 at the age of 78.

mother and held in isolation from the age of three. When he appeared on the doorstep of the town's sheriff, he wasn't able to speak, could barely walk, and knew nothing of the world he had suddenly been thrown into. It was an obvious story for Herzog to adapt into film, because Kaspar, as the ultimate outsider, has a lot to say about our society. In one famous sequence, a child holds up a mirror to Kaspar's face, and he is confused and shocked to see his own reflection for the first time. This is Herzog's way of illustrating the effect Kaspar's presence has on everyone around him. He forces them to see their everyday life with new eyes.

Whereas others have speculated at length on why Kaspar Hauser was imprisoned as a child, Herzog concentrates on his encounter with the world. This encounter prompted several attempts to murder him, and five years later he was indeed killed by a knife through the heart.

Herzog's social critique is to be found in all his works, and over time it has, luckily, grown more subtle than in this early, almost programmatic film. Nonetheless, the film's slightly heavy 1970s air lends itself to a close analysis of what Herzog thinks happens to the individual when he is implanted in a social order based on the truth of accountants.

In the opening scene Kaspar is sitting in his cave, where he is at one with the world. He knows no distinction between himself and the chain that binds him to the cave wall, and he has never seen another living being. Bread and water are provided for him while he sleeps. It's not a particularly nice place but there is a feeling of homeliness, insofar as he has no sense of the existence of anywhere else.

When Kaspar meets another human for the first time, his prison guard, he also learns his first word: 'write'. At the very same moment he is introduced to the logic of exchange, because the guard promises him a toy if he learns to write. This moment introduces the distinction that is pursued throughout the rest of the film: that there is an immediate (pre-linguistic) being in the world, which becomes split in its meeting with language. This hints at the idea that the truth can never quite be expressed. Unmediated being in the world is a utopia and thus not a place we can reach, but an awareness is established that something is lost between being and utterance. The more Kaspar falls into language, the more self-conscious he becomes, but he also notices that the language with which he must express his expanded consciousness is conditioned by discourse. His cave is a very small society structured according to the truth of accountants; he only has one 'father', who, just like Herzog's father figure in *Julien Donkey-Boy*, decides everything.

The next part of the film takes place in Nuremberg, where the prison guard smuggles Kaspar into the city and leaves him to his first real meeting with civilization. On principle, Herzog chooses to refer to the town only as 'N', to avoid the story and its attendant evils being interpreted as specifically German. Stories, and indeed films, about wild or isolated children are far from a German phenomenon. This was noted by the film critic David Overbey when *The Enigma of Kaspar Hauser* was released, and Brad Prager researched the same topic as recently as 2007. Four years before Herzog's film about Kaspar Hauser, François Truffaut had adapted the story of the wild child Victor of Aveyron for the screen in *L'enfant sauvage* (*The Wild Child*, 1970), and Arthur Penn's *The Miracle Worker* (1962) explored how Helen Keller, the famous American blind and deaf-mute girl, broke out of her sensory isolation.

For both Truffaut and Penn, it's communication that is the solution; the isolated are redeemed by love and education. That is not the case for Kaspar Hauser. Herzog was obviously aware of the two earlier films, and incorporates a comment on them into a key sequence in which Kaspar receives his first language lesson at the dinner table. While Victor and Helen both take their respective first steps towards freedom with a revelation about what is *in* their cup (milk), in contrast, Kaspar's first meaningful pedagogical encounter with language comes when he looks into his cup and is told that it is 'empty'.[4] It seems that Herzog wants to make it clear that Kaspar is not like the enslaved boy in Plato's dialogue *Menon*, the boy who is already full of truth, which has only to be recognized and articulated via the Socratic method. Kaspar is an empty cup, or, in more traditional philosophical terms, a *tabula rasa*, a blank slate, upon which knowledge can be imprinted. But every pedagogical impression is also a potential instance of oppression.

Kaspar's entry into society and his education constitute an extended stripping away of this perfect dressage. Herzog allows him to perform as a fool who can, thanks to his strangeness, expose gender norms, religion, science and high culture. The film obliquely develops this critique by detailing two dynamics that discipline Kaspar, both of which fundamentally have the same end: to bring the billowing sail that is Kaspar Hauser under control, and to lash him fast to the mast that is the truth of accountants. *Dissensus* cannot be tolerated, after all.

The first dynamic quite simply wants to position Kaspar within the social order, because his abnormality in and of itself poses a challenge to the dominant order. First, he is put on display in a circus, a freak show, so that he can be of use to the local population in some way or other. Then he is adopted by Professor Daumer, who introduces him to priests, scientists and the educated middle classes, all of whom want to mould Kaspar to correspond to their vision of the world. From beginning to end, the town's notary follows Kaspar painstakingly – so painstakingly that one quickly gets tired of his precise repetitions. He is obsessed with the notion of writing the perfect report. As Jacques Rancière writes: 'The report is an excellent stultifying explication that cannot help being successful.'[5] Appropriately enough, the notary hops around excitedly when the post-mortem on Kaspar's corpse reveals an enlarged liver and brainstem, which 'at last explains this strange man' – that is, it incorporates him into the social order, the self-justifying fiction of the truth of accountants.

The second dynamic is the well-meaning pedagogy that intends to help Kaspar 'make up for lost time', as Professor Daumer puts it. Daumer is the kindest father Kaspar could possibly have, but this well-intentioned educator often adopts methods that perpetuate the hierarchy just as much as the first dynamic does, although in the name of progress. Kasper is a quick learner. When he talks to children and women in the community, he gains knowledge. He learns the language and learns about the world by observing it directly, verifying, reflecting and repeating. He wants to communicate, but in conversations with the pillars of society (all men) a distance is apparent between what he learns through his own intelligence and what it means to understand. It is not enough to grasp new things; one must also comprehend them in particular ways. In one famous scene, Kaspar converses with a professor of logic. The professor proposes a variation of the Epimenides Paradox, or the Liar's Paradox. In Herzog's version, this is a riddle of two cities: one city where only the truth is told, and one city where everyone lies. The professor tells Kaspar to imagine that he meets a traveller and can ask only one question in order to reveal from which city the traveller hails. Kaspar answers that one could just ask the traveller if he is a frog, and then one could immediately tell whether he was lying or not. The professor is enraged because Kaspar has not stuck to the logic of the paradox. Herzog has himself commented on this particular scene to the film critic Paul Cronin:

> In terms of pure logic, the only solution to the professor's
> problem is the one that he himself explains to Kaspar. But,
> of course, the answer that Kaspar gives is also correct. It is
> clear that Kaspar is strictly forbidden to imagine and that his
> creativity is being suffocated and suppressed. We sense that
> everything spontaneous in Kaspar is being systematically
> deadened by philistine society, though people like the
> professor think he is behaving decently with his attempts
> to 'educate' Kaspar.[6]

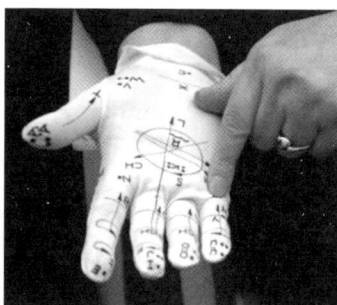

Herzog taught himself tactile sign language using taps on the palm and fingers in order to be able to communicate with the blind and deaf-mute woman Fini Straubinger (left), in *Land of Silence and Darkness*. Straubinger helps others with the same conditions to learn to communicate.

We should not take this statement by Herzog to be a declaration of hostility towards logic, science or rationality in general. He is a declared admirer of mathematics and rational discourse, something he has emphasized by inviting mathematicians and physicists to give guest lectures at several of the Rogue Film Schools. Rather, Herzog is expressing a distrust of the mode of thinking that insists there is a distinction between our own instinctive learning and the established interpretation of the world, one that wants to fix us in place, which insists that a single perspective is the true one. That is not true emancipation but perfect dressage; the truth of accountants.

To envisage Kaspar as a person who has to *catch up* with what he has missed is a pedagogical fiction that paints difference as delay. Kaspar has no right to think for himself, the logic goes, because he has not yet reached the right level.

Is communication not important, then? Of course it is. Three years earlier, in Herzog's film *Land des Schweigens und der Dunkelheit* (*Land of Silence and Darkness*, 1971), the need for communication and community was framed as a basic one. Herzog explores life as a blind and deaf-mute person, largely in conversation with Fini

A dwarf reaches for a door handle in *Even Dwarfs Started Small*. Is it the dwarf who is too short, or the world that is ill-equipped?

Straubinger, who was able to learn to talk a little as a child, but otherwise communicates through touch. Straubinger is, just like Kaspar Hauser, an obviously Herzogian character, an extreme outsider; her separation from the world is sensory, physical. But Herzog shows that those with her disabilities have the desire and the curiosity to engage with the world; our world, however, is inadequate to meet their needs. In the final scene of the film we see a blind, deaf-mute man, who has been living in the corner of a barn for years because no one had any idea what to do with him. In the film he is led out into the open air, and soon he encounters a tree, which he immediately starts to investigate with his hands. We can communicate with blind, deaf-mute people if we adjust to the tactile communication they need – the kind of language Herzog, in fact, had to learn in order to communicate with Straubinger.

Herzog demonstrates a similar point in *Auch Zwerge haben klein angefangen* (*Even Dwarfs Started Small*, 1970), in which all the cast members are dwarfs but the set is built to standard proportions. This consolidates the impression that the actors are vertically challenged and just have to work a bit harder so that they can gradually reach the right height and thus the door handle; as though their height represented a kind of delay. In much the same way, well-meaning pedagogy is revealed to be an endless process of catching up imposed on that which has been delayed, so that the 'delayed' ones are always held in an inferior position, and need the help of their 'superiors'.

'The report is an excellent stultifying explication that cannot help being successful,' writes the philosopher Jacques Rancière. The notary who has pedantically investigated Kaspar Hauser in *The Enigma of Kaspar Hauser* is happy when the post-mortem finds anomalies in the liver and brainstem that 'finally explain this strange man'.

Herzog thus examines in his films how the order of the truth of accountants conceals the notion that things could be different. Just as it does in the documentary context, this truth understood in a broader sense insists that there is one, and only one, truth to be discovered. But the truth of accountants never quite succeeds in its goal of getting everything aligned and stuffing it into the cells on the spreadsheet. It is notable that Herzog consistently engages with people whom societal norms would dismiss as unsuccessful or deformed. All of them display a bodily insufficiency: they are blind and deaf-mute, dwarfs or misshapen vampires. Even the conqueror Aguirre (*Aguirre, Wrath of God*) is hunchbacked, and the world champion ski jumper Walter Steiner in *Die große Ekstase des Bildschnitzers Steiner* (*The Great Ecstasy of Woodcarver Steiner*) is scrawny and so shy that he lives alone in a mountainside hut, his only friend a crow. With these *useless* bodies Herzog demonstrates that we are unsuited to the order of the truth of accountants, in terms of language and in terms of community, and that the order of the truth of accountants is unsuited to these *useless ones* and to the *conquerors of the useless*. After a long learning curve, Kaspar Hauser starts to rebel against all of this. He himself feels an undefined desire for something else, but when he starts to express it, he is killed; on the autopsy bench, he finally fits in.

Time is passing, your perspective is limited, and you're going to die

'I simply do not have goals in life. Rather, I have goals in existence,' says Werner Herzog.[7] The truth of accountants is a much bigger deal than documentary filmmaking methods and oppressive pedagogy. It's not just that people are evil or treat each other stupidly. For Herzog, people are also oppressed by the fundamentals of the human condition. In all his films, he has shown an interest in the existential individual who lives his life in the shadow of death, and is restless under the onus of passing time. This is the tragic and fundamental aspect of the human condition; it makes the limitations imposed by the truth of accountants feel suffocating. We have no time to be oppressed, no time to live in inauthentic ways.

This problem is already apparent in Herzog's debut feature film, *Signs of Life*, which is set in Nazi-occupied Greece during the Second World War and has Peter Brogle in the lead role as the German parachutist Stroszek. However, we see nothing of the war or of parachute jumping in the film. We are told that Stroszek was wounded by partisans on the island of Crete, and that a friendly officer arranged for him to be stationed on Kos. There, he can convalesce and wait out the war, without encountering the enemy again. His only assignment is to watch over a munition store in an ancient mountaintop castle. He lives there with two other German soldiers and a Greek nurse, Nora, whom he marries; but he has a hard time feeling present in his life.

Stroszek is a restless soul who dreams of being elsewhere; he is looking for a kind of meaning that he himself can barely grasp, let alone articulate to the people closest to him. One of his soldier comrades is too hotheaded and the other too pensive, and Stroszek's love for Nora is encumbered by the language barrier. Even his work consists only of waiting. In his quest for meaning, Stroszek sometimes sits on the wall of the fort so that he can be seen from the nearby village, just to make it look as though he has a function; he wants to fit in, but the truth is that even the ammunition he is guarding is useless. It is of a calibre that doesn't match the army's weaponry, and the locals don't seem at all interested in it.

Stroszek feels the need to do something, something he doesn't quite have words for. In the absence of meaning, he starts to obsess about an external enemy. This is a theme that is also apparent in Herzog's short film from the same period, *Die beispiellose Verteidigung der Festung Deutschkreuz* (*The Unprecedented Defence of the Fortress Deutschkreuz*). In it, a group of self-appointed soldiers in an old fort believe they are under siege, but there is no enemy. They need an enemy to give their lives meaning: 'Defeat is better

In *Signs of Life*, the German soldier Stroszek goes mad from living the same life at a standstill, day in, day out. He reacts to the meaninglessness of his life by shooting at random. His challenge is not just to the army, but to all of humankind, all of the universe. The crowd panics, but when Stroszek has been subdued, the world continues as before.

There are very few actual instances of on-screen kissing or physical love in Herzog's films. Those that do occur are anything but clichéd. In *Cobra Verde* (opposite), Kinski is a force of nature that devours everything and everyone – sexually, too. In *Nosferatu*, the kiss of the vampire is fatal. In *Queen of the Desert*, Gertrude Bell (Nicole Kidman) enjoys a romantic desert kiss only to watch her lover die soon afterwards. And in *Bad Lieutenant*, the morality of a police officer (Nicolas Cage) is muddied by his drug abuse. Here (bottom), he intimidates a woman into giving him crack and a kiss by waving his pistol and police badge around.

than no war at all,' as the film's voiceover remarks. The voice seems objective to start with but sounds more and more paranoid over the course of the film, until we're eventually moved to consider whether he might be a ghost from a gloomy past. A relic of past wars? A madman from the period when the fort was an insane asylum? A voice from an all-encompassing, universal void?

Just like the soldiers in the short film, Stroszek in *Signs of Life* starts to go on expeditions to feel active – to feel less useless. On one of those expeditions he arrives at a valley in which thousands of identical white windmills are whirring. This quixotic encounter blows a fuse within him, and in a fit of madness he takes command of the fort and the munition store and opens fire on the village.

Herzog took inspiration from a story by the German Romantic Achim von Arnim, *Der tolle Invalide auf dem Fort Ratonneau* (The Madman of Fort Ratonneau, 1818), in which a wounded French soldier, Francoeur, becomes ill during the Seven Years War (1756–63) in a similar way to Stroszek – perhaps as a result of brain trauma? Perhaps because of his love for a woman whose mother will not consent to the marriage? Or perhaps as a case of demonic possession? Regardless of the reason, all ends well in Achim von Arnim's world, as the woman's love is strong enough to overcome whatever was the cause of Francoeur's problems. The wounded Stroszek also ends up quite mad, but Herzog has no interest in head wounds as an explanation for insanity, and even less belief in love.

Love is too simple an explanation for Herzog, regardless of whether it's good things or bad things that need explaining. There is not much kissing or sex in Herzog's oeuvre, and any exceptions tend to be associated with extraordinary forces. Take, for example, *Cobra Verde*, in which a slave master played by Klaus Kinski impregnates a plantation owner's three daughters pretty much simultaneously, or *Nosferatu*, in which the kiss is of the deadly, vampiric sort.

Madness, on the other hand, is not foreign to Herzog. His films bubble over with it, but it is not the sort of madness that is an effect of clinical insanity or brain damage. 'That kind of illness is sad and prosaic,' says Herzog of his meeting with Mark Yavorsky, the mentally ill actor on whose life story he based the film *My Son, My Son, What Have Ye Done* (2009). In 1979 Yavorksy was playing a role in a Greek tragedy, *Oresteia*, and had trouble distinguishing between fiction and reality. One day he got home from the theatre and killed his real-life mother with an antique sword. Herzog found the story painfully sad, but felt an artistic interest in the insane man's conflation of the aesthetic and the real. This is an interest of his that can be traced all the way back to *Signs of Life*, and which can best be characterized as a *poetic, ecstatic madness*; a greater, all-encompassing insanity that inheres in those who long for another world. In *Signs of Life* the voiceover says of Stroszek's madness: 'In a raging protest, he declared war on the whole world. He even protested against the arc of the sun at daybreak. He screamed that light could be fought with light.'

For Stroszek, it is not the Greeks who seem like the great enemy but time itself. I mean time in both senses, on both scales: the daily grind that bores Stroszek, and deep time, the ruins of civilized history with which the old castle walls were constructed. 'Hasn't it always been like this?', Herzog seems to ask in this film, and he shores up the theme with fragments of stories: the story of a hypnotized hen that stupidly runs in circles until she falls over; the story of a gypsy king who has lost his tribe but retains his joy and dignity as he travels here and there, while the rest of the world moves in ever-decreasing circles. And isn't it the case that circling the same point has always led to war and catastrophe? Even the good old Greeks cheated and bloodied each other at the otherwise peaceful Olympic Games, *Signs of Life* tells us, just as the bored German soldiers in the fort regress to killing cockroaches.

Stroszek notices that something has gone badly wrong, but he doesn't know quite what. When he encounters that circling motion manifest a thousandfold, in the form of the windmill-filled valley, it is too much. He has tried to communicate, but language is insufficient to establish a common understanding or to amply account for his feelings. As the film's title suggests, he produces another 'sign of life': he fires off ammunition like fireworks over the town. However, just as his madness has a poetic character, the battle he has joined is a bigger one than he knows, and it is doomed to fail. The local garrison overpowers him, and, as Herzog has said, the truly tragic thing is not that they kill him, but that they silence him. The order that he managed to shake up for a while is re-established. And perhaps, after all, one cannot hope for more, since, as the voiceover's last remark goes: 'In his rebellion he had challenged something titanic. For the enemy was clearly superior. In this way, he made a miserable mistake, like all the others of his tribe.'

Stroszek yelled that he wanted to battle light with light, but the power was too strong, fundamentally unconquerable, and therefore he was tragically doomed to fail. But something happened anyway. Herzog has often pointed out that film is light – both in the grand sense of enlightenment, and in the more playful sense of a trick show, the manipulation of light in the tents of a market. When Stroszek initiates his struggle, Herzog alters the film's narrative style and tempo. Up to this point, we've seen fragments of stories that didn't quite cohere. There has been no narrative progress; the characters are just present, in one slow scene after another. Nothing has really happened, and no one has seriously intervened in the world.

But now Stroszek begins to take the lead in each scene. He has moved from an interior life that seemed absurd to a dynamic exterior life. It may well be dismissed as symptoms of madness by the world outside, but we, as film viewers, are watching excitedly to see what he intends to do next, and if it will go well for him. The individual in him has escaped, and for a while he is a force that cannot be contained within the accountant's spreadsheet of

In the film *Into the Inferno* (2016), Herzog consolidates his interest in volcanos (they also appear in *La Soufrière*, *Encounters at the End of the World* and *Salt and Fire*). It opens in an indefinable fog, and this metaphor seeps into all the film's encounters. Whether Herzog himself is staring directly down into the volcano, or listening to people who live close to volcanos in Vanuatu, Ethiopia or North Korea; nature people, science people, media people – everyone's knowledge and perspective is limited, foggy.

truth. Goodness knows it's only for a short time, for soon both Stroszek and the film end up back where they started: the shots of landscape with which the film opened showing the wounded soldier being transported into the town, and through which he is now carried away. Like all tragic heroes, he is doomed to fail, and like all human beings, he was born to die (the vampire in *Nosferatu* is, of course, doomed to the opposite fate, eternal life, but in Herzog's interpretation his tragic circumstance is that he cannot himself be allowed to choose death). With light, Herzog has visualized the friction between individual and society, as well as the more fundamental friction between the human and the world in which he finds himself; he has given voice to the feeling of time's merciless march towards human *mortality*.

An unromantic Romantic

People can be cruel to each other. And people die. The individual is limited by culture and by nature. Herzog is also concerned with the further limits of the human: the limits of understanding. He chooses to begin many of his films in different kinds of fog, into which the audience has to move with the camera. Here are seven examples:

a. *Heart of Glass* opens with foggy images of clouds and water, which a prophetic voice asks us to stare into.
b. *Fata Morgana* opens with an aeroplane descending towards a landing strip in the desert, which looks misty in the heat haze.
c. *Lessons of Darkness* opens with the heat shimmer from the burning oilfields in the Kuwaiti desert.
d. *La Soufrière* opens with smoke or heat haze and gases from the volcano La Soufrière.
e. *Aguirre* opens with a shot of a misty mountainside. The Spanish conquistadors dive quite literally into the

mist by moving down the mountainside into the jungle,
where the rest of the film takes place.

f. *Fitzcarraldo* opens with a panorama of impenetrable
jungle shrouded in fog.

g. *Into the Inferno* opens with a hard-to-decode shot of
undefinable fog, smoke or heat haze, into which we
slowly fly on the way up a mountainside, which only
later do we understand is a volcano.

With these images, Herzog establishes a point about the road to
understanding being foggy: we don't know where we come from
or where we're going, but we keep on exploring the mist and
constructing ideas about it.

In *Fitzcarraldo*, the foggy establishing shot of the jungle is
followed by an explanatory on-screen title about local myth:
'Cayahuari Yacu, the jungle Indians call this country "the land
where God did not finish Creation". They believe only after man
has disappeared will He return to finish His work.' In other words,
the people conceive of this land as faulty and understand human
existence to be a form of interruption without purpose or meaning.
What humans know about themselves and the world is in any case
fundamentally limited. Later in the film, we also learn that the
indigenous people believe the world we live in is just an illusion,
and behind it lies a dream world, in search of which they have been
wandering for three hundred years. This echoes Fitzcarraldo's own
worldview and project, as when he says to a rich rubber baron, 'Sir,
the reality of your world is nothing more than a rotten caricature of
great opera,' and goes off to do something about that: to transform
the world into music.

All Herzog's films contain a form of paradoxical nostalgia for a
pre-human or pre-linguistic world, or, alternatively, a longing for
a world in the image of the human, a world in which everything
coheres and corresponds to human feelings. This is what has led
many to write him into the Romantic tradition, understandably

In his documentaries Herzog often finds himself on the edge of an abyss – physically and psychologically. In his fiction films, this is also a recurring motif: the small man in the great span of nature; on the edge. Above we see Josef Bierbichler on a cliff ledge in his role as the Bavarian prophet Hias in *Heart of Glass* (1976).

enough, since many of his films – especially those from the 1970s – are full of images that draw directly on Romantic tropes.

However, it is an interpretation that Herzog has vociferously rejected, not least at the Rogue Film School. 'I am *not* a Romantic,' he says as often as he can. That's true – with some caveats.

Romanticism was an artistic and philosophical movement (active *c.* 1789–1848) that can be hard to pin down, but there *are* a few ways we can connect it to Herzog. He *is* an heir to the Romantics, if by that term we understand the first critique of modernity: a self-reflexivity already inherent in the Enlightenment, which challenges the rational and the reasonable and says that reason is not reasonable enough; that people have irrational feelings, and we must take account of that.

When we use the term 'romantic' today, we tend to mean the idea that has survived in everyday language about love, a Romanticism that stems not from the German Romantic philosophers, but from English poets of the nineteenth century: the irrational, the pathetic, the grandiose; the desire of the subject to reach towards or believe in something greater than itself, and into which it can disappear. It can be the Other, a romance or something religious; a political cause, or a movement.

Herzog acknowledges this impulse – most of his great fantasists cultivate it – and, as many film scholars have emphasized, concrete examples can be found in *Heart of Glass*, *Nosferatu* and *The Enigma of Kaspar Hauser*, all of which directly mimic Romantic paintings, especially Caspar David Friedrich's canvases of lonely men with their back to the onlooker and their gaze fixed on an expansive natural landscape. Images of small human beings in the great, often violent landscapes of Herzog's films are often singled out as some of cinema's most obvious examples of 'the sublime', and it is those images that are most often used to connect Herzog to Romanticism. The sublime (a concept that originated with the philosophers Edmund Burke and Immanuel Kant) is the human sensation of almost being crushed by something greater.

An encounter with a huge mountain, a violent firestorm or some great cruelty overwhelms our perceptual apparatus. We cannot absorb it into our experience; our powers of imagination break down, and the only thing left is a sense of wonder or awe in the face of something essential – something greater than us. We have all experienced the sublime – on a cliff edge, high above an abyss, or in the dark of the cinema watching a terrifying horror film. The sublime is encountered in various forms (jungles, high mountains, volcanos, perilous seas, risky plane journeys and empty deserts) in almost all Herzog's films:

a. In *Fitzcarraldo* and *Aguirre*, humans contend with the great, impenetrable South American jungle.

b. In *Gasherbrum* and *Scream of Stone*, humans tackle the world's highest mountains in the Himalayas and Patagonia.

c. In *La Soufrière*, humans, in this case Herzog himself, visit a volcano in Guadeloupe just before it erupts. This is a subject and a visual repertoire that both *Into the Inferno* and *Salt and Fire* revisit.

d. In *Heart of Glass*, a human sails defiantly out into crashing waves towards the open ocean. In *Encounters at the End of the World*, researchers venture beneath the thick ice of the Antarctic in a dangerous dive without a safety line. Herzog calls this 'ecstatic diving'.

e. In *The Great Ecstasy of Woodcarver Steiner*, the world champion ski jumper Walter Steiner pushes the envelope of human achievement. The human longing to fly has appeared in the shape of an Icarus figure in several of Herzog's films: *Rescue Dawn*, *Little Dieter Needs to Fly* and *Wings of Hope*, all of which are about plane crashes.

f. In *Fata Morgana* and *Queen of the Desert*, humans go into the desert, that great, lonely, dangerous space which also offers, or symbolizes, endless freedom.

Werner Herzog during the filming of *Fireball: Visitors from Darker Worlds* – his third collaboration with scientist Clive Oppenheimer. In a conversation with executive producer Greg Boustead at the premiere at TIFF 2020, Herzog said, 'At its core, Fireball is about the ecstasy of discovery. It's about the pure joy of filmmaking and the pure joy of science.' Herzog's films about science are like no others, more focused on the scientist and the joy of discovery than explaining. 'It's important to remember: a good question is sometimes better than ever finding the answer . . . and this was true throughout antiquity. For instance, if you consider pre-Socratic philosophy, the greatest of all questions we are confronted with is a simple one: why is there existence, rather than nothingness? We will never answer this. But asking it has led to many profound breakthroughs – in science, in philosophy – throughout history.'

g.   In *Fireball: Visitors from Darker Worlds* Herzog – with long-time collaborator Clive Oppenheimer – explores meteors' potential for total destruction and the myths and folklore around them.

Herzog's films, then, are full of Romantic tropes, *but* . . . whereas the Romantic experience of the sublime was often transformed into

Fireball: Visitors from Darker Worlds (2020).

a feeling of awe and impotence – suggesting something larger than humankind, even God himself – on the other hand, the experience of the sublime represents something different for Herzog. It's not just that his characters are rendered small in the face of mighty nature or the universe. They may very well be doomed to lose the battle, but that is not down to a greater divine context; it's down to the indifference of nature. The characters Herzog cares about always end up returning to civilization. They remain within the historical rather than stepping out of it.

When Juliane and Dieter – the main characters in *Julianes Sturz in den Dschungel* (*Wings of Hope*) and *Little Dieter Needs to Fly* respectively – crash in the jungle, it is a combination of rational thinking and the will to live that brings them back to civilization. They don't pray to God or desire to become one with nature; rather, their wish is to make it home to enlightened society. With Herzog, these trials always lead back to the human in history, rather than leading to fulfilment for the character, or their engulfment in some greater power.

At the Rogue Film School, Herzog doubles down on his denial of being a Romantic by declaring: 'Romanticism is an important phenomenon but it does not describe my work.' He wants to borrow from the critique of the reasonable and the rational. He doesn't want this to cross over into a glorification of the unreasonable and irrational, or the worship of the originary, the mythical, the great beyond. Those aspects of Romanticism led to the great 'isms' of the twentieth century, not least Nazism in Herzog's own homeland. When he is interpreted as a neo-Romantic, there is an unspoken hint of criticism from the left that Herzog is a fascist, with his beautiful cornfields and lovely German landscapes in *The Enigma of Kaspar Hauser* and *Heart of Glass*. In my opinion, to interpret those works in such a way entails having drawn the conclusion before even having watched the films. An open mind would be able to see that it is precisely those images in the two films that construct a pastiche of the German 'homeland film' tradition; they are redolent with unease and hardly idyllic. Herzog says that his most important connection to Romantic painting is to Friedrich, but not in the sense of a philosophical Romantic kinship; they are connected through their visual representations of people's inner lives.

The risk of being dismissed as a fascist is one of the reasons Herzog so actively resists the Natural Romantic readings of his films that crop up in the press even today. He is repeatedly prompted to deny any connection to the nineteenth-century Natural Romantic poets who worshipped nature as a divine place where peace was to be found. Another reason for Herzog's stubbornness on this matter is that he has noticed a tendency in our late modern age to elevate the irrational into a form of 'New Age pseudo-philosophical nonsense'. He thinks this neo-Romantic wave has morphed into a new truth of accountants – and Herzog is always willing to come out swinging against stupidity. Actually, it was clearly stated in the welcome letter to the Rogue Film School that despite a very liberal approach to content (see the falsification of filming permits and courses in lock-picking), there was just one thing he would waste no time on: 'Censorship will be in force: There will be no discussion of shamans, yoga classes, dietary supplements, herbal tea, expanding your boundaries or personal growth.'

In *The Minnesota Declaration* there is, similarly, a slightly odd commandment. There is humour in it, but only if you are familiar with the long-running discussion about Herzog's Romanticism:

10. The moon is dull. Mother Nature doesn't call, doesn't speak to you, although a glacier eventually farts. And don't you listen to the Song of Life.

This rule implicitly references Katharine Hepburn, whose most fervent advice to future generations was 'Listen to the Song of Life'. Herzog has remarked that such blatant idiocy has always caused him

Herzog is prepared to travel to any place whatever to find his new images. On the three preceding pages we see images of volcanic eruptions from *Into the Inferno* (2016), and images from the Himalayas in *Gasherbrum* (1984), and free-climbing images from *Scream of Stone* (1991). In *Scream of Stone* the focus is the competition between two famous climbers as to who will be first to conquer the Cerro Torre in Patagonia, which is said to be 'more a scream of stone than a mountain'. Along the way they meet an unfamiliar climber (and passionate Mae West fan), who, without making a big deal of himself, claims that he lost four fingers at the summit of Cerro Torre. The man's nickname is Fingerless, because since his encounter with the mountain he can no longer remember what his name used to be. But he left his mark at the top of the mountain: an ice axe with a picture of Mae West on it. The shooting of *Scream of Stone* was full of perils and challenges, including hard squalls and ice on the mountainside. At the Rogue Film School, Herzog said that he always carries the Book of Job and Titus Livius' description of the Second Punic War with him when he's making films. The former he values for the suffering it describes, and the latter because of the Roman army chief Fabius Maximus, who defeated the powerful Hannibal (and his war elephants) with guerrilla tactics and no heed to honour. 'You have to do whatever it takes to win. A film has to be finished, no matter what,' says Herzog. He encourages all filmmakers to develop their own reading list with the aim of creating a space of resistance during a shoot.

physical pain, and he therefore consistently strives to distance himself and his works from this kind of thinking. While it's always fun to hear Herzog lobbing insults at his enemies, it's also worthwhile diving even deeper into his concern with Romanticism and nature and his rejection of Natural Romanticism, as this enables us to clarify some of his thinking. The discussion of Herzog and Romanticism has occupied the director himself and researchers to a considerable degree, but a more fruitful approach would be to look more carefully at what Herzog is trying to do. He doesn't long for harmony with nature; he doesn't believe that harmony is possible at all.

What Herzog is trying to do is stage the human longing for harmony; to stage human *feelings* and *desires*, the feeling of being distanced from the world and the desire to be at one with the world, or what one can call the human feeling of *discontinuity* and the striving for *continuity*. These drive us into hostility towards *dissensus* and a wish for *consensus*, a dynamic that can often take on a domineering and oppressive character. It is their shared sense of a failed world that moves the fantasist Fitzcarraldo to drag a ship over a mountain in the jungle in order to transform the world into music, and drives the mad conqueror Aguirre to curse God and the world and to recreate it anew. But Herzog gives no indication that there is any kind of redemption to be found on the far side of their projects.

In *The Enigma of Kaspar Hauser*, the eponymous boy is not too satisfied with this world, either. When he learns to speak, 'he feels distanced from everything', expresses his horror that 'people are like wolves', and comments that his 'fall into the world was terribly hard'. At first glance, the film can seem to express a gnostic conception of the world as defiled: only an evil God could have created such an evil world. Gnosticism claims that there is an infinite distance between the good and eternal God and this evil and impermanent world inhabited by confused mortals who have no understanding of their fate. Through insight, humans can liberate an inner spark of the divine and ascend step by step from

The foggy mountain from one of Kaspar Hauser's dreams in *The Enigma of Kaspar Hauser*. One would think that on top of the mountain there would be some kind of overview or clarity, or a kindly god who would explain how the world works, but only the fog persists. The fog also persists in the gaze of the bear in *Grizzly Man*, towards the end of which Herzog says that the argument about whether Treadwell was right or not 'disappears into a distance, into a fog'.

their material prison to return home to the highest spiritual form of divinity. This thinking is another expression of longing for a form of unity, this time through understanding: Herzog focuses on his messianic anti-heroes' attempts to breach the boundaries imposed on them, but real exit strategies are few and far between. Herzog stages this longing for continuity and consensus, yet he always lets his heroes fail. Neither the native people nor Fitzcarraldo find paradise. The tribe has been wandering for more than three hundred years, and it is still wandering at the end of the film. Fitzcarraldo does not succeed in building his opera house – his cathedral of music – to reach a world beyond this one.

Thus Herzog does not aspire to reconciliation. We can see this very clearly in *The Enigma of Kaspar Hauser*. Kaspar becomes sadder and sadder on his path to enlightenment, and starts to escape through dreams. But in one of his dreams he sees humanity moving up a mountain covered in fog, rather than down the mountain, as featured in the opening scene of *Aguirre, the Wrath of God*. Perhaps one might choose to believe that the crowd is climbing towards a form of clear-sightedness, but with Herzog there is no light above the fog, no Paradise – at the mountaintop only Death awaits. As *Kaspar Hauser*'s German title states, *Gott gegen alle* – God is against everyone. In other words, Kaspar's journey into knowledge brings him precisely as far as the wandering tribe. Humanity is still bound by the human condition, and at the foot of the mountain it is 'every man for himself', as the title also makes explicit: *Jeder für sich*.

In Herzog's films, then, there is no Heaven or Hell. We are living in a radical immanence and must work with the world we have at hand, regardless of how meaningless and parenthetical our existence might seem to be.

It's understandable that the many Romantic longing gazes in Herzog's films inspire a superficial analysis. But it is the paucity of exit strategies for his characters that more obviously shifts the critical interpretation towards an understanding of the world as one and irreplaceable; the lack of a possible exit does not hinder people from gazing longingly backwards, forwards or towards the beyond. Near the end of *The Enigma of Kaspar Hauser*, a high-society lady asks about Kaspar's life before he encountered civilization, and, with bitterness, he describes his cave as a better alternative to that civilization. The theatrical scenes in which the nineteenth-century bourgeoisie frolic in extravagant robes and adhere to strict etiquette are contrasted with extended, calm shots of the wind rustling the corn or a swan gliding majestically across a lake. It is such landscape shots that have inspired the Romantic interpretation of Herzog's work. He uses landscape in all his films, and has often drawn on Romantic landscape painting. In *Heart of Glass*, it's almost as though we are roaming around in pictures by Friedrich. But it is too often overlooked that although society is depicted in the films as a man-made hell, nature is no paradise – and even if it were, it is irrevocably lost anyway. Although Kaspar Hauser, in his feeling of discontinuity, longs for the cave that offered continuity, a return to imprisonment is no solution for Herzog. It is too easy to resort to reading Herzog's entire oeuvre as an homage to nature on the basis of his critique of civilization and his beautiful landscape shots. Nowhere, neither in his films nor elsewhere, does he suggest that humans can throw off the chains of civilization and return to nature. If we can identify a state of nature in his work, it is definitely not Jean-Jacques Rousseau's harmonious picture that Herzog is thinking of when he declares that 'our civilization is like a thin layer of ice upon a deep ocean of chaos and darkness.'[8] Here he is more in line with Thomas Hobbes's gloomy state of nature in which men seem to resemble wolves, just as Kaspar Hauser comments, and in which all nature around the human seems to be a kind of hell. As the twelfth and final point of *The Minnesota Declaration* muses:

> 12. Life in the oceans must be sheer hell. A vast, merciless
>   hell of permanent and immediate danger. So much of
>   [a] hell that during evolution some species – including

man – crawled, fled onto some small continents of solid land, where the Lessons of Darkness continue.

In his more recent films there are also strong indications that Herzog does not see the state of nature as something we ought to be casting longing glances at. Just as we see the wind rustle the corn in *The Enigma of Kaspar Hauser*, so too do we see it rustle the long grass in *Grizzly Man*. This film features the bear whisperer Timothy Treadwell, who, like Kaspar Hauser, regarded humans as wolves. Treadwell was a wounded person, full of anger and disgust towards a society in which he could not find his place. He had sought recognition through a glittering media career, and when that failed he achieved fame by pursuing his passion for Alaska's wild nature and great bears. Whereas Kaspar Hauser became an object of fascination for nineteenth-century high society, Treadwell the bear whisperer featured on the more modern phenomenon of David Letterman's talk show, and there he told stories about dangerous people and sweet grey bears that were really just big pets. For thirteen summers he romanticized the wilderness and sought a feeling of continuity with the bears, until eventually they ate him. He believed in the harmony of the universe, a harmony that humans had destroyed – but here Herzog puts his foot down in the voiceover: 'I believe that the common denominator of the universe is not harmony, but chaos, hostility and murder.' While we watch footage of the bear that probably killed Treadwell, Herzog says:

> In all the faces of all the bears Treadwell filmed, I discover
> no kinship, no understanding, no mercy. I see only the
> overwhelming indifference of nature. To me, there is no such
> thing as a secret world of the bears. And this blank stare
> speaks only of a half-bored interest in food. But for Timothy
> Treadwell, this bear was a friend, a saviour.

Herzog is not indulging in simple mockery of Treadwell, for even though Treadwell had only pseudo-philosophical nonsense to impart regarding the bears' nature, his life provides an insight into human nature and our communities. Although there is a tendency in Herzog's early works to create an idyll out of the landscape, I think we should see them with *Grizzly Man* in mind. We long nostalgically for pre-human continuity but Nature is indifferent to humanity, and we cannot turn to it for help, even if our longing seems to offer a short respite. The author Emmanuel Carrère wrote in 1982 of Herzog's Kaspar Hauser that as a person he was in an '*eternal* prison' in his mortal body, and the sequences showing nature are mere 'transient nostalgia just like a corner of the sky seen through the prison bars'.[9]

Thus Herzog's landscapes are not dreamy romanticizations, but instead show human communities as constructions, fictions of continuity, laid over the state of nature like a thin layer of ice. We get nothing out of wishing we could revert to such a state, but the landscape images do offer the possibility of *something else* by revealing civilization as a construct that could potentially be constructed differently. When we see and consider the possibility of something else in Herzog's films, or perhaps the possibility of an *outside*, what is being gestured to is not something beyond this world, but this *one and only* world: the world that is to be found among our linguistic predicates in the tiny invisible and inaudible gaps in the spreadsheet of the truth of accountants. This distinction is essential if we are to understand Herzog's new images, the aim of which is not to suggest any kind of concrete solution that would only develop into another accountant's truth.

All the actors in *Even Dwarfs Started Small* are dwarfs. The film depicts a rebellion at an institution on the island of Lanzarote, but the chaotic revolt of the dwarfs lacks clear direction. Both the dramaturgy and the images are full of circular motifs, such as the motorbike above, which drives in circles without ever leaving the premises of the institution.

FOUR
THE IMPOSSIBILITY
OF DIRECT REVOLT

Even dwarfs start small

It all seems hopeless: for Kaspar Hauser, for Timothy Treadwell and for all the others in Herzog's gallery of characters, both the *useless ones* and the *conquerors of the useless*. If it's true that we are tragically condemned to fail in the existential scheme of things – we are going to die, and our potential for understanding is limited – one would think that Herzog would devote himself to fomenting a real social revolution here on Earth. We might expect him to throw in his lot with the left-wing filmmakers and students of the 1960s and '70s who shared his scepticism towards modern rationality and his anger at the oppression of weak minorities. But no: 'I never had an affinity for student revolts. They usually involved upper-class kids who were supposedly speaking for the working class,' he said in a German interview in 2010.[1] This was when the Germans were starting to rediscover him in earnest and to look back on his career. When I interviewed him after the Rogue Film School and asked him if his critique in the Kaspar Hauser film, for example, really had nothing in common with the wider left-wing project, he expanded on this point:

> Yes, okay, but my critique is more subtle and when I wasn't willing to say that I agreed with everything, I was quickly condemned as a fascist. And I disagreed with their analysis on a basic level. I had visited most parts of Germany, and it wasn't my impression that the whole nation was completely permeated with fascist sentiment. It was more complicated than that. It didn't seem like those students had any experience of the real world. They were all talking about liberating the working class. I asked: have any of you ever worked in a factory? Even for just an hour? No, none of them had. They just talked about their collective fantasies and had no idea about the reality.

Herzog had travelled too widely and seen too much of the world to romanticize the lower classes. He'd worked too hard to romanticize manual work, and he didn't believe in the hard-left analysis of Germany as a police state that had to be won over through a socialist revolution. In 1968 he refused to fall in line with the students' call for a boycott of the film festivals in Oberhausen and Berlin, and he screened *Signs of Life* there. While other directors supported the boycott of Cannes the same year, Herzog chose to write a short essay, 'Howling with Wolves' (Mit den Wölfen heulen), which was published in the German journal *Filmkritik*. In it, he called out what he saw as a herd mentality in politics that was trampling on a nuanced understanding of the world and of art; that people were being forced to choose sides in the name of a glorified truth. Those who elected not to howl with the wolves were counted among the sheep.

But Herzog also provoked his critics with a filmic riposte to his indictment by the left wing. While May 1968 was in full swing,

Herzog shot *Auch Zwerge haben klein angefangen* (*Even Dwarfs Started Small*), which quirkily parodies the sectarian milieux and political dreams of the left and right wings alike. In the film, a group of dwarfs at an institution on the island of Lanzarote foment a rebellion.[2] Laughing crazily, they carry out their revolt, but it proves to be meaningless, incompetent and, most of all, destructive. It is hard to see what the rebels are revolting against, because the head of the institution is also a dwarf, and they never leave the grounds of the institution. Instead, they drive the getaway vehicle around in circles in the middle of nowhere and carry out grotesque, meaningless actions such as smashing things up and starting fires. Eventually the meaninglessness descends into ritual, with the crucifixion of an ape. Slowly, the revolution devours its own children, as the revolutionary dwarfs demonstrably lack solidarity: they force the two smallest among them to get married and have sex, and they humiliate and kill a blind dwarf. At the other end of the political spectrum, the head of the institution has barricaded himself into his office with a hostage. He yells threats at the mob: they had better behave themselves and restore the semblance of order that reigned before the rebellion. It is also made clear that there is no help to be had from the world outside the complex. At one point a car drives past, but the driver turns out to be a dwarf who is lost and looking for directions. In the end, the head of the institution resorts to violence and turns out to be just as unreasonable and violent as the rebels.

Even Dwarfs Started Small led to death threats from the right wing and accusations of fascism from the left wing, which saw the film as ridiculing the Revolution. (It was around this time that Herzog began to be referred to as a fascist. Or rather 'fascistoid', as he corrected me in conversation: 'They had to invent a new word, because it was really difficult for them to paint me as a member of the right wing.')

Both right- and left-wing critics were justified in feeling that they had been targeted. The senseless insanity depicted in the

Images from *Even Dwarfs Started Small.* Werner Herzog points out that dwarfs have played an important role in German and Nordic folk tales from the Old Icelandic *Poetic Edda* and the earliest German heroic songs (*Heldenlieder*), to the opera of Richard Wagner and Günter Grass's *Die Blechtrommel* (*The Tin Drum*, 1959). At the Rogue Film School, the *Edda* is on the reading list – and in *Into the Inferno*, which was in post-production at the time of the Sixth Rogue Film School, Herzog travels to Iceland to read the original manuscript of the *Edda*.

film demonstrates that it is not just a question of supporting one political conviction or the other. The two political wings resemble each other in their unflinching demands that society be ordered in particular ways.

Bearing in mind its circular motifs and lack of resolution, it makes sense to read *Even Dwarfs Started Small* as a revolt against all forms of grand construction that purport to lead us towards a defined future social order. The film ends with a caricature of the truth claims of both political currents, when the head of the institution makes a megalomaniacal attempt to bring nature itself into line. He raises his arm in a fascistic salute that points towards a tree, whose branch extends in a similar gesture. It is an absurd competition to determine who can hold their arm up for longest, to determine who is in possession of power and truth. The scene ends without a winner. Instead, we see complete social breakdown in the image of a pathetic camel whose utter confusion about which leg it should stand on is resolved when it shits itself in a panic, soundtracked by the manic, ear-splitting laughter of a dwarf. When *Even Dwarfs Started Small* is over, we understand that the establishing shots with which the film initially mapped out the various shooting locations were just an ironic gesture: there is no panorama, no correct position from where we can direct the spotlight of knowledge. The same strategy also makes it clear that there is no easily identifiable locus of power that we can rebel against, nor a grand, pure form of freedom that we can ever hope to achieve. Herzog's works speak of freedom, but in a voice that trembles, because there are no absolute solutions, and no 'outside' of the system.

Woyzeck and Stroszek

In the films he made in the 1970s, Herzog continued his exploration of the complexities of power. With *Even Dwarfs Started Small* he had rejected overarching solutions and grand narratives (or perhaps in this case 'big' narratives), and in particular he opposed the Marxist historical philosophy that insists history has an inherent intentionality or meaning that is fulfilled when we are ready for it, at the end of history. With his films *Woyzeck* (1979) and *Stroszek* (1977), he shows how power operates on the micro level and how difficult it is to revolt against it directly, because both power itself and the possibility of resistance to it are more complex than they seem.

Woyzeck is about a good-hearted nineteenth-century soldier who, in order to feed his family, volunteers to participate in a medical experiment that has a severe impact on his health. The little man is broken by the system (science and the social order), while his wife, Eva, throws herself at a handsome major who can pay her more attention than the ailing Woyzeck. The penny finally drops for the little soldier and he confronts the major, but instead of winning his desired vindication he is beaten and left humiliated. In his frustration, he ends up stabbing his wife to death in a fit of rage.

Stroszek centres on the harmless lunatic Bruno Stroszek, whose name was abbreviated by the justice system to Bruno S. The character is played by the real-life Bruno S. (Bruno Schleinstein, 1932–2010), and the fictional story draws on real elements from the street musician's own life. Ever since Bruno was abandoned at the age of three by his prostitute mother, he had ricocheted between the assorted social institutions that define modernity: special schools, juvenile detention centres and psychiatric institutions. As a child during the Nazi period, he experienced how the mentally ill and disabled were subject to forms of treatment that were directly disciplinary; as an adult, his body and mind were subject to the more indirect forms of discipline of the post-war era. *Stroszek* opens with Bruno being released from prison – again. But this time, he decides, it's going to be different. He moves to the United States with his girlfriend Eva, a prostitute, and a friend, the old eccentric Scheitz. The trio dream of freedom, but the dream proves much harder to realize than they had expected.

Whereas Herzog's version of *Woyzeck* is very faithful to the drama of 1837 by Georg Büchner that inspired it, *Stroszek* can be regarded as freestyle Herzog. But the two stories play off one another as two different perspectives on a broader theme of the little man who gets clamped in the vice of existence and throttled until he can take no more. (In the foreword to the Danish edition of Büchner's *Lenz & Woyzeck*, the latter is described as the first example of a representative of the masses in literary history. It's argued that Woyzeck should actually be read not as a name, 'but as a sign; even more modern than Kafka's K, Woyzeck is an X, an *anybody*, a soldier in the service of the state and a guinea pig in the service of science', an idea that is updated by Herzog for the present day with the figure of Bruno S. in *Stroszek*.[3])

Bruno S. does not commit murder, but he arguably goes further than Woyzeck. While he doesn't fall into the clutches of science and the old hierarchical social order, he does get trapped on a capitalist merry-go-round, and the American dream becomes

Klaus Kinski as the eponymous little soldier in Herzog's film adaptation of Georg Büchner's drama *Woyzeck*.

a nightmare when he can no longer pay the bills. His girlfriend leaves him and the bank repossesses his trailer. Despite his kind heart, there is no place in society for Bruno S; that is made very clear when his possessions are auctioned off by the bank, in a sale conducted by the real-life world champion auctioneer Ralph Wade.

Herzog met Wade in the context of the documentary *How Much Wood Would a Woodchuck Chuck . . .* (1976), a film that betrays a fascination with what we could call a *poetry of capitalism*, whereby the auctioneers have refined their sales lingo into such a high-tempo form that it is more or less a song. Herzog recounts how the best auctioneers perform lung-expanding exercises no less demanding than those undertaken by opera singers, and that the best of them would be able to perform the whole of *Hamlet* in under fifteen minutes. It is at this grotesque tempo that Bruno's things are snatched away from him, bid by bid, leaving him entirely without possessions and thus worthless as far as capitalism is concerned. When Bruno and Scheitz protest, or rather question the etiquette, the auctioneer shakes his head and says he cannot understand them. Bruno's feelings and dreams cannot be expressed within the prevailing discourse and are dismissed as noise or babbling. The bailiff and the auctioneer accept no responsibility for the dissolution of the little German community: it's out of our hands, they say. They gloss over their quite concrete lack of compassion by referring to social structures that they say they cannot change.

Film researchers in the United States such as Timothy Corrigan see *Stroszek* as a critique of the American Dream and the ways in which the forces of capitalism smash the dream to pieces. That kind of interpretation seems sound enough, but, just as *Woyzeck* is about more than the miserable conditions of the nineteenth-century working class, so too does *Stroszek* offer insights that have more universal resonance. The film is about how people's illusions are shattered when they try to operate within structures that neither accommodate them nor let them go.

Entangled in life – and the rejection of the idiot

Woyzeck experiences the kind of direct discipline that was more prominent in nineteenth-century Eastern Europe than in 1970s America. He is moulded by school and by the military and potentially for factory work, so that even his movements have something forced about them. He is crushed and crushed again in a deliberate process of humiliation, and eventually explodes. In *Stroszek*, Bruno is also crushed, but by a different technique of regulating power that seems much harder to react against. When Eva, his girlfriend, starts selling her body again, and the bailiff bangs on the door, Bruno says that it feels as though he is being excommunicated; that he is being treated as though he doesn't exist. Eva retorts that here in the United States no one is kicking him. 'No, not physically,' answers Bruno, but mentally, he is still being trampled on. In the institutions where he was placed during the Nazi period, the violence was at least direct and the attacks were obvious and intelligible. If Bruno wet his bed, the staff would make him stand with arms outstretched, holding the sheet out of the window until it was dry. If he got tired and his arms drooped, they would beat him. But at least that was an explicit kind of punishment; everyone could see what was going on. These days nobody hits you, but the same damage is done in a quiet, polite, insidious way, and 'it's much worse,' as Bruno says.

It is remarkable that at the very same time that Herzog was making films about the complexities of power and resistance, the French philosopher Michel Foucault was writing his major works (*Discipline and Punish* and *The Will to Knowledge*). These books deal with the development of techniques of power starting from the explicit exertion of power in the Middle Ages, with the sovereign's cruel, corporal punishments of his inferiors in show trials; over time these were superseded by a more internalized discipline, whereby power does not punish with death, but shapes life using techniques of the self, to enhance productiveness. Foucault rejects the juridical theory of power typical of grand narratives, the most marked trait of which is perhaps a negative view of the concept of power. Instead of being something concrete and substantial that a class or person has and can wield over others, thinks Foucault, power in modern society is exercised in a network of productive relations, in which cause and effect are rather complex and diffuse phenomena. Thus power does not have a clearly localizable centre, from where it functions hierarchically upwards and downwards. Rather, it is a ubiquitous strategy of rationalization in society, within which one is always situated. These techniques of power have moved outwards from the military, where *Woyzeck* plays out, and from the institutions where Bruno S. grows up in *Stroszek*, into the rest of society, permeating every aspect of life.

Foucault's example of the techniques of power par excellence is the panopticon, a prison construction designed by the philosopher Jeremy Bentham (1748–1832). Within it, the inmate can potentially be surveilled at all times, with the effect that the inmates start to surveil themselves, because they never know when someone might be watching them. They get a modern soul installed, so to speak, which enables them to control themselves. This is a form of control and oppression that is difficult to resist. Foucault writes of 'bio-power'; whereas explicit punishment and possible death were important tools in earlier eras, in the modern period of bio-power this shifts to a focus on keeping the body alive and regulating it. He writes in *The Will to Knowledge*: 'The old power of death that symbolized sovereign power was now carefully supplanted by the administration of bodies and the calculated management of life.' For the power that takes charge of life is concerned with 'distributing the living in the domain of value and utility. Such a power has to qualify, measure, appraise, and hierarchize, rather than display itself in its *murderous splendour*.'[4]

While the prison is the most effective modern institution of discipline, in principle the same observations can be made of other social institutions. We surveil, illuminate and investigate every corner. Werner Herzog is not a poststructuralist. He is sceptical of most theory, which can after all very easily descend into just another example of the truth of accountants, and can overshadow life if left to its own devices. However, some of his analyses of the essence of power resemble Foucault's, and while Foucault's scholarship on the history of ideas is now standard reading for university students, Herzog's very similar social analysis and critique actually pre-date Foucault's.

Herzog's critique of modern surveillance culture is expressed cinematically in both his exploration of the entanglement of power and knowledge in repressive pedagogy in *The Enigma of Kaspar Hauser* and his examination of disciplinary power in *Woyzeck* and *Stroszek*. Recently, he has taken a more direct approach to this kind of critique; for example, in a conversation with Paul Holdengräber at New York Public Library in 2007, under the rubric 'Was the Twentieth Century a Mistake?', he discussed the catastrophes of the two World Wars, over-population, the climate crisis and the extinction of languages and cultures, but also the overexposure both of the world and of people's interior lives. He picked up this theme again in a similar public conversation in 2008 in Valencia, where he was preparing a production of Wagner's opera *Parsifal*. There, he compared the interrogation of the modern soul to the Spanish Inquisition and identified the advent of psychoanalysis and excessive introspection in the service of truth-seeking as the single greatest catastrophe of our catastrophic century:

> I think that the development of psychoanalysis was a huge mistake. A mistake of such amplitude that in many ways it can be compared to the Spanish Inquisition. The goal of the Spanish Inquisition was to root out the last pockets of non-Christians, Muslims, Moors, etc. To interrogate them and torture them to reveal the most essential truths about their faith. The results were catastrophic. One should not do

such a thing. If you carry a conviction or a deep faith,
I could never countenance doing anything to persuade you
to reveal it to me. I would never challenge you in such a
way. On the contrary, I would respect who and what you
are. I would let what you are stand absolutely untouched.
One must never try to expose the darkest nooks, the deepest
crannies of our souls. This was one of the greatest wrongs
of our civilization. There's a metaphor I have often used: if
you live in an apartment, and every single corner of it is lit,
that apartment becomes uninhabitable. Those humans who
expose the darkest corners of their souls to the light become
uninhabitable humans. I've never been able to be with a
woman who didn't have some kind of secret or mystery.
I've never been able to live with anyone who strives to say
it all, who thinks that this is the basis of a relationship. On
the contrary, that's the basis for murder. That's how it is.
Faced with that kind of attitude, the only answer would
be *murder*.[5]

This is in the same oppositional spirit in which we have to understand the oft-cited Herzog dictum that he never dreams – and
when he occasionally does, it's about something prosaic like eating
a sandwich, nothing that can be analysed with any degree of seriousness. Another Herzog dictum is that he never looks at himself
in the mirror: 'Yes, of course, I do when I'm shaving. But never to
study my identity or my soul.'[6]

Herzog is sceptical about the increased focus on the Self that
makes it possible to administer people in a way corresponding to
the truth of accountants. Just as *cinéma vérité* strives for objective
truth in the context of documentary, the psychologist is a kind
of modern priest, drilling into the individual person in search of
truth. As always with Herzog, it's paradoxical that he himself is
such a skilful interviewer (we'll come back to that in the next chapter). But if we read his critique in the spirit of Foucault, on the one

hand, the intensified knowledge of the subject and the illumination of its deepest recesses facilitate an increased individualization. On the other hand, such knowledge also entails an increasing objectivization of the subject, because it becomes easier to classify and fix individuals within clearly defined identities, which in turn can be arranged in a binary schema: productive/unproductive, sick/healthy, good/evil – and, in practice, the Herzogian distinction between *useful* and *useless*.

Even allowing for the vociferous accusations of fascism from the left wing in the 1960s and '70s, and the criticism of Klaus Kinski's superhuman characters in *Aguirre* and *Fitzcarraldo*, my overarching impression of Herzog's oeuvre is that it is the *useless ones* that he cares about. He is also all too painfully aware that they have no chance of direct revolt, nor does he harbour any illusion that the minorities would prove to be any nicer than the majority, should they come to power. The two categories are interrelated; in terms of identity, the useless ones are inextricably linked with the useful ones.

In *Woyzeck*, science, the army and the upper class are ostensibly responsible for Woyzeck's problems, and he is also guilty of reacting to his defeat with passionate aggression. He challenges the army major directly, but the point here is that Woyzeck weaves himself even more tightly into the identification mechanisms of bio-power through his own counter-reaction. His aggression makes him a criminal, or at best a revolutionary, but it is only in relation to the extant power that such a revolutionary identity exists. Thus Woyzeck does not break free through his revolt, but entangles himself even more inextricably in the mesh of the truth of accountants in which he feels so trapped.

In *Stroszek*, Bruno S. has no desire for confrontation, at least to begin with. He has travelled to the United States precisely to extricate himself from the oppression he experienced in Europe. He tried to create a parallel society that was not in opposition to

Crushed by the capitalist system, Bruno S. and little Scheitz in *Stroszek* go straight into battle against what they believe to be the system: a bank. But, since the bank is closed, they rob a barber's. Bruno S. and Scheitz escape with $32 and go straight to the supermarket across the road to buy groceries. The police arrive and arrest Scheitz, but Bruno gives them the slip with his frozen turkey under his arm.

Some very well-known Herzogian motifs pour forth in the grand finale of *Stroszek*. On the run from power, Bruno S. steals a pick-up truck and drives to a remote Native American reservation that has its own amusement park. The car he is driving resembles the car from *Even Dwarfs Started Small*, the one that the dwarfs leave to drive in circles within the grounds of their institution. Bruno drives his truck in the same pattern, and sets fire to it. In the background is a chairlift into which he climbs and rides round and round – until eventually a gunshot is heard. Bruno S. has committed suicide.

the established one, and which only wanted to be allowed to exist without conflict. But this kind of liberation is not possible, either. As the Italian philosopher Giorgio Agamben points out:

> The state can recognize any claim for identity . . . What the State cannot tolerate in any way, however, is that singularities form a community without affirming an identity, that humans co-belong without any representable condition of belonging . . . For the State, therefore, what is important is never the singularity as such, but only its inclusion in some identity, whatever identity.[7]

Agamben, who has built on aspects of Foucault's work on bio-power, claims that it is a fundamental task of Western political communities to distinguish between naked life and politically qualified life, where the latter is the right and the good life. All Herzog's *useless* figures are, just like anyone else, naked life – simply physically existing, as an animal or a plant does – but in order to qualify to take part in the political community, the community demands that one distance oneself from the singular and accept the definitions of the good life set by the truth of accountants. Conceptually, says Agamben, it is a matter of an *inclusive exclusion*,

Chickens, according to Herzog, are the stupidest and most wicked of all animals: 'Try looking intensely into the eyes of a chicken, and intense stupidity will stare right back at you.'[8] In his early films chickens are often humiliated, and a detail of the Herzog Myth is that one of his films, *Spiel im Sand* (*Game in the Sand*, 1964), has never been screened in public because the child actors in it were too cruel to a hen. This sequence in *Stroszek*, claims Herzog, was invented during the shoot – right at the last minute. None of the crew members liked the idea of filming animals in cages, so Herzog had to shoot the scene himself. It remains one of the more famous and affecting scenes in his oeuvre. It has also become notorious as allegedly the last film the Joy Division singer-songwriter, Ian Curtis, watched before he took his own life in 1980.

whereby the political life is defined positively in relation to the life it is not. It is thus crucial to distinguish between right and wrong lives, between the useful and useless; *the useless ones* are included in society only by virtue of their exclusion.

Herzog also investigated this idea in his short film *Massnahmen gegen Fanatiker* (*Precautions against Fanatics*) as early as 1969. In quasi-documentary fashion, we explore life at a horse-racing track, where the horse owners feel it is necessary to protect the animals against fanatics; from our point of view, though, the owners themselves seem to be the fanatics, conjuring up an imaginary external enemy. We meet a man who sneaks in to protect the horses. He seems nice, very much like Kaspar Hauser and Bruno S., but the horse owners do not understand his apparently unmotivated deed. What is he up to? His motives cannot be discerned, and thus he seems to be a fanatic. We meet other people at the racecourse who may have permission to be there, or maybe they don't. They all make claims about why they are there and what they are doing. They all have a place to stand, a function, and an identity to defend: for example, a man who is defending the racecourse's fence from fanatical spectators, although we can't see the threat he describes. Their community revolves around the imaginary perils and safety measures that all the characters feel are necessary. Now and again a one-armed man appears who asks people to go away; he is trying to protect the horses and the track, too, but in his last remark he reveals that the intense focus on well-defined identities and positions trumps real presence and insight: 'You're going to have to admit that I'm here too,' he says (although without any trace of hope in his voice). The various individual lives disappear into the crude categories of the truth of accountants, the categories that constitute community, and those people (and things) that fall outside the spreadsheet's cells are included only insofar as they are excluded.

Bruno S. in *Stroszek* is able neither to break free nor to become a properly included member of the community. When his last remaining possession, the trailer, is towed away before his eyes and before the camera, his life, and the image itself, are stripped of their central motif. But Herzog holds the shot, which is now an empty frame suggestive of a mental landscape: naked life mirrored in the denuded flatlands of Wisconsin.

At first, Bruno and his friend Scheitz make the same mistake as Woyzeck. They obviously think they can react by wresting themselves free. When they start to notice the net of power around them, they go right into battle with what they *think* constitutes systemic power: they decide to rob a bank.

They are destined to fail. With Bruno sporting a laughably oversized Stetson and little Scheitz wielding a rifle that is far too long for him, they look exactly like what they actually are: partners in incompetence; inadequate in the face of the world they have to live in. Anyway, the bank is closed for lunch, so they are reduced to robbing a barber's for a measly $32, and then they visit the supermarket across the road. The police arrive and arrest Scheitz, but Bruno manages to escape (with a turkey under his arm). Woyzeck's next step was to murder his wife, Eva, but Bruno's Eva is long gone, and his reaction seems more like an act of defiance against the universe. In the wake of the failed robbery it dawns on him that he has no chance of escape, but nor is he inclined to let power conceal its murderousness under a facade of administrative procedures. As Herzog said in Valencia, all-encompassing illumination, and the ensuing administration of the individual, inevitably leads to murder. And, as the philosopher Gilles Deleuze writes in his book on Foucault, 'Life becomes resistance to power when power takes life as its object.'[9] Bruno S. stages his own idiotic sacrifice.

In a stolen breakdown truck, Bruno drives to a Native American reservation that has been converted into an amusement park. One of the amusements is a doll's house containing hutches with animals in them. When money is inserted into the slots the animals are forced – through reward or punishment – to perform excruciating circus tricks. He stuffs coins into all the slots. A chicken plays the piano with its beak (when grains of corn fall on to the keys); another dances (on a hot plate) to a looped recording of a manic harmonica.

It's a trailer park version of a Dionysian orgy, with substitute maenads raving in their hutches. Bruno S. climbs into the chairlift and rides round and round, until at last we hear a shot. We already recognize that tragic revolving dynamic from *Even Dwarfs Started Small*. For Bruno, it all ends with an idiotically circular rejection of the society that ostracized him. We could say that his revolt is more successful than the others – not only because Eva doesn't have to die, as her namesake does in *Woyzeck*, but because the forces of order arrive and are revealed as embarrassingly inept. A life has been lost (a life that ought to have been allowed to continue, either as a productive life or as an inclusive exclusion), yet they cannot even manage to stop the chairlift or get the chicken to stop dancing. Maybe they're even going to have to temporarily cut the power to the amusement park?

In any case, the revolt seems hopeless. Power has been challenged and even made visible for a moment, but the electrical power will soon be restored; meanwhile, Bruno has lost his life. In his works, Herzog applauds the urge to revolt. He embraces his characters' sense of a world that often *ought* to be different, but he refuses to accept that the great, direct revolutions are the way forward. He wants something more than merely to replace one truth of accountants with another. Bruno's revolt is the closest we get to rejecting the premises of the truth of accountants, but, since his story seems to present suicide as the only viable exit strategy, we urgently need to identify other forms of resistance.

Shoes à la Herzog in Les Blank's film *Werner Herzog Eats His Shoe*, 1980.

FIVE
ECSTATIC TRUTH:
A COOKBOOK FOR
THE REVOLUTIONARY
FILMMAKER

Eating a shoe – fomenting disorder

Herzog's films are full of rebellious souls. The most famous of them is Timothy Treadwell in *Grizzly Man*, whose revolt against modern civilization in its entirety is driven by his sense of being sidelined by it. In mainstream society he is *useless*, a failed actor and an alcoholic. In his fantasy world he is a 'kind warrior', who not only fights for the bears, but fights *with* the bears, and wants to *be* a bear. His fight for the bears is an example, in its own way, of a *useless conquest*, since Herzog makes it clear in the film that there are no poachers in the area. But the desire to be a bear is a pure Herzogian *conquest of the useless*, a project so ambitious as to be ungraspable. Of course Treadwell can't become a bear; like Stroszek's revolt in Herzog's debut feature, *Signs of Life*, this ambition is 'tragically doomed to fail'. But Herzog sympathizes with the compulsion; it reminds him of his own obsession with cinema, and he knows only too well that sense of longing for escape from a world full of chaos, hostility and murder.

In *Gasherbrum – Der leuchtende Berg* (*The Dark Glow of the Mountains*), one of his many films in which mountains play a prominent role, Herzog says he sometimes wishes that he could just start walking and walk to the ends of the Earth, with only a couple of good dogs for company. The final images of *Grizzly Man* are reminiscent of that vision of escape. In his rage at an unjust world, Treadwell consoles himself with a long walk, completely alone, away from the camera. With only a couple of good grizzly bears for company. For a time, he can imagine a world free of man-made problems, existing in harmony with nature. But in the real world, bears are not good; they *are* nature, and are therefore beyond good or evil. They're not interested in morals, ethics or fame. They're only interested in food. And in the end they eat Treadwell, too.

Treadwell's project was doomed to failure, just like Fitzcarraldo's desire to disappear into a world of music deep in the jungle. You can't escape just like that. We see the same in *Woyzeck*, *Stroszek* and *Even Dwarfs Started Small*. It's simply not possible to revolt and escape the human condition and the power relations within which we are situated. But what can we do, then? How are we to challenge the truth of accountants? Is all resistance futile? Perhaps. But nonetheless, Herzog has a recipe to offer. It goes like this:

Cookbook for revolutionary filmmakers
Chaussures Confit (Slow-roasted Shoes)

Ingredients
1 pair of leather shoes, preferably worn-out walking boots
of Bavarian origin

2 bulbs garlic
4 red onions
1 bunch fresh parsley
1 bunch fresh rosemary
duck fat

water

salt

hot sauce (Tabasco can be substituted with a strong
Mexican salsa, for example Cholula or Valentina)

Method

Brush any dirt off the shoes and remove the laces (but set
them aside). Stuff each shoe with 1 bulb of garlic, 2 red onions
and a handful of parsley. Season with generous quantities of
hot sauce. Lace up the shoes again and tie them tightly. Place
the shoes in a heavy-based pot. Add equal quantities of duck
fat and hot water until the shoes are completely covered by
the liquid. Add a bunch of rosemary to the liquid and season
with salt and more hot sauce to taste. Cook on a low heat for
around five hours.

To serve

The shoes can be served like pig's trotters – with beans, chilli
and lots of chopped onion on top, seasoned with garlic and
herbs. Or they can be eaten straight from the pan, in the
presence of an audience if wished, served with a cold beer.
The soles should not be eaten; treat them as the equivalent of
bones in poultry.[1]

If the shoe fits – eat it? In 1978, with help from the chef Alice
Waters of local restaurant Chez Panisse, Werner Herzog cooked his
Bavarian walking boots in duck fat, hot sauce, garlic and herbs and
ate them on stage at the University of California Theatre, watched
by an audience of UC Berkeley film students.

The shoe-eating stunt was an homage to Herzog's protégé
Errol Morris, who had completed his debut film, *Gates of Heaven*
(1978), but was struggling to get it distributed. The 'happening'
was an indirect revolt against the inflexible U.S. film distribution
system, and can be seen as a clarion call for the film industry to

mount a more effective resistance. As a performance, it can be reconstructed via Les Blank's short film *Werner Herzog Eats His Shoe* and a few articles.[2]

It's hard to pin down the persona that Herzog adopted up there on the stage at the UC Theatre. With his receding hairline, grey suit and moustache, he looks like a mixture of a mad scientist, a porn star and a 1970s FBI agent. But he also exudes a kind of messianic charisma, and he tries to instil some audacity in the young students: 'Give us adequate images. We need adequate images,' he says. 'Go out and steal film stock, steal a camera, and sneak into a film lab. Just do it,' he instructs them like a guerrilla leader, while bite-sized chunks of the roasted shoe are passed round the auditorium like communion wafers of courage to a congregation of revolutionaries.

In many ways that's exactly what the gathering was, although cinema's war is not one that can be won with guns and explosives. That said, Herzog once suggested, with a glint in his eye, that 'our grandchildren will blame us for not having tossed hand-grenades into TV stations' to protest against the tired images of adverts, series and talk shows that bombard our collective consciousness.[3] But even the most powerful weapons in this battle are 'not of significant calibre': the endgame of the battle is to expand the colour spectrum on our shared palette of images and languages, so that we have more nuances to choose from when we paint our self-image as individuals and as a society.

There are various accounts of how Herzog came up with the idea of eating his shoes. He himself claims that he had promised Morris that he would do it if Morris ever succeeded in converting his creative ideas into a concrete project – and Herzog is a man of

Werner Herzog after the happening at the University of California Theatre, eating the leftovers of his shoe in a more relaxed outfit. Herzog reminisced that cooking in duck fat made the leather too hard, so it had to be cut up with poultry shears.[4]

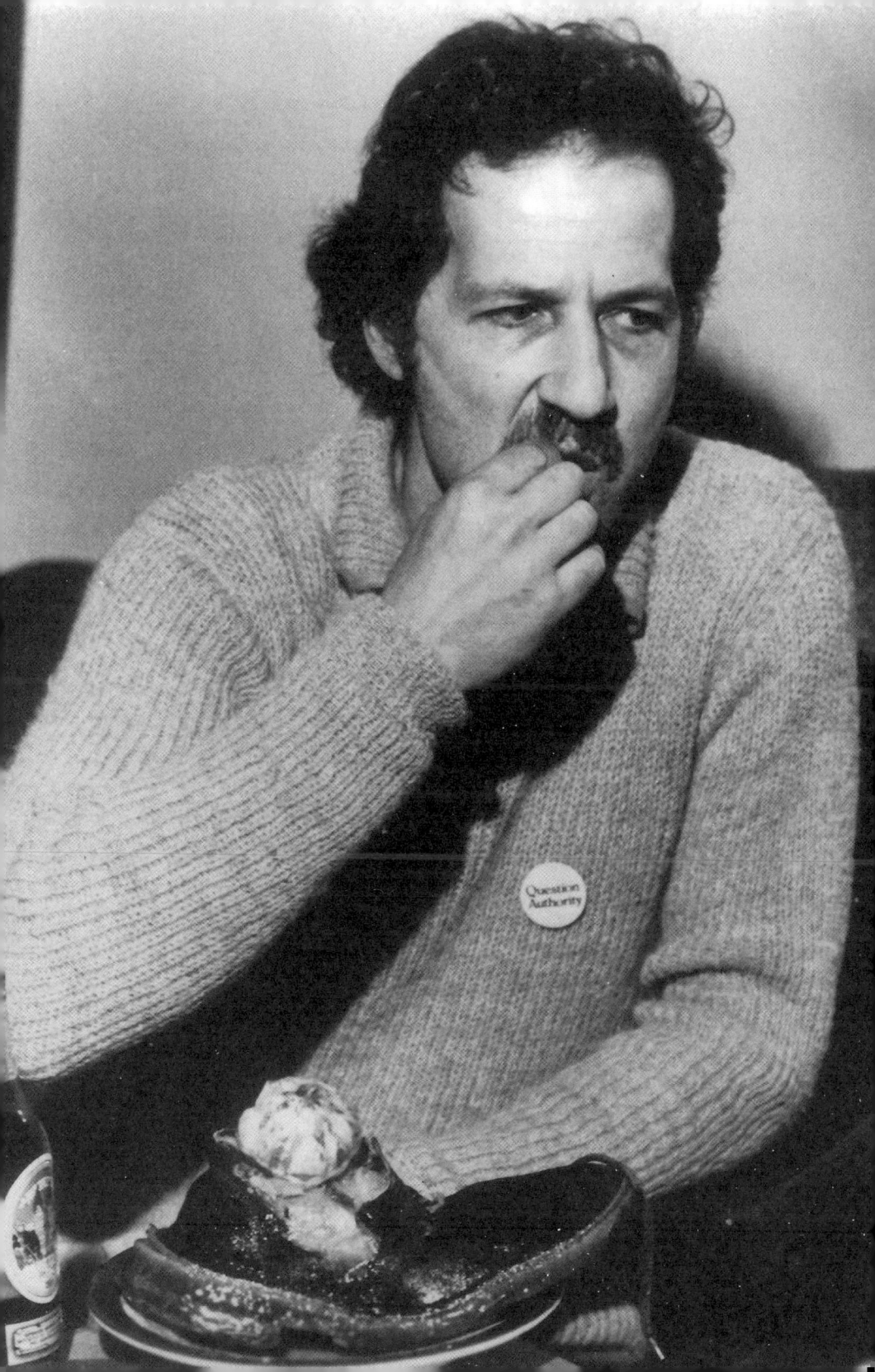

his word. Over time he has refined his absurd promises and quid pro quos into one of his methodologies, a form of performance in the art project that his persona has become. Let's take three examples:

a. *A university essay in exchange for immortality*
Signs of Life is based on a story by Achim von Arnim, in which the main character is called Francoeur. In Herzog's film he is called Stroszek. Herzog has said that the name stems from his time at university in Munich, where he once asked a fellow student if he would write his history essay for him. Why should I? asked the other student. What's in it for me? 'I have no money,' replied Herzog, 'but I will make your name immortal.' The student agreed. His name was Hauke Stroszek, and Herzog repaid his debt twice over, since he also made Stroszek the title of his cryptic film of 1977.

b. *Total anarchy in exchange for a dive into a cactus*
During the shoot of *Even Dwarfs Started Small*, Herzog made and kept a promise to throw himself from a ramp down onto a large cactus, if all the extras could manage to get through the challenging take featuring flames, violence and manic anarchy without further casualties (one dwarf had already caught fire). Whenever Herzog reminisces about this incident, he explains laconically that the problem with diving into a cactus is not the jump itself, but having to live with the spines afterwards. It was never possible to have them removed, and he has had to accept them as an integral part of his body.

c. *Elevating the banal*
One winter morning on the banks of the river Vils, during the production of *Heart of Glass*, one problem

after another arose during the shooting of a scene that should have been straightforward. Herzog promised the tired film crew that if they got the difficult take in the bag then, in exchange, he would dive into the freezing water and swim under the ice to the far bank and back again. Their energy restored, the crew renewed their efforts to complete the scene, and Herzog immediately stripped off and kept his promise. The American author Alan Greenberg, who was there at the time, knew that Herzog was not a particularly strong swimmer and asked him quietly how he had managed it. Herzog revealed that there was a layer of oxygen between the ice and the water, so luckily he hadn't really needed to swim. He just made his way across by grappling with the underside of the ice and keeping his nose in the narrow pocket of air.

A barter completely out of proportion. An absurd vow fulfilled. A dangerous reward assayed to elevate a banal situation into a matter of life or death. These are all exaggerated promises that have the air of *conquests of the useless*, and they also throw into sharp, shivering relief the distinction between speech act and performance. It is in relation to these stories that we should understand Herzog's roasted shoes.

Herzog eats his shoes, or, more precisely, his walking boots. In his opinion, it is when walking that a person is most present in his own body and in the fabric of the world; it is in such situations that the human has the greatest freedom to think independently. More cinematically, the shoes are a reference to one of film history's best-known scenes, from *The Gold Rush* (1925), in which Charlie Chaplin eats his shoe. The shoe eaten by Chaplin's little tramp was a prop made of soft liquorice, whereas Herzog couldn't have made it more obvious that he was eating a real shoe. If Chaplin's shoe was melt-in-the-mouth, Herzog's was as hard and sharp as plastic,

In 2003 Timothy Treadwell was killed by the bears he loved. He filmed more than 100 hours of his own video footage, which Herzog used as the bulk of *Grizzly Man*. At the Rogue Film School Herzog told us that the film took 29 days from the first day of filming to the first rough cut, then only nine days to edit. 'Make decisions fast, don't let waste accumulate: we're filmmakers, not garbage collectors.'

and had to be cut up with poultry shears. There is no doubt that it was quite a mouthful, and a painful one at that.

To eat the inedible is to tear up our ideas about the relationship between language and the world. It scrambles the connections between concrete reality and the words and images we use every day without thinking about them. In our approach to language we are just as naive as Timothy Treadwell, striking out towards the horizon with his bears, blithely assuming a seamless bond between his perception of the world and the world as it is.

All grown-ups ought to eat a shoe every so often, Herzog has said, or do something along the same lines, something that society sees as crazy – because it's good for the heart.[5] We call it 'making a scene' when we break the agreed norms of proper behaviour in public; making a scene is irritating, or may perhaps provoke laughter, but in any case it poses questions about the way we have organized our community. When we say 'I'll eat my hat if . . .', we are preparing to make a scene. We're betting our communicative honour that the words we use about the world correspond to the actual world. And if it should transpire that we are wrong, then we've offered a humiliating, masochistic, public spectacle as penance. The expression 'I'll eat my hat' suggests that linguistic credibility can be re-established only if we use a daft physical act to bind the statement up with the world again. After the ritual speech act we can say: Well, he's a man of his word, and let's say no more about it.

Herzog tries to push this move to extremes. By making a scene he has no wish to reconnect the statement with the world, but rather to shake up the relationship between them and to reveal that there is always a gap between words and things; that language is inadequate in relation to the world, much as Treadwell's conception of the bears' world was inadequate. And if language is not naturally anchored in the world, what does that say about our social order and social systems?

But is Herzog's performance even successful? Isn't it the case that the world just stays exactly the same afterwards, and let's say no more about it?

Even during the project, Herzog already had his doubts. This is making me look like a clown, he says to Les Blank in *Werner Herzog Eats His Shoe*. That was not meant as an attack on Blank's filmmaking, just a recognition that when the documentary images of Herzog's shoe-eating reach the mainstream media, he will be assigned to the boxes on the accountants' spreadsheet of truth: either as a weird countercultural phenomenon or just as the clown of the day indulging in a media stunt. This was what had happened with his cactus dive. The nuances get lost if taken out of context: nuances such as humour and seriousness, sincerity, love, the critical sting in the tail.

If direct revolt is impossible, and if even well-executed, critically engaged filmmaking is not enough, where does that leave cinema? Blank asks Herzog about this. What do you want with your art? What can it do?

Herzog is surprised by the direct line of questioning and mumbles a bit under his moustache. He eventually formulates an answer: film can't start a revolution, but it can change our perspective on things, give us the kind of insight from which something valuable might grow. Twenty years later, in *The Minnesota Declaration*, he had a better answer: 'There are deeper strata of truth in cinema [than the truth of accountants], and there is such a thing as *poetic, ecstatic truth*. It is mysterious and elusive, and can be reached only through fabrication and imagination and stylization.' This poetic, ecstatic truth is, like the shoe-eating, a kind of awareness that the truth of accountants is not the only or final truth. That the way we have organized our society, the ways in which we have identified positions and characters, is not determined by some natural order of things, but could be otherwise. But we cannot reveal this by revolting directly, because our resistance would then be identified *qua* resistance, and thereby rendered harmless. We must therefore create disorder through 'fabrication and imagination and stylization'.

In the modern period, art has been regarded as having particular potential to create this kind of disorder. Theodor W. Adorno has been an influential advocate of this idea, and his writings were quite literally proclaimed as key texts underpinning the New German Cinema by its leaders, Alexander Kluge and Edgar Reitz. In §143 of his *Minima Moralia*, Adorno writes, 'The task of art today is to bring chaos into order,' and in the same paragraph: 'Art is magic, delivered from the lie of being truth.'[6] According to Adorno, then, art offers a distinctive space in which what Herzog calls a more poetic, ecstatic truth can play out, because it does not have to be truth. In his *Ästhetische Theorie* (*Aesthetic Theory*, 1970), Adorno writes that art is both 'autonomous and *fait social*'; it is both an independent sphere that evades society's tendency to think in terms of the truth of accountants, and historically conditioned, just like everything else in this world (*fait social*).[7]

The composer Florian Fricke (Popol Vuh) worked closely with Werner Herzog during the first twenty years of Herzog's career. Here he is seen in a cameo role as a pianist in *Signs of Life* (1968).

In *Signs of Life*, the existential soldier Stroszek is seen walking down the street. He feels lost, uneasy, but doesn't understand why. After all, he is stationed in a quiet, peaceful place well away from the war. He suddenly hears music – Chopin – from behind a door, opens the door a little and looks in. A German soldier is sitting there playing, without his boots on.

The soldier invites Stroszek inside. For a time, we enter a world that is separated a little from the one outside the open door. The music being played resonates with Stroszek, who has difficulty finding words to express his feelings and is misunderstood by his comrades. 'Perhaps you think this music is not appropriate for this place,' says the pianist, whose role is played by the composer Florian Fricke. 'It is different, it is dangerous. Chopin himself was wicked. He was unreliable. The only thing one could be sure of was that he coughed up blood.' Stroszek leaves. Perhaps he has gained some kind of insight, but he is not sure what it is.

'Art works detach themselves from the empirical world and bring forth another world, one opposed to the empirical world as if this other world too were an autonomous entity,' writes Adorno.[8] Art is autonomous because it is subject to its own law of form, such that the empirical material from this world undergoes a restructuring in the artwork. This restructuring reveals the mendacity of existence, that gap between words and things – the gap in which Herzog ate his shoes. In its critique, art gestures towards a closing of this gap, a reconciliation of the divide. That is of course what Timothy Treadwell and Stroszek alike are dreaming of when they foment rebellion, but, just as they are tragically doomed to fail, the artwork's potential to heal the world is also a mirage. The reconciliation can never be achieved. Nonetheless, Adorno thinks that art, as the negation of society's dominant order, can say something objective about that society. Like the incomprehensible music that Stroszek encounters in *Signs of Life*, art can give voice to what is silent – the suffering and liberation that are not unique to the experience of a particular German soldier during the Second World

War, but universal conditions for modern humanity. It was these conditions that Treadwell rebelled against in vain, and, as Herzog says in *Grizzly Man*, it is witnessing human pain that gives his films value:

> Treadwell is gone. The argument about how wrong or right he was disappears into the distance, into a fog. What remains is his footage. And while we watch the animals in their joys of being, in their grace and ferociousness, a thought becomes clearer and clearer: that it is not so much a look at wild nature as it is an insight into ourselves, our nature. And that, for me, beyond his mission, gives meaning to his life and to his death.

With his artwork *Grizzly Man*, Herzog restructures Treadwell's footage, so that it becomes less a direct criticism of poaching and more a broader, but oblique, critique of the modern human condition. Herzog does not burst the balloon of Treadwell's project just for the sake of it. He applies the same puncturing technique to his own works; a good example is *Glocken aus der Tiefe* (*Bells from the Deep*), a film that is, unfortunately, often overlooked because it dates from 1993, when the world was not so enamoured of artistic documentaries. If part of Herzog's project is to drive holes into our conception of what documentary film is, and can be, this film is an interesting hammer in his toolkit. It cracks open a useful point of entry into the work that Herzog does with the form and function of art.

The invisible city

In *Bells from the Deep*, Herzog undertakes a journey through Russia, not long after the collapse of the Soviet Union. Belief and superstition are bubbling up through the cracks in a society where they had long been held down by totalitarianism. Herzog

This image of the pilgrims in *Bells from the Deep* is one of the most famous examples of staging in Herzog's documentary films. In order to illustrate the legend of the Russians who seek out the mysterious city on the lake bed, he paid three alcoholics to crawl around on the frozen surface.

does not take a stance in relation to the Russians he meets. He faithfully follows one of Russia's many incarnations of Jesus, and describes him with respect as the best of the 110 Second Comings living in Siberia. He also follows the healer Alan Chumak, a former television star who now uses his powers of suggestion to bless water in Pepsi bottles, among other things. The quackery is obvious in each case, but Herzog's remit is not to expose them (they do a perfectly good job of exposing themselves). Rather, his interest is in the sentiments that were suppressed for so long and for which the Russians were now fumbling.

At the climax of the film, Herzog depicts faithful Siberian pilgrims searching for the invisible city of Kitezh. According to Russian legend, in the thirteenth century Kitezh was an extraordinarily rich and lovely town, peopled with good townsfolk, on the edge of Lake Svetloyar. When the Mongolian chief Batu Khan heard about the city, he set off with his army to conquer it. On arrival, he found a town without defences, and all its citizens on their knees in prayer. When the Mongols attacked, God defended his kneeling flock by transporting the beautiful city to the bottom of the lake, where the townsfolk peacefully continued their lives. Just as the myth of the model city of Atlantis still resonates in the West, Kitezh remains a utopian dream in the Russian collective imagination. There is a persistent myth that in the winter, if the weather is clear and one's heart is pure, the town can be glimpsed on the lake bed and the church bells can be heard ringing from the depths. Herzog stages this myth and persuades his pilgrims to crawl out onto the white ice, from where they peer down towards something the camera cannot capture – the city is invisible, after all.

Although Herzog is not in the business of exposing con merchants, he doesn't glorify the Russians' superstitions either. On the same lake where the pilgrims are seen crawling around on the ice and peering down into its mysterious depths, Herzog also films locals cutting holes in the ice to fish, as well as a couple of competitive skaters who glide over the ice in modern sportswear. This is a way to puncture the superstition and reveal it to be a version of the truth of accountants, but it's also a way to puncture the film *qua* art. From Adorno's perspective, the artwork is a mysterious cipher that has to be decoded if society is to progress in the right direction. Enlightenment's only hope is the feeling that strikes the beholder of a genuine artwork, the feeling that there is something compulsive and incomprehensible that insistently waits to be grasped. The enigma of the work of art, however, must not be glorified or worshipped like an icon that can be physically seen, apprehended and touched – no more than the Russian superstitions should be glorified. There is no other world beyond the empirical world that art mediates, but there is something ineffable in the empirical world, and this is what art articulates – the same thing that Herzog's pilgrims on the white ice are trying to glimpse.

With Adorno, we can say that the artwork gestures to the non-identical – something that is not picked up by the *identity thinking* of the truth of accountants. Identity thinking has to do with reducing things and facts to general concepts, just as the accountant assigns items to her cells on a spreadsheet. The peculiarity of the individual thing is reduced to a predetermined category. This kind of identity thinking is, for Adorno, an expression of violent mastery. 'Brutality towards things is potentially brutality towards people,' he writes in *Aesthetic Theory*.[9] Herzog remarks that when you're a German with an awareness of the national past, you pay careful attention to this tendency. Art negates brutality by finding its own form, and it is through this form, rather than by direct revolt or by preaching moral theses, that it points to the *non-identical*. The non-identical is not the romantic idea that all individual phenomena in their particularity ought to have their own names and not belong to any category. That kind of nominalism is so closed that it exempts itself from any power to determine, and thus can only remain a pure abstraction. The non-identical is not something that lurks intact under the surface layer of culture. It is not lurking intact under the ice, at the bottom of the frozen lake in *Bells from the Deep*, because it does not exist; it is created only when it is set free.

If one sees the non-identical as an intact unit, one has succeeded only in identifying it with the label 'non-identical', to the exclusion of other possibilities, just as Herzog feared that the media would reduce his shoe-eating to countercultural clowning. Rather, the non-identical should be understood as an aspect of things that cannot be translated into a general concept, but obtains ecstatically in little pockets of air between the crudely drawn cells of the spreadsheet of the truth of accountants. And in modernity, says Adorno, it is precisely the non-identical that art manages to sustain. This is because art does not *identify* the non-identical but identifies *with* it and allows it to express itself. In his documentaries, this is precisely what Herzog has pursued with a range of strategies.

Mysterious realism: death, distance and friendship – encountering white elephants with Mozart souls

In Herzog's diary novel *Conquest of the Useless* (written during the shooting of *Fitzcarraldo* and first published in 2004), a young man asks whether filming or being filmed can be harmful: can it destroy a person? 'In my heart the answer was yes,' writes Herzog, 'but I said no.'[10]

We have all had the experience of seeing a photograph of ourself and feeling that it doesn't represent who we are. Or a picture of a loved one that makes our love seem banal, because it doesn't capture the complexity of emotion. Every picture of a person or of the world is a possible identification that runs the risk of excluding the non-identical and fixing the subject as being identical with the image – and it's no use shouting: No, that's not me, that's not all I am. Or: That's not my loved one, or my love for them. But when the young man poses the question, Herzog answers no anyway, because ceasing to make films is not a solution. We can only try to do it better.

In the documentary *The White Diamond* (2004), Herzog filmed in the Guyanese jungle in South America. The crew reaches the great Kaieteur waterfall, whose inaccessible abri or undercut is home to thousands of birds that dive through the torrents of water to build nests. Herzog sends a free-climber out with a camera on a dangerous mission to film in the abri, and he succeeds. But the waterfall's undercut is not just a nesting ground; it is also a place that is sacred in the local religion because of its inaccessibility. Herzog therefore decides not to show the footage, but it is not a matter of a simple, private ethical boundary. Herzog has staged the sequence and shows us both the free climber and the scene when the decision is taken not to use the images from within the abri.

The same stylistic restraint is in evidence in *Encounters at the End of the World* (2007), when he interviews the Czech mechanic Libor Zicha about the bleak circumstances of his flight from the

Eastern Bloc during the Cold War. When the interview begins to touch on the most dreadful aspects of the story, and the blood-thirsty viewer is hoping to hear more about how it really was, and Zicha is squirming uncomfortably, Herzog says: 'You don't need to,' and Zicha answers, 'Thank you.' Instead, Zicha demonstrates how incredibly quickly he can inflate a rubber dinghy and escape with a small bag. Enough has been said between Herzog and Zicha and between the film and the audience. It is a lightly disguised commentary on the kind of investigative journalism that has led to some languages adopting the term 'interview *victims*' for what we refer to in English as interviewees. Herzog takes this metaphor very seriously. He is conscious that every exposure can turn into a kind of assault, and he tries to emphasize distance over disclosure – his respect for Zicha's need to guard his secret is an example of this.

Cinéma vérité and investigative journalism would aim to illuminate all the nooks and crannies of these lives under the spotlight of a truth that they believe exists and can be tracked down. They wouldn't hesitate to reveal any and every secret, certain that the whole story can be told if they are just honest enough and drill down deep enough. In contrast, Herzog has no wish to engage in exposures and justifications. He does not want to brutally 'identify' everything (in Adorno's sense) and thereby risk destroying people or facts. Instead, he has developed a documentary style that can be termed *mysterious realism*, in which the non-identical is safeguarded through a practice of mimicking, instead of exhibiting and identifying. In *Minima Moralia*, Adorno writes: 'What would hope be, without distance?'[11] To maintain something mysterious – to be discreet, to be secretive, to hold back – in relation to people and to the world is to refuse the all-pervasive identity thinking that strives to flood every corner with light. What is mysterious enjoys a stealthy triumph over power. In his documentaries Herzog sustains a profound concern with the details of life, without dishing up intimacy. Instead of aggressively going head-to-head with the other, mysterious realism aims to enact concrete encounters with inner

Three examples of stylistic restraint. The Kaieteur waterfall in *The White Diamond* (top). In the bottom right corner, a figure can just be glimpsed, a photographer hoisted down on a rope to film behind the waterfall. But Herzog never shows the images: the waterfall's abri – which is important in the local religion – is allowed to keep its secrets. The mechanic Libor Zicha in *Encounters at the End of the World* is allowed to withhold the story of how he fled from East Germany. And Jewel Palovak in *Grizzly Man* – Timothy Treadwell's friend, who is in possession of the recordings of the moment of his death. Here Herzog is listening to the tape, but he never passes on what he hears – and thereby draws a line.

and outer landscapes, maintaining a discreet distance from what is secret. This anticipative form is able to say something ecstatically true that would never come to light under the punctilious gaze of the accountant.

A photograph can make us look dead, because we think it hasn't captured our life. In the documentary *Into the Abyss* and the television series *On Death Row*, Herzog visits American prisons to film a few prisoners who are facing execution. They stare into the abyss that is the human condition, and Herzog stares into the abyss that is the human soul. As with Zicha in *Encounters at the End of the World*, Herzog doesn't use classic interview techniques. 'I'm not a journalist; I'm a poet. I had a discourse, an encounter with these people, but I never had a list of questions,' he has commented.[12] This was a lesson he learned when he met Errol Morris and found out that they shared a fascination with evil and murder. Many years before *Into the Abyss*, this shared interest led them both to death row.

Herzog met Morris for the first time in the early 1970s. The precise date is lost in the mists of time for both filmmakers, but it was after Herzog's cactus dive had left his body peppered with spines, and a few years before he ate his shoes. It was Tom Luddy, head of the Pacific Film Archive in Berkeley, California, who introduced them; he knew that Morris, a cinephile and student of philosophy, was thinking about writing a PhD on murderers and psychiatrists, and had a hunch that Herzog would like him. He did, and the first picnic they ate together took them to Vacaville prison, where the serial killer Edmund Emil Kemper III was incarcerated.

In 1972–3 Kemper had murdered at least six women hitchhikers in Santa Cruz, and raped their corpses. Moreover, he had killed and dismembered his mother, her friend and his grandparents a decade earlier. Kemper phoned the police and confessed everything on 20 April 1973, and was, as he himself wished, condemned to death. But because the U.S. Supreme Court had suspended the use of the death penalty at the time his sentence was handed down, he had to make do with life imprisonment with no possibility of release on probation. On the bright side, now he had visitors: a Jewish philosopher and a German filmmaker. Or rather, Dr Morris and Dr Herzog. (Herzog has since related that the only reason Kemper's lawyer agreed to disguise them as psychiatrists was probably that he wanted to increase his own chances of getting out of there alive. Kemper was well over 6 ft/2 m tall and weighed 330 lb/150 kg, and if he killed again in prison he could fulfil his ambition of being sent to the electric chair.)

Herzog admits that they were all shitting themselves in fear, but Kemper turned out to be an intelligent and very sensitive person: his hands were 'like the hands of a violin player. I remember he looked like an elephant with a Mozart soul.'[13] It's a description that could also apply to Herzog and Morris, who tend to operate like bulls in a china shop but always manage to stop and appreciate the china. They learned an important lesson during their meeting with Kemper. He had confessed to the murders in impressive detail, and had a great talent for concocting rational explanations on the basis of his sick view of the world. Here are two examples:

a. Kemper's mother, he claimed, had always wanted people to look up to her. So he buried the head of one of his victims in his mother's back garden, positioned so that the eyes were gazing up towards her bedroom window.

b. After Kemper had killed his grandmother – because she was always on his case, just like his mother – he felt it was necessary to shoot his grandfather as well, because he suspected that he would be very angry about his wife's death.

Dr Herzog and Dr Morris did not formulate a diagnosis of their patient's state of mind, but they were fascinated by this paradox of a man. He was walking proof of the depths of evil a human being

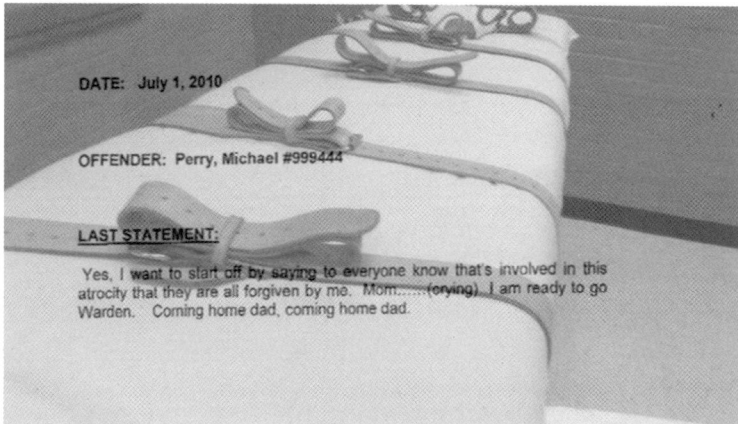

DATE: July 1, 2010

OFFENDER: Perry, Michael #999444

LAST STATEMENT:

Yes, I want to start off by saying to everyone know that's involved in this atrocity that they are all forgiven by me. Mom.......(crying) I am ready to go Warden.   Coming home dad, coming home dad.

In the film *Into the Abyss* and the television series *On Death Row*, Herzog interviewed prisoners condemned to death in Texas. Given his German origins, he feels he cannot pass judgement on any other nation. But for exactly the same reason, he cannot accept that a state has the right to take the life of its citizens. Here we see Michael Perry, who was executed by lethal injection eight days after this interview. The other image shows a shot of the relevant paperwork dissolving into an image of the execution trolley.

can accommodate, but he also taught them something about the fundamental difficulty of achieving certainty. Facts are inaccessible in direct form, given how the world and human experience are constructed. What we do have is individual stories. Herzog and Morris were also fascinated by Kemper's confession, which was a six-hour monologue, whereas the initial plan had been for the psychiatrists to declare him insane after just a few minutes. He was certainly mad, but to force Kemper's thoughts into an analytical straitjacket and believe that was enough to understand him was to render banal the mystery of the man.

For what if . . . as Herzog and Morris philosophized afterwards:

What if he was presenting himself as considered and rational after the fact? What if he committed murder in a fit of affect, but was now living out a fantasy of control over his own self-image, and the legal system was the perfect framework for this? These questions are not meant to sow doubt about Kemper's guilt or how dangerous he was, but they raise some points concerning how humans formulate questions, get answers and construct explanations and narratives.

. . . What if the psychiatrists were living out a fantasy about their own elevated positions of power? And what if society's conception of true and false was influenced by the desire to distance Kemper from humanity, ostracize him as a monster and thus exonerate ourselves from the possibility that we harbour the same forces?

In the fourth episode of the television series *On Death Row*, Herzog talks to the murderer Linda Carty, who allegedly killed a pregnant woman with the intention of stealing her baby. She likes to sing, and she has a lovely voice that Herzog records at some length. At the end of the episode – and thus towards the conclusion of the project that *Into the Abyss* and *On Death Row* together constitute – the public prosecutor argues that Herzog can try to humanize Carty as much as he likes; however much he might wish she was a good person, she simply isn't. Herzog answers: 'I'm not humanizing her. And I'm not trying to humanize her. She simply *is* a human being. Period.'

This fundamentally respectful stance is already given expression in the very first interview on death row in the film *Into the Abyss – A Tale of Death, a Tale of Life*, and it influences how the interview is set up. When the murderer Michael Perry launches into his rehearsed presentation of himself and his case, Herzog interrupts him to make one thing clear: 'When I talk to you, it does not necessarily mean that I have to like you, but I respect you, and you are a human being, and I think human beings should not be executed.' This jolts Perry, who has spent ten years on death row and has got used to arguing his case on the basis of a grim premise: he may not have any right to life. It's as though this is the first real conversation he has had in many years – the first time in a decade that his right to life and his humanity were not up for discussion – and after a moment's hesitation he accepts the new principle that the interview is not about arguing for or against his actions, but is a conversation that should encompass far more. This is a story about both death and life, as the film's title suggests, and a story about what people are capable of under certain circumstances. By holding back a little in the interview situation, by not arriving armed with a list of questions or an explanatory model, and with no particular goal in mind, the world and human experience in all its myriad nuances of good and evil can perhaps be allowed to swim more clearly into view.

Afterwards, Morris continued his project about serial killers, delving into the stories about one of America's most famous murderers, Ed Gein, who inspired the character of Norman Bates in Alfred Hitchcock's *Psycho* (1960). Gein had an unhealthy relationship with his mother. Apart from the many murders he committed, he also dug up graves in a churchyard in Plainfield, Wisconsin, to find the corpses of women who corresponded to his mother's profile, which he then took home and stuffed. Morris realized that no one had investigated whether Gein had exhumed his own mother's grave. Plainfield's local psychiatrist thought Gein's logic was too twisted for him to undertake something so obvious, but perhaps he had dug tunnels from the other graves to his mother's grave? Morris was doubtful, so he phoned Herzog – and that always has consequences. Herzog was in Alaska shooting landscapes, but he drove to Wisconsin right away, and had agreed to meet Morris in the Plainfield graveyard at night. But when Herzog arrived, Morris got cold feet and didn't show: 'In my mind's eye I saw a full moon. I saw Plainfield police station. I saw the forensic photographers. I saw myself being led away in handcuffs beside the German – the ultimate disgrace to my Jewish family,' Morris explained later.[14]

Herzog was annoyed, but he decided to creep around a bit in the graveyard by himself with his ear to the ground, listening for hollow areas that could reveal the truth. He has commented since that Plainfield is a mythical place in American culture, along the lines of the stock market on Wall Street and the jail at San Quentin: places where dreams and nightmares coalesce. The image of himself lying on the ground and listening for the mystery in the graveyard has become a signature motif in several of his films, not least the pilgrims on the ice in *Bells from the Deep*. Today, Herzog admits that he's glad that Morris never turned up and they didn't carry out their planned dig, because it would have been a violation to cross that boundary: 'Sometimes it's better not to know, to ask the question, but not to get an answer.'[15]

Death also plays a key role in *Grizzly Man*, but as a *mysterious realist*, Herzog dances around death instead of tackling it directly. We know from the start of the film that Timothy Treadwell lived with the wild bears in Alaska for thirteen summers before they eventually ate him. There is a basic fascination in looking at a dead man's footage of himself; to see a human life in the shadow of death is like attending a cinematic funeral during which we ponder our own fate, the human condition. It's even more alluring that we know he was killed by the creatures he loved more than anything else in life, the bears – and that it was a very violent, gruesome death. So says a dramatic coroner who (when Herzog tracks him down) provides a lively description of the moment of death: the first thing the bear did was to flay the skin off Treadwell's face, the essential signifier of the human. But we are privy to more details; it transpires that there is an audio recording of Treadwell's death, because his camera microphone was switched on during the bear's attack and feeding frenzy. Throughout the film, Herzog ensures we are aware of the existence of this tape, but when the film nears its gory epicentre, he doesn't play it. He *holds back*, so that we're left with our own thoughts about whether we want to hear it or not, and with our thoughts about what that curiosity says about us. Instead of playing the sound recording, Herzog himself appears in a scene where he sits with his back to the camera across from Treadwell's friend Jewel Palovak, whom he treats as his widow.

Herzog listens to the recording, which is clearly very unpleasant, and can't bring himself to listen all the way through. He then warns Palovak, who has the tape in her possession, that she should never listen to it, and that she should never seek out the post-mortem images of Treadwell's corpse. Herzog has since said that the film's American investors pressurized him to use the material, but that he refused to cross that line and make an exhibition of a man's death. *Cinéma vérité* would have regarded it as a kind of duty to use the sound recording and thereby come closer to reality as it *really was*. But Herzog's point is that he would then run the risk of the tape overshadowing the whole story and thus destroying the in-between spaces where the audience has a chance to think, and destroy the nuanced story that Treadwell's life *also was*. Both for Palovak and for the film viewer, there would be a risk of reducing Treadwell to his moment of death. Herzog says that this can become a 'white elephant' in her life; warns her that it can grow into an obsession that will destroy her – and destroy her feelings for Treadwell. To cherish the mysterious is also to cherish friendship: friendship as something greater; as the possibility of communities that are better at embracing the non-identical, and have no urge to flay off the face of the other.

Form under pressure

The mysterious realism in Werner Herzog's documentary films attempts, through its form, to identify itself *with* the non-identical. In so doing, it seeks to open up the possibility of a more capacious, ecstatic truth than that of the accountants who try to *identify* everything. If we look carefully at Herzog's fiction films, whose form is ostensibly more classical, we can see that here, too, he seeks to engage with the form of the artwork in the spirit of Adorno, and to avoid the standard forms of dramaturgy. The form of these artworks identifies itself *with* the non-identical, insisting that reality is not a closed space, and that the characters cannot be trapped within simplistic action schemas.

The classic film (the Classical Hollywood model) is action-orientated and follows two standard models that are both closed structures moving towards a goal, in the tradition of Aristotle's *Poetics*. This is the famous pattern with a beginning, a middle, an end, and a turning point along the way.

There is the large, grand, epic form that we know from melodramas, great war films and westerns. A particular starting point entails a problem or challenge that requires action, so that it leads to a new situation. This is a strict composition in which the plot proceeds in causal and logical ways towards its goal.

In the small or minor form we have an action that provokes a situation which then requires another action. We see this with the little man who is unwillingly forced into situations to which he must react. The minor form can seem less closed than the major one, but this is not the case in practice. In this type of film from Classical Hollywood the phrase *rise to the occasion* is often used about the little man who was just minding his own business, but shows what he's made of when the need arises. The little man can be found in many guises, from the victim of bullying who fights back, to Clark Kent, who walks into a telephone box and is transformed into Superman when the situation demands it.

These two forms are just schemata, and it can be hard to distinguish between them: when little hobbits have the whole world to save, or when the president's love life is a mess. The key point, however, is that all action is subject to a predetermined meaning and processual logic that moves inexorably towards a goal once it has been set in motion.

Herzog deliberately pushes these two models to the extreme. As previously mentioned, he operates primarily with two different character types. They are either little *useless ones*, like the foundling Kaspar Hauser and the psychiatric patient Bruno S. in *Stroszek*, or grand *conquerors of the useless*, like Klaus Kinski in the lead roles in *Aguirre* and *Fitzcarraldo*. To start with they fit the patterns, but they try to evade the order of the truth of accountants by being smaller or greater than the classical narrative schema.

In *Fitzcarraldo*, the challenge the opera-loving title character sets himself is infinitely larger than the narrative scheme can accommodate. His conquest of the useless is so meaningless, so exaggerated, that no obstacle that Hollywood could place in his way would be able to overshadow the project's fundamental madness.

The little characters like Kaspar Hauser are infinitely smaller than the everyday little man. When the going gets tough they do not react as they should, and, as we have seen, their revolts are never successful anyway. Woyzeck attempts a rebellion, but is quickly put in his place, and most of Herzog's other little figures don't even try, but just keep on confusedly keeping on, without ever letting their inner Superman fly. When the situation requires action, they fail to enact the deed that the standard model prescribes; they take *evasive* action.

Herzog brushes cinema's classical scheme of action against the grain and thereby reveals his characters to be greater or smaller than it. Just as he does with the two wordless war victims in *Lessons of*

Darkness, he allows both the great and the small to stand out. They refuse to disappear like dust strewn on the roadway of history, but instead emerge as singular events.

A ski jumper makes the leap

Probably the most successful example of evasive action is to be found in *Die große Ekstase des Bildschnitzers Steiner* (*The Great Ecstasy of Woodcarver Steiner*, 1974), Herzog's film about Walter Steiner, the world champion of ski flying, an extreme form of the ski jump. This film includes many Herzogian calling cards. It is the first film in which Herzog himself appears unequivocally before the camera, and he combines the mysterious realism of his documentaries with an interrogation of fiction's little and grand forms alike, all in one film.

Walter Steiner is a real person, but this documentary film about him is so stylized that it is impossible to distinguish it from fiction. Playing with the caricature of a sports reporter, Herzog follows Steiner during a competition, but the beautiful cinematic images express something other than the norm at that time, and Herzog is far from a normal reporter. Whereas the rest of the world is concerned with performances and world records, Herzog is interested only in his own film, which he discusses several times. He maintains a distance that also opens up the possibility of the non-identical. His mysterious realism creates space for Steiner to show various sides of himself beyond the world champion Steiner. It actually seems as though he doesn't care that much about the competitions; he just wants to take off from the Earth and fly away like a bird.

Steiner is unique in Herzog's universe because he is an amalgam of the two Herzogian figures. On the ground, he is spindly, goofy and a bit helpless, and his best friend is a crow – he is *useless* (pressured small form). In the air, he executes great *conquests of the useless* and floats further than any other person, but his project of becoming a bird is, from the outset, just like Fitzcarraldo's project, itself a hindrance greater than any other (pressured grand form). As world champion, he is already a success, measured in terms of the truth of accountants, but his behaviour is designed to avoid all demands. He doesn't care about the world championship. He only wants to float like a bird far away from the community structured by the truth of accountants, in which he feels less than comfortable. Each time the public and the media challenge him to achieve a new world-record jump, he inexplicably chooses to start from a lower position than the other competitors. The accountants' truth is that the real Steiner adopted this strategy to protest against the conditions of the competition. He could jump so far that he was frightened of flying further than the length of the slope and ending up dead in a landing on the flat. So he started lower down, and still won the competition. Conversely, the ecstatic truth is that Herzog stages Steiner's strategy in the film as though he is trying to evade worldly notions of success, but without confronting them directly.

Walter Steiner is reminiscent of the little evasive figures that often appear in the fiction of Robert Walser, of which Herzog is an enthusiastic reader. To this day, Herzog claims that the draft of his book *Conquests of the Useless* is written in miniature script, just as Walser wrote. Herzog wrote his diary novel during the long, hard shoot of *Fitzcarraldo*, when territorial wars, accidents and a critical press combined to create an insuperable set of challenges. Perhaps the miniature script was a way for Herzog himself to evade the great film project and the very idea of the great auteur in the jungle, and seek out a smallness akin to that of his useless characters?

It's probably a lie that the book was written in miniature script, but it's a constructive lie that contributes to the truth. In fact, it invites us to look more closely at *The Great Ecstasy of Woodcarver Steiner*, and if we do, we notice that Steiner more or less speaks with Walser's literary voice, and, more concretely, that the film features passages from Walser's 'Helblings Geschichte' ('Helbling's Story', 1915). The character Helbling is a goofy clerk who is very

Walter Steiner in *The Great Ecstasy of Woodcarver Steiner*. This was the first film in which Herzog appeared before the camera and adopted the on-screen persona that has become his signature.

reminiscent of Steiner on dry land. Helbling talks himself down all the time, makes himself little. He feels that he is useless, but does not dream of greatness; he dreams of being alone in the world and free from the restrictions of bourgeois society, of which he observes: 'Oh, what a talent people have for giving the wrong labels!'[16] At the end of *The Great Ecstasy of Woodcarver Steiner*, we watch as Steiner floats in the air, and the closing words from 'Helbling's Story' are superimposed on the image. The only difference is Steiner's name:

> I ought really to be quite alone in the world, me, Steiner [Helbling] and not a single living being besides me. No sun, no culture, me, naked on a high rock, no storms, not even a wave, no water, no wind, no streets, no benches, no money, no time, and no breath. Then, at least, I should not be afraid any more.[17]

In the course of 'Helbling's Story', there is only one context in which Helbling does not feel fear. He feels a form of ecstasy in dance. There, in physical communion with the world, he is not afraid but instead escapes society's identifications: 'When I dance I forget that I am Helbling, for I am nothing but a happy floating-in-the-air. I am flying: can one imagine oneself happier?'[18] This is what Adorno in *Minima Moralia* calls a line of flight away from productivity, planning, egoism, oppression, towards being 'without any further definition'.[19] When Helbling forgets who he is, for a time he escapes the categories of the truth of accountants, and arising from this ground zero of forgetting there is the possibility of a new beginning, one in which the non-identical is part of the equation. Walter Steiner could say the same thing as Helbling, but his joyful floating-in-the-air entails sliding down the white slope, escaping the Earth and taking off like a bird. We could say the same of Herzog's art, which in its form mimics the non-identical, and lets it float happily for a short while. This is ecstatic truth.

SIX
A NEW GRAMMAR
OF IMAGES

Moments of truth

In Wim Wenders's *Tokyo-Ga* (1985), featuring Werner Herzog, the two former New Wave directors rendezvoused at the top of the Tokyo Tower in 1983.

The film is an homage to the Japanese director Yasujirō Ozu (1903–1963), as well as an exercise in creating the kind of image that Wenders and Herzog found so inspiring in Ozu's work. In his voiceover, Wenders describes the images in question – and thus describes indirectly the kind of image that Herzog promises to deliver later in the film:

> Each person knows for himself the extreme gap that often
> exists between personal experience and the depiction of that
> experience up there on the screen. We have learned to con-
> sider the vast distance separating cinema from life as so per-
> fectly natural that we gasp and give a start when we suddenly

discover something true or real in a movie: be it nothing
more than the gesture of a child in the background, or a bird
flying across the frame, or a cloud casting its shadow over
the scene for but an instant. It is a rarity in today's cinema
to find such moments of truth.

Ozu was a true master of this kind of moment of ecstatic truth,
when the film image escapes from the unyielding frame of the
classical cinema and gestures to something that the classical film
image found it difficult to include. With Herzog's help, Wenders
tries to investigate this image and to capture it on his trip to Japan,
but the two filmmakers don't find anything there that reminds
them of Ozu.

Ozu made his films in a very quiet, pre-Second World War
Tokyo, but the Tokyo of today is a modern city offering a sensory
bombardment that would have been unimaginable even for the
sociologist Georg Simmel, who tried a century ago to define the
lifeworld of the city dweller: buildings, trains, cars and people
tightly packed together in a blinking neon cityscape of adverts,
every square metre meticulously covered in signs. There is no
longer any trace of the world that Wenders and Herzog discern
in Ozu's images.

In *Tokyo-Ga*, the trip to Japan is staged as an oblique criticism
of the homogenization of everything at the expense of the unique,
of the fact that the variety of the world is being reduced. Post-war
Japan has developed into a carnival of simulacra, a country that
has lost itself and is orientated only towards the Western market.
The Japanese now watch dubbed American cartoons, play baseball
and whack golf balls out across the rooftops. They have even built
a branch of Disneyland precisely like the one in California.

As Germans, Wenders and Herzog recognize in these aspects
of Japanese culture the shameful self-regard of a defeated military
power. Shaken, they gaze out over these 'embarrassed landscapes
. . . where new images are hardly possible any more'. But Herzog

Wim Wenders and Werner Herzog during shooting of *Tokyo-Ga* (1985), on top of Tokyo Tower – the broadcasting station that was at the time the tallest building in Japan. Here Herzog delivers a speech: a kind of practical poetic in which he promises to do anything and go anywhere needed to find new images. Years later, in 2019, at the European Film Awards in Berlin, it was Wenders who presented Herzog with a Lifetime Achievement Award.

insists that we need at least to try to find them, for 'we absolutely need images that correspond to our level of civilization and to our inner, deepest nature.' That is, we have a desperate need for new images that break with the truth of accountants, are open to what is excluded and try to bring it to attention: all the material, all the feelings that are not accommodated by our forms of expression; the voices that are drowned out in all the noise.

Wenders wants new images in the style of Ozu, who, he says, managed to do more than participate in a homogeneous 'empty form'. At the top of the Tokyo Tower, Herzog agrees to carry out a rescue action, and in a long monologue he declares himself willing to do whatever it takes and to go to any place whatever to find new images.

> Often it's a question of taking risks . . . That can compel
> us to go right into a war zone or wherever necessary. I will
> never complain that it's too difficult to climb 8,000 metres
> up a mountain to get pictures that are pure, clear and trans-
> parent . . . I will go immediately to Mars or Saturn . . .
> I will go any place whatever.

Herzog's declaration in this speech is an interesting example of how he always takes what he says and makes it literal. He did indeed later head into a war zone (*Lessons of Darkness*, 1992) and up a 8,000-metre-high (26,000 ft) mountain in the Himalayas (*Gasherbrum*, 1984), and he even brought images home from space in collaboration with NASA (*The Wild Blue Yonder*, 2005). But Herzog's monologue in *Tokyo-Ga* is about something more than just being brave enough to set out into concrete landscapes.

We've seen how Herzog's *Stroszek* (1977) anticipated the philosophical discussion of power and surveillance that the historian of ideas Michel Foucault was formulating at almost the same time. Similarly, Wenders and Herzog's conversation on film art took place at the same time that the French philosopher Gilles Deleuze was writing his philosophical tomes on film, *Cinéma 1: L'image-mouvement* and *Cinéma 2: L'image temps* (in English, *Cinema 1: The Movement-image* and *Cinema 11: The Time-image*). In his painstaking theoretical account of film history – in which Herzog himself is highlighted in some rather important and memorable passages – Deleuze gets his teeth into the same images by Ozu that Wenders and Herzog discuss in Tokyo. Deleuze agrees with our German filmmakers that Ozu has a special status in film history, and claims quite simply that Ozu is the inventor of the kind of film image that transcends the classical model; as such, for Deleuze, Ozu is a forerunner of neo-realism and of the French and German New Waves, not least Wenders and Herzog themselves.

Deleuze highlights Ozu's sequences of images because of their ability to create examples of what he calls *any-space-whatever* (*espace quelconque*). These are in-between spaces within the narrative logic of a film, where the image lingers and is caught up in itself rather than progressing to the next shot. So this entails working down at the micro level of the film: there, the form of the artwork can create a freer space for thought, a kind of thought that is about potentials, and among the potentials is this cryptic concept that insists thought is not subject to control but can move any place whatever. An *any-space-whatever* thus corresponds to *ecstatic truth*, because it shows us that there is something in the individual sequence of images that cannot be reduced to a mere element in the entity of the film. When Herzog declares at the top of the Tokyo Tower that he'll go to *any place whatever* to find new images, his ultimate goal is to create precisely this *any-space-whatever* with the results.

Many of the directors of the German New Wave were interested in both philosophy and film theory. For the first generation it was more or less compulsory to know their Adorno, and the philosopher Alexander Kluge in particular was a pioneer in terms of connecting theory with practice. Today, Kluge is probably best known for his writings with Oskar Negt and the concepts

Family Romance, LLC, is a truly herzogian hybrid of documentary and fiction. The main character, Yuichi Ishii, is the real-life CEO of the company Family Romance, LLC, in present-day Japan. The service offered by Mr Ishii and his many employees is to act as friends or family members for the clientele. Some use the service to re-enact a certain moment or feeling in their life, others rent a father for their child for several years. Herzog hired Mr Ishii to act out his everyday life.

Herzog explains: 'Everything in the film is false. Everything is invented, a game, a performance. But the funny thing is that the feelings are real enough; they don't have a hollow ring. And I think that Ishii compels us to consider our own lives and ask ourselves to what extent it's all a performance, how authentic our own families are, and how much play-acting we all do. And whether that matters?'

'The film is essentially about loneliness and about the longing for connection with others. It takes place in Japan, but we all know that the trend is the same all over the world. More and more artificial products are being designed to help us to feel. What's scary is not that someone invented a robotic pet fish that alleviates loneliness, or a company that hires out actors to play missing friends or family. What's scary is that there is enough existential loneliness out there to create a demand for these things.'

In a crucial scene in the film, Mr Ishii visits the observation deck of Tokyo's Skytree, the television tower that superseded the Tokyo Tower not only in terms of its function, but as the highest landmark in Japan. This is a clear reference to the scene in *Tokyo-Ga* in which Herzog talks about going any place whatever to find new images. But this time, there is no monologue about climbing mountains or venturing into war zones or outer space. What the camera captures is a man giving a young girl an affectionate hug.

proletarian public sphere and *counter-public sphere*, which advocate for creating small pockets of resistance in the public discourse. But his films were interesting, too: *Abschied von gestern* (*Yesterday Girl*, 1966) and *Die Artisten in der Zirkuskuppel: ratlos* (*Artists Under the Big Top: Perplexed*, 1968).

Wim Wenders has also explicitly worked philosophically and theoretically with the medium of film. In his writings and in his metafilms he seeks out his heroes and tries to understand on a more rarefied level what cinema should and can do. But Herzog is arguably the German filmmaker who has reflected most deeply on the film medium since Kluge. He often tries to distance himself from theoretical discussions by saying that 'cinema is athletic' and requires 'courage and strong thighs', but at the same time he writes manifestos on ecstatic truth, and over the years he has written articles on subjects ranging from the American avant-garde to Greek philosophy.

Herzog's love for certain big names in film studies is also well known. His book *Of Walking in Ice* is primarily a love letter to the Jewish film historian Lotte Eisner. She played an important academic role in the reconstruction of German film culture, which the Nazis had rendered suspect with their exploitation of media. He named his son Rudolph Amos Achmed Herzog, after the American film theorist Amos Vogel, and he dedicated *Encounters at the End of the World* to the film critic Roger Ebert. It is difficult to believe that a man who reads ancient Greek, Latin, Spanish and French (not to mention German and English) doesn't keep abreast of what's happening on the film theory scene, and in his rebuttals

Werner Herzog with mountaineering equipment, ready to go any place whatever. This image and the image opposite were taken by the photographer Beat Presser, who worked closely with Herzog in the 1980s.

After *Fitzcarraldo*, Herzog began to receive invitations to stage operas. The two portraits on this and the preceding page were taken in conjunction with the staging of Ferruccio Busoni's *Doktor Faust* in 1986.

of this or that interpretation of his work, he is always extremely precise in his choice of words.

We cannot know for sure whether Herzog was well-versed in French philosophy in the 1980s. Herzog would always deny it, but it seems pretty likely that some of these thoughts have found their way into his work. Films such as *The White Diamond* and *Encounters at the End of the World* are both very Deleuzian in terms of their style, and even their titles. In any case, the interesting coincidence of Wenders's, Herzog's and Deleuze's interest in a specific type of image in the films of Yasujirō Ozu is testament to an affinity that in and of itself makes it worthwhile to delve into the tricky metaphors of what is, to my mind, some very intricate French theory. This should help us to advance our understanding of what Herzog is up to with his new, ecstatic images, and what the grammar of those images looks like in more concrete terms.

According to Gilles Deleuze, the peculiarity of cinema as an art form is that it consists of moving sequences of already moving images – hence *the movement-image*. This observation seems obvious now, but in the 1980s it was a seminal intervention in film theory, which until then had regarded film images as photographs lined up and set in motion, or the illusion of motion. Philosophically, this shift is part of a broader revolt against thinking in terms of stable identities, and a move towards thinking in terms of processes and relations. Here, I want to linger a little on Deleuze's objection to the established models of thinking, because later on I will show how these correspond to dramaturgical models in relation to Herzog's grammar of images.

Just as Herzog has consistently been concerned with creating new images, liberated from conventional templates and visual clichés, so too has Deleuze always focused in his philosophy on blowing up restrictive structures and setting thought free. In his monstrous masterpiece *Mille Plateaux* (*A Thousand Plateaus*, 1980), he and his co-author Félix Guattari use the concept of the *rhizome* as a liberating figuration of thought. Whereas *any-space-whatever*

'Films require strong thighs,' says Herzog. This picture of the director running has been adopted as the logo for Werner Herzog Filmproduktion, his production company. He has written books as well as film criticism, so those strong thighs do sit down once in a while, but he is always on the hunt for direct engagement with the world. 'If an actor knows how to milk a cow, I know he won't be difficult to work with,' he says. He claims that he can always tell within a few seconds if a person can milk a cow: 'I can see it from several kilometres away. Woody Allen will never milk a cow.'[1] In his own film criticism, Herzog has often adopted distinctly physical forms of expression. For example, when the German distributor of the Taviani Brothers' Cannes-winning *Padre Padrone* (1977) decided not to give the film a theatrical premiere, Herzog chained himself to a Munich cinema in protest – together with a sheep, since the film is about a shepherd. It was a concrete, physical act in defence of film art. As he says, 'all I want to be remembered for is being a good soldier of cinema.'

is a conceptual metaphor for a break with the classical film's stringent logic of progress, the *rhizome* is a conceptual metaphor that functions on a more general philosophical level to break with the models of thought of the philosophy of identity.

'Rhizome' is a term borrowed from biology. It is a term that describes the complex subterranean root system of plants such as couch grass. The root stalks grow horizontally, weaving in and out of each other, and sending shoots and roots in all directions. The rhizome is used as a metaphor for life and for thought in order to create a concept that can counter the philosophy of identity's classic models: the tree and the root. These models, according to Deleuze and Guattari, are not adequate to the constitution of the human, and thus hinder us from thinking and living freely: 'We're tired of trees. We should stop believing in trees, roots, and radicles. They've made us suffer too much. All of arborescent culture is founded on them, from biology to linguistics . . . Many people have a tree growing in their heads, but the brain itself is much more a grass than a tree.'[2]

The familiar tree-structure of thought is vertical and communicates hierarchically. It is rooted securely and branches out into dichotomies: subject-object, body-soul, and so on, always outwards from a centre or an entity. The other model of the philosophy of identity is the root structure, which is centred on a taproot from which other roots grow. This can seem more multifarious than the tree structure, but is just a variant of the same idea, since all the roots are still connected to a centre. As models, the tree structure and the root structure function as closed systems of thought just as they do for film narrative, reducing diversity and creating the illusion of a locked-down meaning. If we return to Herzog's own conceptual apparatus, the tree and the root correspond to the truth of accountants in thought, in life and in cinema. In contrast, the rhizome has an ecstatic character, whereby *any-point-whatever* in the story can be connected to any other point. There is life in the in-between spaces, a multiplicity of entrances and lines of flight out again. This is quite different from the tree, which from one dominant centre predetermines and fixes a particular order.

Ozu's birds, Herzog's butterflies

The classical film is characterized by a logic of progress that is reminiscent of the closed forms of the tree and root structures. The tree structure equates to the Hollywood model's grand form, and the root structure to its minor (small) form. These two forms, and the way Herzog plays with them, were described in the section 'Form under pressure' in Chapter Five, but to sum up briefly again: the *grand form* is the epic drama in which everything is subject to a tight plot and moves towards a clear goal. Often, big personalities have to do something equally big, such as winning a war or saving a princess. Individual stories and characters are there only as small pebbles in the river of the action, which flows towards a goal. On the other hand, the small form can seem less closed, since it starts with a man who was not part of a story, but who experiences something that kickstarts the same schema. The small form, which deals with little, ordinary people, can seem less closed than the grand form, but on closer inspection this is not the case; the sole function of the individual actions and images is still to work in unity to move the film forward.

According to Deleuze, Ozu crafts visual compositions that have a rhizomatic character. As Wenders says in *Tokyo-Ga*, Ozu creates 'moments of truth', which we could interpret to mean moments when the audience realizes that the tree and root forms, the forms of the Hollywood model, do not correspond to reality; that there is not one single truth but truths, plural. Using Deleuze's metaphor, we can say that we realize through these images that reality is more like grass.

In Ozu's work these truths manifest as simple image sequences where, for example, a bird crosses through the frame. These are moments when the rhizomatic nature of reality makes itself felt, and Ozu allows it to do so. He gives space to this interruption, this in-between space, which erupts from the forward motion of the plot.

There is a similar sequence in Herzog's essay film of 1999, *Mein liebster Feind* (*My Best Fiend*), which concerns his love-hate relationship with Klaus Kinski. We hear about Kinski's insanity, how he smashes up hotel rooms and gets into fights with theatre audiences. We see archive footage from the shoot of *Fitzcarraldo*, in which Kinski screams at everyone around him in an uncontrollable rage. This is the Kinski we know; this is what we're used to hearing about him. But Herzog has also dug up another recording from the archives. In this one, we see Kinski in a film scene that is suddenly transformed by a tropical butterfly fluttering into the frame. It ought to fly off, but it seems fascinated by Kinski's blonde locks, and flies around him in circles. Eventually Kinski gives up trying to continue with the take as scripted and starts playing with the butterfly. The creature has broken into an otherwise closed space, and, as Wenders says in *Tokyo-Ga* about the effect of the bird in Ozu's film, we gasp and give a start, because suddenly we notice something true or real in a film. The butterfly (Herzog) and the bird (Ozu) are random events, but they make themselves felt in the film frame, and the directors manage to incorporate them in a way that makes the viewer conscious of the breach in the films' closed logic of progress.

Any sequence of shots in a film (even a Hollywood film) contains moments that are present and full of possibility. There is an actual image and a virtual image. In classical film, the actual image slides quickly over to the next. The in-between spaces are obscured. The individual sequence is insignificant outside the film as a whole. But when this whole is breached, we linger in the virtual. In this lingering the image is, for a short time, set free (*ek-stasis*) and can potentially move any place whatever. This nascent moment is what Herzog calls an ecstatic truth, and what Deleuze calls an *any-space-whatever*. Thought is incited to consider the potential

A butterfly is attracted to Klaus Kinski, and the furious blonde actor softens up and forgets both himself and the performance he was in the middle of – giving himself over to the randomness of the moment. In the film *Mein liebster Feind* (*My Best Fiend*, 1999), made many years after the shoot in the jungle, Herzog discusses this clip. The film is both an homage to and a portrait of Kinski, and is also the last word in their long-running saga.

of the individual image or the individual situation, all the possible ways that story and thought could rhizomatically spool out from the moment in question. And, as a further corollary: whether the narratives of our lives and our society could be different.

Bergman's faces, Herzog's landscapes

The butterfly and the bird might seem to be random banalities, and, if so, Herzog's, Wenders's and Deleuze's interest in this type of image could be considered somewhat exaggerated. But a wingbeat in the East can whip up a storm in the West, and after Ozu, modernist cinema began to occupy itself more deliberately with these situations of *breach*.

Breaches start to be created with the help of what Deleuze calls *pure optical and sound situations*, that is, situations where the particular image or sound sequence stands purely outside the narrative. This turn of phrase might seem inappropriate, since 'purely' might be taken to indicate a completely liberated image that no longer has anything to do with cinema, but is perhaps closer to something we would see in video art or installation art: an interminable lingering on patterns on a screen. A more strikingly poetic formulation is that the image is left dangling, flapping amid the film's dramaturgy, like a door that has fallen off its hinges but is still swinging in the door frame. It sways blithely as potential, but is still attached to the film narrative. Deleuze thinks these situations are characterized by their *pre-linguistic affect*. They communicate with us outside our established systems of language. Herzog's early experimental documentary *Fata Morgana* can serve here as an example.

In 1968 Herzog travelled to Africa with the photographer Jörg Schmidt-Reitwein, in order to film mirages in the Sahara desert. Initially, the intention was to use the images for a science-fiction film about aliens who visit Earth and are surprised by the desolate landscapes inhabited only by dead animals and broken machinery.

Herzog returned to that idea later and used it as a framework for *Lessons of Darkness*, but in *Fata Morgana* he threw away the screenplay in order to focus on these prelinguistic visual phenomena, the mirages, images whereby the thing we see is present to the eye, but its real spatial location is diffuse. It can be that the car we see is actually 80 km (50 mi.) away and is being projected into the frame only by the heat and the play of light in the desert landscape. Maybe the lake we see doesn't exist, but is actually a reflection of the sky.

Back home, the images were edited together by Beate Mainka-Jellinghaus, one of post-war Germany's best editors. She wove the images together into a loosely structured essay film in three acts. It is the optical situations that emerge as the main character: we see a bus driving through the desert, although there is no bus for miles around. We see strange pink streaks, which are probably flamingos somewhere else entirely. And so on. The title *Fata Morgana* refers to these mirages, but probably also to the mythical figure Morgan le Fay, a sorceress from the time of King Arthur, who appears in both Wolfram von Eschenbach's epic poem *Parzival* (1200–1210) and the myth of the Flying Dutchman, which inspired the opera by Richard Wagner. Morgan le Fay could shape-shift and lure travellers off the beaten track, down to her underwater kingdom. In the same way, the desert mirages disorientate the traveller, and they leave the viewer of Herzog's *Fata Morgana* mistrustful as to whether what we see chimes with reality. Is there a bus before the camera or just a simulacrum, a representation of something that does not concretely exist, or at least is nowhere near the eye of the camera? For a moment, we might think back to *Tokyo-Ga*, as Herzog stands at the top of the Tokyo Tower and shakes his head at the Disneyfied culture of modern Japan.

There is a critique of civilization hidden in *Fata Morgana*, but let us for now, like Herzog, restrict ourselves to the optical situation. The first time we see the mirage images, we catch ourselves and ask whether this is a reliable picture or not. Once we've

Fata Morgana is Werner Herzog's homage to the African desert that he journeyed in so much as a young man. The film is experimental from beginning to end, a study of mirages, strange people and visual musicality. It opens with eight aeroplanes landing in slow motion in the heat haze of a runway. 'I had the feeling that audiences who were still watching by the sixth or seventh landing would stay to the end,' he says.[3] We are then taken on a slow tour of the desert landscape. The film is full of moments of uncertainty. An image crops up, but is it genuine, or a *fata morgana*? We view a person standing before the camera without any possibility of decoding what will happen next. The white desert fox is held up to the camera in a chokehold, for no apparent reason, and we have no idea what is about to happen.

Klaus Kinski, as the mad conquistador Aguirre, treks through the jungle and down the river on a raft in *Aguirre, the Wrath of God*. For both Kinski and Herzog, *Aguirre* and *Fitzcarraldo* were films that defined their public image – including in real life. Herzog's own artistic obsession would be connected forever after with Kinski's temperamental character.

experienced that doubt, we realize that we must look carefully at every single image and assess it, instead of naively accepting it as part of the film's onward progress. Herzog spices things up with long sequences of the desert sand, shot from the back of a truck driving slowly through the desert. The length of these tracking shots was very important to him, and he explained later that it took huge effort to dig a flat road into the sand to make it possible to hold the shot for so long. The duration of the sequence has the effect that we eventually stop expecting it to end, and we just let the image hang on the hinges of the dramaturgy and start to sense the drifting of grains of sand across the desert. Later in the film, there are long compositions featuring people whom Herzog meets in the desert. These are not interviews, nor are they what we would recognize as film performances; they are just people who return the gaze of the audience, probably desert folk who are amazed to meet a German with a camera. For example, there is a young boy who stands completely still, holding a desert fox in a stranglehold. We don't know what he's up to, or whether he intends to kill the fox or set it free; he just stands there, and no one says anything that explains the images. Herzog calls this kind of thing 'moments of uncertainty', when the image alone has to speak for itself, and we don't know where the film is going next.

Fata Morgana's form was so experimental that Herzog did not dare to release it immediately: 'I felt that people would ridicule the film. I felt *Fata Morgana* was very frail – like a cobweb – and I did not consider it a robust piece of work that could be released.'[4]

A couple of years later the film historians Lotte Eisner and Henri Langlois persuaded Herzog to let them have a copy, and arranged to have it screened – initially without his knowledge – at the Cannes film festival. *Fata Morgana* is the film by Herzog that comes closest to the avant-garde film tradition. It is probably the strangest of all his strange works, and with its cobweb-like air it is a film that demands patience, and an openness to optical situations.

Mirages are of course pure optical situations par excellence, but such a degree of experimentation is not always required. It could also be a very fine close-up of a face that moves us to consider the face in a purely optical way, without thinking about the context, or who the face belongs to. The Swedish director Ingmar Bergman was the master of such images. In his films, faces often slide into a zone of indistinguishability, where they become themselves and another – to such an extent that the actors sometimes couldn't tell which face on the screen was their own during the editing of *Persona* (1966), as Bergman has recounted. Whereas Bergman's faces wrest themselves loose from the story, and the face of the subject becomes an any-face-whatever, Herzog prefers to generate affect with decontextualized landscapes. He has highlighted this difference in conversation with the film journalist Paul Cronin:

> it seems that for Ingmar Bergman his starting point is a human face. The starting point for many of my films is a landscape, whether it be a real place or an imaginary or hallucinatory one from a dream . . . the landscapes are not so much the impetus for a film, rather they become the film's soul . . . The landscapes in *Aguirre* are not there as decoration or to look especially exotic. There is profound life there, a sensation of force, an intensity that you do not find in movies of the entertainment industry.[5]

The conqueror Aguirre in *Aguirre, the Wrath of God* betrays God, king and fatherland in a fit of megalomania and feverish delirium. He declares a form of all-encompassing independence, from a little raft on his way downstream through a series of waterfalls in the Amazon. Aguirre's dream of the ultimate treason and a possible new world order is just as tragically doomed to fail as is Stroszek's revolt in *Signs of Life*, and ends with a total dissolution of meaning, as did the rebellion in *Even Dwarfs Started Small*. As we shall see in what follows, Herzog used his experience with *Fata Morgana* to crystallize pure optical situations in *Aguirre*'s images of junglescapes.

The great traitor Aguirre

Aguirre, the Wrath of God tends to be regarded as the major work of the early part of Herzog's career. The film was not an immediate commercial success when it premiered, but after a few years it began to acquire cult status, especially in the United States. Francis Ford Coppola singles it out as a major inspiration for *Apocalypse Now*, and today it is the Herzog film that most often features on 'world's best film' lists. The American professor of philosophy and film Noël Carroll and the film critic Roger Ebert both include *Aguirre* in their Top Tens when they contribute to *Sight and Sound* magazine's occasional surveys of the best films ever.

Werner Herzog made the film at a point in his career when he was desperately hoping that the international audience would give him a warmer reception than the Germans had. He intended *Aguirre* to look ambitious and expensive, and wanted it to conquer the world, rather than just the niche audiences his films had hitherto reached, and in many ways *Aguirre* is Herzog's most American-looking film. Indeed, the first time Ebert included it in his list of the 100 best films, he remarked that he had had no idea it was not a normal commercial film. Actually, it is possible to watch *Aguirre* as a relatively normal film about a soldier who goes mad during a campaign and slowly loses control over himself and his troops. It ostensibly has a classical narrative shape, but, as one would expect with Herzog in the director's chair, there's something else afoot, too; through pure optical and sound situations during the film, he creates little spaces in which the audience is encouraged to think beyond the classical models of film and of thought.

The film was shot in Peru and centres on the Spanish conquistador Lope de Aguirre, who, as we are told in the opening titles, took part in an expedition in 1560 in search of El Dorado, the mythical city of gold. Herzog was attracted to the story because the real Aguirre was thought to be the first to defy Spain and declare South America's independence – and also because Aguirre was clearly stark raving mad, dubbing himself 'Wrath of God' and revolting not just against political power but against the whole world, even nature itself. For the same reasons, Kinski was the obvious choice for the lead role.

I use the term 'lead role', but at the start of the film Kinski's Aguirre is just one among many minor characters. The film opens with an expansive landscape shot – perhaps the most impressive of Herzog's career – in which hundreds of soldiers, pigs, llamas and chained tribespeople are moving like ants down a very narrow path in a mountain pass in the Andes, near Machu Picchu. They move slowly through the fog and into the jungle. We don't see any faces clearly, not even Kinski's. What we see is an undifferentiated mass of people in the magnificence of nature, and nature gives not a whit for whoever is moving through it. A cage of live chickens tumbles (like a reality effect) down the mountainside. A cannon follows and explodes, but the procession continues unabated. There's something tragic and gloomy about this march. The film's introductory title has already stated that the myth of El Dorado is just that, a myth, so we know from the start that the expedition will fail, but this nonetheless piques our interest in how exactly things will go wrong.

After the long opening shot we find ourselves in the depths of the jungle, and it's still hard to decipher whom we are supposed to be following. The actual leader of the expedition is Gonzalo Pizarro, but Herzog's camera does not follow this dominant subject for long. Instead, it joins the expedition's vanguard, led by Don Pedro. Don Pedro finds the terrain impassable and gives up, where-upon the hunchbacked lieutenant Aguirre rebels and stubbornly drives his men further down the river – and the camera tags along with them. Even here, though, it is not Aguirre who is the focus of the film, but the weak-willed priest Gaspar de Carvajal; he, or rather the content of his diary, is the film's narrative voice, trying to hold the story together.

The audience knows, not just from the film's title but also from our knowledge of the conventions of film drama, that it is Aguirre we should eventually expect something from, but we have to wait quite a while. Each shift between apparent lead characters is a breach that creates an any-space-whatever in the film's forward thrust, indicating that the hero could be someone else, and that the film could be about something else. Herzog consciously sub-verts the classical plot schema by hesitating to reveal who is the hero of the story and what kind of man he is. A true protagonist corresponding to the Hollywood model never really emerges. For a long time Aguirre is a small and *useless* character, but then there is no external situation that pressures him to act. No one has asked him, or forced him, to do anything. When he finally comes into his own it happens spontaneously, and he becomes the great traitor who wants to change not just the situation at hand, but the whole world in his voracious lust for power. His project is so crazy, such a *conquest of the useless*, that the standard model cannot keep pace.

One after the other, the men on the raft are lost – to fever and hunger, but mostly to the ugliest side of human nature, the dream of moulding the world to one's own will. Some of them dream of money and status, others of spreading God's word. Many of the other characters are Herzog's discreet nods to the Old World's assault on the New, but the main theme is the lust for power itself, rather than particular concrete or historical expressions of it. Aguirre is the one who most desires power, and he is willing to betray them all and do anything to get it. When he finally comes out on top his megalomania is inextinguishable, and he starts delivering wild speeches. Herzog took inspiration from the mad Field Marshal John Okello, who came to power in Zanzibar in the bloody coup of 1964, and during his short period in charge was known for such excesses as handing down sentences of 218 years' imprisonment for the theft of a bar of soap.

> I am the great traitor. There must be no other. Anyone who even thinks about deserting this mission will be cut up into 198 pieces. Those pieces will be stamped on until what is left can be used only to paint walls. Whoever takes one grain of corn or one drop of water more than his ration will be locked up for 155 years. If I, Aguirre, want the birds to drop dead from the trees, then the birds will drop dead from the trees. I am the wrath of God. The earth I pass will see me and tremble. But whoever follows me and the river, will win untold riches. But whoever deserts . . .

Aguirre ends with an image that is even more famous than the opening shot. Kinski is completely alone on the raft. All the others are dead. He still cannot let go of his crazy vision, and makes a magnificent speech about his plans for future world domination, and how he will found a new race, purer than ever before, by marrying his daughter, whom he seems not to have noticed has died. Neither does he seem to have registered that all his men are dead, or that they may have been transformed into a troupe of small monkeys that are bobbing around the raft.

Animals always have a role in Herzog's films. For the role as Aguirre, he and Kinski agreed on a distinctive crab walk, and the crab has since played a role in both *Invincible* (2001), which is set in 1930s Nazi Germany, and *Echos aus einem düsteren Reich* (*Echoes from a Sombre Empire*, 1990) about the despot Jean-Bédel Bokassa of the Central African Republic, in which Herzog uses thousands of crabs. They scuttle over the land, symbolizing that the most evil aspects of the human have crawled up from the dark depths of the sea, breaking through the thin layer of ice that Herzog thinks of as civilization. *Echoes from a Sombre Empire* ends, just as *Aguirre* does, with a monkey: a chain-smoking chimpanzee as the embodiment of a country where all civilized behaviour has turned to ashes.

In *Aguirre*, Kinski hunts the monkeys around the raft, yells at them, fishes one out of the water and throws it away. This is a madman who has uncompromisingly battled his way to the top, casting aside everything and everyone in his path, and is now incapable of letting go, even amid his resounding defeat. It is a leader who has no one left alive to lead, is cut off from the world on his raft, yet who in the final hours of defeat is still contemplating new territorial conquests and the sacrifice of more young men. 'I am God's wrath. Who is with me?' he shouts at the monkeys and the camera.

Aguirre is clearly a film about the most destructive sides of human vitality, but if the film refuses to adhere to classical cinema's standard models for plot and hero, it also negates categorization as

Monkeys, chickens and crabs all appear repeatedly in Herzog's films. The chicken is stupid, and the crab is a cipher for a dark past constantly threatening to crawl out of the sea. But the monkey or ape always appears when human nature has degenerated into its most atavistic forms. In the end, Aguirre is alone on his raft except for a troupe of monkeys. One of Herzog's most famous apes is to be found in the closing scene of *Echoes from a Sombre Empire*, which takes place in the dictator Jean-Bédel Bokassa's private zoo. The chimpanzee has been made to smoke by its owner and is now an addict.

The monk Carvajal (bottom) has the function of a chronicler in *Aguirre, the Wrath of God*. But slowly, any classical fixed points of narrative start to float around like the raft on which Aguirre and his followers are drifting. Along the way, we shift between main characters and points of focus, and finally the whole story descends into a fever dream, with severed heads that talk, ships in the crowns of the trees, and Brechtian dialogue on the respective lengths of the arrows that the local tribespeople are shooting at the company on the raft.

a portrait of an insane man whose interior world must be revealed and explained. It is not a straightforwardly political film warning against totalitarianism, either. Herzog is concerned with form. Neither the dramaturgy nor the characters are furnished with stable identities, and no one gets to lay claim to himself, to a final truth or to a linear narrative. Rather, the camera starts drifting away from Aguirre and the irresolute priest's narrative voice. Instead of illustrating Carvajal's stories or examining Aguirre's face, Herzog shows us landscapes. The camera wanders towards waterfalls and lingers on them much longer than makes sense for the film's forward impetus. Even after extended shots of the middle distance, Herzog cuts to a tighter close-up on the currents in the river, and the rivulets pirouette in little eddies, just as the images do in a way. Nothing in the soundtrack supports the story. The music lives out its own life in little loops. With his landscapes and sound, Herzog creates pure optical and sound situations, in Deleuze's terms, 'tearing a real image from clichés'.[6] The 'real image' is that neither life nor cinema can be accommodated in the spreadsheet of the truth of accountants.

From around the middle of the film, any fixed coordinates are abandoned, and the film's elements start to busy themselves with their own potential, each of them heading away from the tree structure's coherence and dichotomies. From the eddies under the waterfalls, a new perspective emerges: fever dreams, unbridled lust for power and megalomania merge imperceptibly. Unreal boats are suddenly hanging in very real ways from the trees, and all-too-real killer arrows are commented on in unreal ways, almost in Brechtian style, by the crew on the raft: 'Oh, long arrows are in fashion again,' says a dying man with his last breath. Then another one dies, still denying the very existence of the arrow that has pierced his heart. It all becomes an edited field of tension that oscillates between the subjective and the objective, until the whole plane of reality buckles and even the film's narrator must give up: 'I can write no more. We are going in circles.'

Thereafter, the camera's privileged perspective is consigned to the currents and circles the raft, which itself spins senselessly on the water around a point of emptiness. These are the circling motions we know from almost all Herzog's films, their role being to insist that there is no centre to be found. Herzog has made it impossible to differentiate between images that are subjective feverish visions, a madman's fantasy or an objective external gaze. But crucially, in the form of these sequences full of pure optical situations, he has crafted an any-space-whatever in which the viewer no longer feels that distinguishing between these perspectives actually matters. This breaks the habit of thinking in terms of the fixed identities of the truth of accountants. While the figure of Aguirre articulates absolute lust for power in its most perverse form, the filmstrip speaks to an evolution of thinking and an opening up of new paths.

The B-movie's crazy talk

A number of the modern directors of the 1960s and '70s played with pure optical and sound situations, but for many of them these were experiments that doubled down on their own predetermined agendas: a new truth of accountants. Such films often descended into forbidding abstractions, and Herzog has not been able to resist comparing them to his own work, suggesting that they have lost touch with audience and reality alike. He has never backed himself into a corner by essentializing pure optical situations as a cinematic truth. 'I love making that type of film, but please don't forget that I'm essentially a storyteller. The kind of storyteller you find in a marketplace in Marrakesh with a crowd around him, and he needs to tell them a story, or they'll leave.'

Perhaps that's one of the reasons why Herzog's work continued to seem accessible even after the New Wave period. One of the ways he ensured that his films did not get sucked into the elitist culture of the New Wave was to adopt the crazy language of the B-movie, incorporating lots of physical and sensory elements into

All Herzog's fiction films are typified by his distinctive direction of the actors, emphasizing slow movements and dialogue. But nowhere is this so pronounced as in *Heart of Glass*, in which he hypnotized all the supporting actors. The effect is to make them seem to react slowly and oddly to the clairvoyant prophet Hias.

Werner Herzog delights in finding skewed bodies and using strange gestures – a delight he shares with his American friends such as Harmony Korine and David Lynch. Since moving to the United States and having his American breakthrough, Herzog has used both his friends and his friends' actors in his own work. Here we see Michael Shannon, Grace Zabriskie and Chloë Sevigny in Herzog's *My Son, My Son, What Have Ye Done* (2009), which grew out of a collaboration with Lynch. This moved one journalist to write that 'The potentially insane David Lynch is finally teaming up with the certified insane Werner Herzog.' Herzog has always insisted that he is the sanest man in Los Angeles, at least in a clinical sense.

his films. The twisted bodies and strange gesticulations are formal experiments in their own right, but they stem from a popular culture that punctures the modernist pure optical situations. Just as he keeps the form of his works susceptible to butterflies, he tries to incorporate a high degree of physical experience into them, and in terms of methodology this means that he consistently eschews the closed space of the film studio and never uses special effects or storyboards:

> The world of the film studio seldom offers surprises to the filmmaker, partly because you only meet people who are being paid to be there. There is no environment, just four solid walls and a roof. Another thing I never do – which unavoidably kills off the necessary spontaneity of a film set – is to storyboard the plot. Accidents always occur if you keep your eyes open, but storyboards are just a tool for cowards, who have no faith in their own imagination, and are like slaves to the template.[7]

This must not be confused with *cinéma vérité*'s idea of going out into the world and being a fly on the wall. Being a fly on the wall is in itself a privileged position associated with the truth of accountants; it is being a slave to the template. Nor is it just a matter of going to the jungle and 'trying to be honest', as Herzog put it sarcastically in *The Minnesota Declaration*. It's about creating a form that breaks with the forms of the truth of accountants, but never closes in on itself as a new truth – as many of the 1960s art films ended up doing.

In a film such as *Woyzeck*, in which Herzog exclusively uses a stationary camera, it is up to Klaus Kinski to confront the closed space. There is a manuscript from which Kinski improvises, constantly aware of the camera's position. In the scene where Woyzeck (Kinski) tries to flee from the major, he does so by leaping straight towards the camera, startling the viewer. The dynamic physical factor that suddenly challenges the static narrative style has the effect of making us aware of our own physicality and that of the film. Initially we just manage to formulate the thought that Kinski is going to end up on top of us, and then we realize where the camera is and think: He's going to knock over the camera! Kinski neither knocks over the camera nor ends up in the viewer's lap, because the major pulls him back at the last moment, but an any-space-whatever has been created, a space that in a very physical way extends beyond the film frame and the logic of the plot and opens up room for thought. Kinski has crafted an ecstatic truth: for a short moment, in an otherwise normal film, we become aware that the fixed filmic settings are only perspectives and not a privileged truth.

Another way in which Herzog has always ensured that his works are not locked into a high-modern New Wave project has been to play up to the media machine that has tried to pin him down and label him in line with the truth of accountants. He says that he first began to grasp the dynamics of the media towards the end of the *Fitzcarraldo* shoot. Lots of stories were circulating about how wild, fascistoid Werner Herzog was violating the local population and devastating the South American rainforest. The tabloid press revelled in the knowledge that Herzog, Mick Jagger, Claudia Cardinale and Klaus Kinski were working together, but it was tricky to report on a project based deep in the jungle, so various papers started to invent stories. Herzog says he learned an important lesson: that he would have to come up with counter-stories himself.

At one point, the Italian press began to push a rumour that Cardinale had been run over by a truck and badly injured. Herzog debunked the story in a call from the jungle to an Italian journalist, but that didn't help, and the rumour spread to the international media. So Herzog revised his strategy and told the journalist that the rumour about Cardinale being hit by a truck was true, but that the details were much worse than reported. The lorry driver had been a barefoot drunkard who leapt out of the cabin and raped his unconscious victim. The reporter slammed down the receiver and the rumour died out. Ever since, Herzog has tried to take control of stories about his films. Instead of shutting the media out, he has continuously bombarded them with incredibly wild stories, so wild that in some cases even the tabloids have given up on him, ostensibly marking Herzog as too dishonest to slander. But a lot of material does seep into the media mill, and then back into the films as active ingredients, and this phenomenon can actually serve as a point of entry into some otherwise quite difficult works.

When *Aguirre* premiered, it was common knowledge that Kinski was also insane in real life, and that Herzog had found it necessary to have a gun in his hand while directing, to force him to finish the film. Before *Stroszek* everyone knew that Bruno S. really was a psychiatric patient, and in the years leading up to the launch of *Fitzcarraldo* it was stressed again and again that the ship was a real ship dragged over a real mountain, and that several real tribespeople had tragically died in the process. All these facts were true, but this is less interesting than their impact: they function as ecstatic interventions that offer a kind of access route into the films, so that the films can unfold in exchange with the extra-filmic world instead of closing in on themselves. If the films were allowed to close in on themselves completely, this would only invest them with a self-righteousness, just another variety of the truth of accountants.

In the case of *Heart of Glass*, in order to open up a work that is otherwise inaccessible Herzog uses B-movie gestures alongside this kind of extra-filmic ecstatic intervention. *Heart of Glass* consists almost exclusively of pure optical situations; it makes *Aguirre* look like a Hollywood classic. For example, many of the shots are produced by stop-motion, whereby pictures of cloud formations were taken every ten seconds over a period of eleven days. This results in a sense of flow, which is actually choppy if you look closely enough. It is a challenging film to relate to, so, before it was released,

Herzog told anyone who would listen that all the actors had been hypnotized before shooting started. Even today, you cannot pick up a DVD version of the film without that snippet of information featuring heavily in the paratext. This ecstatic intervention outside the work compels the viewer to look closely at the bodies. Every single one of the actors has a distinctive physical feature: large noses, deep-set eyes or extremely pale skin, and they move with awkward, absent gestures that are very different from the normal logic of movement. During a serious conversation a hand will begin to twitch, as if the actor suffered from Tourette's syndrome. The twitching does nothing to contribute to the scene in question or to move the plot forward, and it doesn't seem to be a gimmick. Rather, it seems as though the hand has detached itself from its moorings and from the force of the story. It no longer serves the unity of the film, but lays claim to its own heterogeneity. The viewer is jabbed at by the stories about hypnosis that pre-empted *Heart of Glass*, and by the strange glitches and twitches in the work. They breach the static frame of the film and an ecstatic truth swims into focus: that there is more than one way to give bodies and circumstances the once-over.

The documentary art of the 'And'

Werner Herzog does away with the idea that there is one, and only one, truth to be grasped. There is no *actual* story that is just awaiting excavation, and there is no one definitive identity that can easily be portrayed. In his cinema books, Gilles Deleuze comments on this as the shift in modern film culture away from a stable identity, Ego = Ego, and towards the poet Arthur Rimbaud's famous phrase *Je est un autre* (I is an other). In the context of documentary cinema, Rimbaud's grammatical displacement of identity entails film breaching the stable points and identities of classical dramaturgy as well as our notions about what a documentary is, genre-wise, and focusing instead on what it *can* be.

As a genre, documentary can be loosely defined as film whose content is based on this world rather than another world, but Herzog's documentaries feel no compunction to stay in this world or to live up to requirements about objective versus subjective, or true versus false. Rather, they undermine themselves with detours and breaches that blast open the narrative. Deleuze would say they were rhizomatic. Any proclivity for the idealism of the tree structure is abandoned, which opens up the possibility that neither subjects nor documentaries should be looked at essentialistically – as something clearly defined and goal-driven – but should be seen instead as changeable things, a medley of creative forces, always in the process of becoming something other than they were before. A key quotation about the rhizome is: 'A rhizome has no beginning or end; it is always in the middle, between things, inter-being, *intermezzo*. The tree is filiation, but the rhizome is alliance, uniquely alliance. The tree imposes the verb "to be", but the fabric of the rhizome is the conjunction, "and . . . and . . . and . . ."'[8] This more or less describes Herzog's *The White Diamond* of 2004, a film that pre-dated his comeback with *Grizzly Man* and is thus somewhat overlooked, especially considering how important it is for an understanding of his method.

The White Diamond is so far from a classic documentary film that it's almost impossible to describe what it is about – so quickly does it abandon the carabiners of its plot. Instead of mimetic reproduction, it focuses on the life force of the event, which opens up to the other routes that the story could have taken. The film opens in the middle of its own story and propagates wildly outwards in a myriad of directions.

When we as the audience step into the narrative, we encounter a sequence about the engineer Graham Dorrington, who is constructing a special air balloon formed like a raindrop or a diamond (the white diamond) that can hover silently. The hope is that the balloon can be used to dive into the rainforest to film animal and plant life without disturbing it. From the start of the film,

Herzog and Dorrington vie for the status of main character, but the film project itself slips from the construction of the vessel to Dorrington's dream of filming the mystical abri behind the Kaiteur waterfall to a story from the past about Dorrington's friend Dieter, who crash-landed and died in another of Dorrington's inventions. The vessel seems to be unusable, and perhaps an act of penance, but the film does not linger on this psychological revelation.

Every time the film finds a new story, it starts off down a new path. Eventually we leave Dorrington in favour of his assistant Yhap and various local people, who are abandoned in turn for Yhap's red rooster. For a time, Herzog leaves the whole project behind and travels back to the Kaieteur waterfall. He sends an experienced free-climber into the cave behind the waterfall with a camera to film the mysterious space, a feat that turns out to be feasible and thus renders Dorrington's balloon totally pointless – perhaps it was a *useless conquest*, just like Fitzcarraldo's impossible project? We simply don't know, and the film has no intention of telling us. Neither, as we have seen, has it any intention of showing us the footage shot in the cave. *Mysterious realist* that he is, Herzog chooses to safeguard the waterfall, which is a mystical site in the religion of the local people. In the end, the film slips through our hands. The viewer leaves the film behind without it ending as such. Instead, we step out of it in the middle, while it is still becoming.

It is no coincidence that the air balloon and the film are named after a white crystal. In all Herzog's films, white appears as the colour of possibility. Just as many Herzog films open to fog, white often crops up at crucial moments. In *Fitzcarraldo* the ship is painted white, and Kinski wears a white suit when he embarks. In *Bells from the Deep* the pilgrims crawl out on to the white ice to peer down to the bells on the lake bed. In *Grizzly Man* Herzog uses the term 'white elephant' about the secret sound recordings of Timothy Treadwell's death. In *The Great Ecstasy of Woodcarver Steiner* the white snow forms the backdrop to Walter Steiner's metamorphosis into a bird. In *Fata Morgana* it is a little white

The White Diamond is Herzog's most daring documentary in a dramaturgical sense. The title refers to the special airship in the film (illustrated on the facing page) – a sort of small Zeppelin that can navigate soundlessly over the jungle to film inaccessible areas. But the film moves curiously on from science and aviation to the scientist Graham Dorrington and to the great Kaieteur waterfalls in Guyana, which play an important role in the local religion. The film is also about the people Herzog (or perhaps, rather, the film) happens upon, not least Marc Anthony Yhap and his red rooster.

desert fox that the boy is possibly choking, and so on. In these *white events* all possibilities stand open – for better and for worse. They are, in Herzog's words, 'moments of uncertainty'. The many stories in *The White Diamond* are like light that hits a white crystal and is scattered in all directions. Every time the story is stopped by a plane of the crystal is an any-space-whatever and pure potential.

In powerfully staged documentaries, what is important ceases to be the identities before the camera; instead, it is what arises in relation in a zone of indistinguishability, very much like the one we experience at the end of *Aguirre*. A documentary such as Herzog's *The White Diamond* never really coalesces into a form, but remains in a state of becoming, and every sequence thereby constitutes an event in its own right: that is, something concretely singular that evades a general identification with the truth of accountants and is always in the process of becoming something. The film ceases to think in terms of stable identities, but focuses on spaces in between. These in-between spaces become *a cinema of the And* that rhizomatically and unhierarchically and in a potentially infinite series shows this *and* this *and* this *and* . . .

The White Diamond is a metafilm about truth in documentary: an essay film that researches a method Herzog would later use in *Encounters at the End of the World* (2007), a film in which we find ourselves in the Antarctic and meet a researcher *and* a researcher *and* a researcher, each of whom is their work *and* something else. PhD *and* dishwasher; philosopher *and* truck driver; and so on.

In *Cave of Forgotten Dreams* (2010) Herzog perfects his *cinema of the And* and combines it with his *white events*. He was the only filmmaker ever to be granted entry to the Chauvet cave in the south of France, which is home to cave paintings that are 32,000 years old. Herzog calls this a glimpse into the awakening of the modern human soul, a cradle of our civilization that demonstrates that who we are has been determined by the development of cultural systems and artistic expression. Herzog also finds it interesting that the artistic thinking evinced by the paintings seems just as

Herzog prefers to work with people who are more than one thing. Here we see Stefan Pashov in *Encounters at the End of the World*, who is a philosopher *and* drives a forklift truck at the McMurdo research station on Antarctica.

advanced as it is today. They contradict the notion that history necessarily develops towards greater sophistication. This indirectly supports his argument that civilization entails constantly being on guard for the evil and murky aspects of the human and the world; they will always be lurking below the surface, at least as long as we humans are as we are.

In terms of style, *Cave of Forgotten Dreams* consists of sequences in which Herzog alternately films the cave paintings and interviews archaeologists and scientists, while the soundtrack features him philosophizing about the nature of historical narrative and truth. It is a story *and* a story *and* . . .

Herzog is at least as interested in the people who are obsessed with the past as he is in the cave paintings themselves. Why do these archaeologists stare so intensely into the depths of time? What does it say about the human race that we do such things? In this film, as in *Encounters at the End of the World*, he makes a blatant point of not assigning the people he interviews to identity categories fixed by the truth of accountants. They are not just their work. Take, for example, Gilles Tosello, archaeologist *and* painter, and Julien Monney, archaeologist *and* circus artiste. The conversation between Herzog and Monney is particularly interesting, not just because Monney is a circus performer and the conversation is a charming collision of German-English and French-English pronunciation, but also because it clearly demonstrates Herzog's project and his method. Monney works with the laser scanning technology that generates 3D computer representations of the cave; before the interview (see below) we have just been shown the model of the cave, precise to the nearest millimetre. Monney explains that all of this is a means to understand what happened in the cave. Herzog interrupts with a turn of phrase he has used before in his criticism of the filmmakers of *cinéma vérité*, who he thinks only produce the truth of accountants and behave like tourists taking pictures of ruins.

> Herzog: It is like you are creating the phone directory of
> Manhattan. Four million precise entries, but do they dream?
> Do they cry at night? What are their hopes? What are
> their families? You'll . . . we'll never know from the phone
> directory.
>
> Monney: Definitely. We will never know, because the past
> is definitely lost. We will never reconstruct the past. We can
> only create a representation of what exists now, today. You
> are a human being. I am a human being. And here when
> you come to the cave, of course there are some things.
> I have my own background.
>
> Herzog: What is your background, if I may ask?
>
> Monney: Well, I used to be a circus man before, but now
> I've switched to archaeology.

I asked Werner Herzog what difference he thought it made that it was he and not a more traditional director of science documentaries who got permission to film in the Chauvet cave with its 32,000-year-old paintings. He answered: 'It would have been a bad film otherwise.' In one of the key scenes in *Cave of Forgotten Dreams*, he converses with the scientist *and* circus artist Julien Monney about lions – on the walls of the cave and in our dreams.

Herzog: Circus? Doing what? Lion tamer?

Monney: Well, mostly . . . no, not a lion tamer [laughs], mostly the unicycle and juggling, yeah.

At this point Herzog cuts away from the interview and briefly shows Monney inside the cave, while the interview continues on the voiceover. The cut most likely hides the fact that Herzog has asked him to include lions in the dreams he relates, since a lion tamer is a more suitable and indeed funnier image in relation to the cave paintings than a unicyclist.

Monney: The first time I entered to Chauvet Cave, I had a chance to get in during five days, and it was so powerful. Then, every night, I was dreaming of lions. And every day was the same shock for me. It was an emotional shock. I mean, I'm a scientist but a human too. And after five days, I decided not to go back in the cave, because I needed time just to relax and take time to . . .

Herzog: Absorb it?

Monney: Absorb it, yeah.

Herzog: And you dreamed not of paintings of lions, but of real lions?

Monney: About both, both, definitely.

Herzog: And you were afraid in your dreams?

Monney: I was not afraid. No, no, I was not afraid. It was more a feeling of powerful things, and deep things, a way to understand things that is not a direct way.

Herzog cuts next to a scene inside the cave, where the senior scientist asks everyone to stay completely quiet, so quiet that one might be able to hear one's own heartbeat. But Herzog doesn't turn down the music, a high-flown cello composition by Ernst Reijseger (who is a guest lecturer at the Rogue Film School). Herzog does not want to listen to the heartbeats of the scientists; he wants the audience to feel their own hearts beat, while he shows images of the scientists' faces as they stare at the cave paintings and directly into the camera, at us. What is it that they are looking for? What are they listening to? What are we staring at as viewers? What are *we* listening to?

The camera glides towards the cave paintings: 'These images are memories of long-forgotten dreams,' says Herzog in voiceover. 'Is this their heartbeat or ours? Will we ever be able to understand the visions of the artists across such an abyss of time?'

This is twenty minutes into the film. For the next hour, Herzog shows sequences with different scientists, one *and* another one *and* another one, each of them pursuing their charming obsession with the past. At first glance, *Cave of Forgotten Dreams* could seem to be an entirely normal scientific documentary, spiced up with humour. But when Herzog reveals in his voiceover that plans are afoot to build a precise replica of the grotto, a kind of theme park, and that replicating even the smell of the cave is under consideration, one can almost hear the sneering tone from *Tokyo-Ga* when he complains about people mutilating the landscape with numbing neon signs. At the very end of the film, an hour after we have listened to our own heartbeat, Herzog's *white event* takes place, in the form of an ecstatic truth, an epilogue about albino crocodiles, an addendum that has sparked both outrage and joy.

Herzog relates that only 100-odd miles (160 km) away from the Chauvet cave lies a nuclear power station. Waste water that has been used to cool the reactors is let into a series of large greenhouses, where the warm water has created a tropical climate – and the facility is constantly being expanded. At some point crocodiles were

As an epilogue to *Cave of Forgotten Dreams*, Herzog shows these albino crocodiles. The last time I asked about them he said: 'Yes, it's pure fiction of course. They're not even crocodiles, they are caimans. But they're what most people remember about the film. And people love them.'

released into the water and they started to breed in the favourable environment of this artificial jungle. Unsurprisingly, mutations have occurred because of the radioactive water: albino crocodiles.

'A thought is born of this surreal environment,' says Herzog in voiceover, while we watch the white crocodiles swim around and stare at us and at each other. Only a few tens of thousands of years ago there were kilometre-high (⅔-mile) glaciers here, but now a new climate is on the way. Are the white crocodiles perhaps the start of a race that will be dominant thousands of years from now? And what will *they* think, when they see the paintings in the Chauvet cave?

'Nothing is real, nothing is certain,' says Herzog poetically in his voiceover. Perhaps he means his own science-fiction epilogue, or perhaps the many theories about the past that we've heard over the last hour. We see an albino crocodile approach what looks like its mirror image. It's hard to know if it is seeing the other or just looking itself in the eye. 'Do they really meet, or is it just their own imagined mirror reflection?' asks Herzog. The two albinos get very close to each other in precisely the same pose, their lips almost meeting in a kiss. It looks like a reflection, but then one of them swims away. Nothing is certain, not even Herzog's metaphor about humans seeing only their reflection in animals and in the people of the past. But the shots of the white crocodiles have punctured the documentary idea of an objective gaze, and in their ecstatic truth they question our assumptions: who are we, and from what podium do we hand down our cocksure judgements about the past? Are they more valid than Herzog's playful prediction about the race of the future? 'Are we today,' he muses in the voiceover, 'possibly the crocodiles who look back into an abyss of time when we see the paintings of Chauvet cave?'

Herzog with Bruce Chatwin's old rucksack during the shoot of *Nomad: In the Footsteps of Bruce Chatwin*. On his deathbed Chatwin gave the rucksack to Herzog, who has kept it ever since. It appeared in *Scream of Stone* as a quiet tribute, but not before Herzog made a film about his friend, with whom he shared an idea about walking as a poetic activity.

(overleaf) *Where the Green Ants Dream* dives – like Bruce Chatwin's *The Songlines* – down into the Aborigines' mythical songlines in Australia, songlines that are threatened by the settlements of modern civilization.

SEVEN
THE NOMADIC
ALTERNATIVE

Bruce Chatwin's rucksack

When the writer Bruce Chatwin (1940–1989) was on his deathbed, he summoned Werner Herzog and handed over his famous rucksack with the words: 'You're the one who has to carry it on now.'[1]

Chatwin was ill with AIDS, and Herzog was visiting to show him his new film *Wodaabe*, about the nomadic people of the Sahel region in Africa. The film made Chatwin long to go exploring again, but his legs could no longer carry him. Herzog picked up where he had left off, and has since identified the rucksack as his most treasured possession. 'I still carry it, and I had it with me in the snow storm in Patagonia, sitting on it for fifty hours dug into the snow. It is much more than just a tool to carry things. If my house were on fire I would first grab my children and throw them from the window. But of all my belongings it would be the rucksack that I would save.'[2]

Herzog and Chatwin first met in Australia, when Herzog was filming *Where the Green Ants Dream* (1984) and Chatwin was writing *The Songlines* (1987). In their respective art forms they were exploring Aboriginal mythology, which is not written down, but is passed down from father to son in the form of song on the basis of lines in the landscape – songlines – while out walking. This common interest in the nomadic was the basis of Herzog's and Chatwin's friendship and their intellectual affinity. In the posthumously published *What Am I Doing Here?*, Chatwin writes: '[Herzog] was the only person with whom I could have a one-to-one conversation about what I could call the sacramental aspect of walking. He and I share the idea that walking is not simply therapeutic for one's self, but that it is a poetic activity that can heal the world of its ills.'[3]

Herzog inherited Chatwin's rucksack because of this common understanding, and he took the responsibility of carrying it very seriously. His works are full of nomads, pilgrims and other wanderers, who in Chatwin's words are pursuing a form of poetry. Walking – whether in nature or as a flâneur in the city – is a

Herzog's documentary *Wodaabe - Die Hirten der Sonne* (*Wodaabe - Herdsmen of the Sun*, 1989) is about the nomadic Wodaabe herdsmen of the Sahel region. They consider themselves the most beautiful people in the world, and hold ceremonies celebrating beauty and love, in which the criteria for loveliness are height and white teeth and eyes. The women select the most attractive men and spend a night in the desert with their chosen beaus. Herzog took the raw footage with him to Chatwin's sickbed and showed him the film in short segments, when he was awake. In this image, Chatwin can be seen during the shooting of *Cobra Verde* (1987), an adaptation of Chatwin's novel *The Viceroy of Ouidah* (1980). Chatwin is on the right holding his notebook, in which he wrote the essay 'Werner Herzog in Ghana' (from *What Am I Doing Here?*). In this photograph by Beat Presser, alongside Herzog and Chatwin, the photographer Viktor Ružička can also be seen (he broke his leg during the shoot), as can Mikhelina, the daughter of the executive producer Walter Saxer. In 2019 Herzog made a documentary, *Nomad: In the Footsteps of Bruce Chatwin*, about his friend.

romantic notion in the culture of modernity, lauded by thinkers who subscribed to the idea that it cultivated gainful philosophical activity or brought one closer to the nature of the Divine. In the hippie era the same wanderlust lured Western youth around the globe, and more recent youth culture has the phenomenon of the gap year, backpacking to Southeast Asia or on the highways of America. Understood in relation to Herzog's aesthetic as I have described it in the previous chapters, walking[4] – travelling on foot – is a form of artistic activity that deviates from the usual processual logic of life and creates one of Herzog's ecstasies; in this sense it is analogous to the new images that spawn any-spaces-whatever in his films. This is a matter of extremely physical any-spaces-whatever – so far from theoretical constructions, so concretely sensory, that in Herzog's walking films we glimpse an ethics in the aesthetics. I use the word 'glimpse' advisedly, since Herzog treats this subject just as poetically and evasively as he does any other, and even Chatwin's more explicit theory is fuzzy at best. Nonetheless, it is worth trying to grasp their ethics of walking, because it can add nuance to our understanding of Herzog's new images.

Herzog's pilgrims

In *Pilgrimage* (2001), Herzog follows various Russian and Mexican pilgrims. The images focus on their wandering rather than the point of origin or the goal, and the only words in the film are in the form of a faked quotation from the medieval mystic Thomas à Kempis: 'It is only the pilgrims who in the travails of their earthly voyage do not lose their way. Whether our planet be frozen or scorched, they are guided by the same prayers, and suffering, and fervor, and woe.'

Herzog is not interested in the pilgrims' God. This is made very clear in *Rad der Zeit* (*Wheel of Time*, 2003), in which Herzog follows a Buddhist pilgrim on his 3,000-km (1,800 mi.) walk to reach the Kalachakra initiations presided over by the Dalai Lama

A dedicated pilgrim in *Wheel of Time* travels on foot to the Dalai Lama's ceremony in India. For every step the pilgrim takes, he lies down prostrate with his forehead against the earth.

in India. The trek is extremely physically demanding. Each time the pilgrim takes a step, he lies down prostrate with his forehead touching the ground and prays. The journey has taken him over three years, but when he reaches the religious ceremony, Herzog punctures the reverence of the moment with a dancing monkey performing for a musician.

Herzog is excited about the pilgrim's walk, but it is 'the travails of their earthly voyage' and not the religious goal that interests him. It is in the intense transit between A and B, between things, in the gap between categories in the truth of accountants, that we should look for the poetic and liberating activity of travelling on foot. This is very obvious in Herzog's three films about plane crashes: *Little Dieter Needs to Fly* (1997), *Julianes Sturz in den Dschungel* (*Wings of Hope*, 1999) and *Rescue Dawn* (2006). Despite the fact that all three films are built around almost miraculous events, they focus not on divine intervention but on individual people, and the anguish of their earthly journeys.

The documentary *Wings of Hope* is about a German woman, Juliane Koepcke, who at the age of seventeen was a passenger in an airliner that crashed in the Peruvian jungle. It was Christmas Eve 1971 and she was travelling home with her mother from Lima, where she was at school, to visit her father, who was working as a research biologist in a small research station in Pucallpa in the east of the country. There were 92 people on the aircraft when it exploded at an altitude of 3,000 m (10,000 ft). Juliane was the only survivor. Twelve days after the accident, and two days after the search teams had given up trying to find the wreckage in the densest jungle, the young girl walked out of the rainforest.

In 1971 Herzog was working on *Aguirre* in Peru, and had himself planned to be on board that same flight together with a group of actors, of which one was Kinski. But the plane was overbooked and there was not enough room for everyone with a ticket, and to their great annoyance Herzog and his companions were left at the airport. In the documentary, he flies the same route with Koepcke, who sits in the same seat, 19F, that she had been assigned when her plane went down.

Wings of Hope was made as part of the television series *Höllenfahrten* (Trips from Hell) for the German station ZDF. The producers demanded that all the films in the series include re-enactments of historical events, but Herzog thought that was a terrible TV cliché. Instead of using actors on a set, he pushed the notion of re-enactment to its furthest extreme. He flew with the actual person to the concrete geographical spot where the event took place.

Herzog and Koepcke head into the rainforest, where they find the wreckage of the plane and talk about the accident, their conversation structured by the crash artefacts they find. Then they walk out of the jungle, taking precisely the same route that Juliane did in 1971. Along the way she explains how she managed it: with a broken collarbone, concussion, one eye swollen shut, one shoe missing and only a bag of sweets to eat, she remembered the survival tips she had gleaned from her scientist father and followed a watercourse until she encountered people.

For Herzog, Koepcke's journey in *Wings of Hope* is a methodical do-over of *Little Dieter Needs to Fly* (which itself is a feature-length version of *Flucht aus Laos*, which was made for the same ZDF series). Herzog tells the story of the pilot Dieter Dengler, who grew up in the ruins of post-war Germany and was obsessed with flying. When he was eighteen he left the country, which did not have an air force, and moved to the United States to become an army pilot. He succeeded, and in 1966 he was sent to Vietnam, where he was shot down on a secret mission over Laos. He was taken prisoner and tortured, but managed to escape and walked (missing one shoe, just like Koepcke) through the jungle to freedom.

Herzog's re-enactment in this case was more extreme than what he put Koepcke through. Dengler is first led through the jungle in handcuffs, as happened in 1966, and then put in prison; only then does Herzog have him walk out of the jungle.

Werner Herzog takes a radical approach to re-enactment in *Wings of Hope*. Juliane Koepcke, who survived a plane crash in the Amazon in 1971, is filmed making precisely the same journey that she did back then. She flies the route in the same seat, and walks on foot out of the jungle, just as she did in 1971. Herzog used the same method in *Little Dieter Needs to Fly*, which he later remade as the feature film *Rescue Dawn* (2006), starring Christian Bale.

Dengler's and Koepcke's respective treks away from death and imprisonment towards freedom and life both have the air of useless conquests, quite impossible projects, but as people they are very different types. They both experienced a childhood that inured them to hardship, but they handle supposedly insuperable hurdles differently – Koepcke has a cool, scientific approach to the world, while Dengler lives life with an indomitable optimism and joy – but what they have in common is that they refuse to be knocked down, either by nature or by civilization. They accept the rough conditions as premise and overcome them, and overcome themselves, too. They do not deposit their fate in the hands of a god or other beliefs about how the world works. They take action – and action is, as indeed it so often is for Herzog, to travel on foot.

In 2006 Herzog directed *Rescue Dawn*, a feature-film version of Dengler's story with Christian Bale in the lead role. Perhaps this seems unnecessary, when he had already explored the topic in two excellent documentaries, but at least in theory the repetition has the advantage of making Herzog's point clear. Dengler's fellow prisoners who opt to stay in prison and hope for mercy or a diplomatic solution end up dying; those who flee also risk death, but at least they enjoy the possibility of staying alive.

In his book *In Patagonia* (1977), Bruce Chatwin expands on the sacramental but non-religious aspect of walking: 'My God is the God of Walkers. If you walk hard enough, you probably don't need any other God.'[5] The walker does not need a God on high, for by keeping himself in motion he himself penetrates the space between world and word, a gap that God or other overarching explanatory models fill in or cover up. By keeping oneself moving, one avoids stagnating in one single explanation; one holds oneself open to the world, showing that this world could be different. To travel on foot is therefore to breach the identities of the truth of accountants, just as Herzog's new images break with the processual logic of the classical film. If the walking is concerned with itself as form, with its movement, it becomes a poetic act that can create an any-space-whatever. As such, walking is an *ecstatic truth* and an expansion of Herzog's new images towards a nascent ethics, an ecstatically true form of life.

Breeding pigs

In Herzog's first feature film, *Signs of Life* (1968), the German soldiers who are stationed in Greece during the Second World War meet a nomad, a gypsy king who has become separated from his tribe and is travelling through the world alone. The soldiers ask whether he and his tribe are perhaps walking in circles and that's why they never find each other, but the gypsy replies: 'No, I'm not moving in circles, other people do that, my people are always changing direction.' Already in his first film, then, Herzog establishes this conceptual opposition, an idea that runs like a red

Gertrude Bell – played by Nicole Kidman in *Queen of the Desert* – flees her homeland's conventions of gender and marriage. In the desert, with the Bedouin, she finds a freedom she can have nowhere else.

thread through all his work: the person, or the thought, that is permanently settled, versus nomadic movement and changeability. The wandering gypsy king is a serene, polite man. The German soldier is a restless soul who feels out of place and needs to break free or trample something under his feet. In *Queen of the Desert* (2015), Nicole Kidman, playing Gertrude Bell, says it plainly: Far from the British middle class, with the nomads in the desert, she finds a kind of freedom.

In Chatwin's draft of his unpublished work *The Nomadic Alternative*, he maintains that the great vertically structured (or tree-structured) religions first arose when humans began living in permanent settlements. He praises the lifestyle of the nomads as less hierarchical, less tree-like, and thus more life-enhancing in the way they lead their herds towards life-giving oases and new pastures with no heed to property deeds or fences. Chatwin argues that the nomads' horizontal movement and concrete link to the empirical shape their way of thinking, such that they are more open to displacements, changes and loose connections than are sedentary cultures, which in turn are characterized by closed social structures and develop a need for the thought frameworks of the tree structure. Chatwin talks about an *horreur du domicile* of which the modern Western lust for travel is a symptom.[6]

Herzog carries Chatwin's rucksack with him. In his science-fiction film *The Wild Blue Yonder* (2005), an alien visits Earth and seems inspired by Chatwin's thoughts on the nomadic and the sedentary. The alien is a thoroughly Herzogian alien, unsuited (or *useless*) in every possible way for conditions on Earth, which he freely admits, and thus Herzog punctures any fantasy of redemption on the far side of the Milky Way. But he gives the alien time to talk anyway, because as an outsider he can offer a critical appraisal of our earthly community:

> Breeding domesticated pigs. This was mankind's first heart sin. Why? Because in order to breed animals you have to become sedentary; this begat settlements, which begat towns which begat cities, which begat all the problems that will be mankind's destruction. Breeding dogs is not a sin because they all go with you on your nomadic hunts. But pigs, that was the sin.

The alien's outburst against sedentary culture seems vitriolic, and Chatwin's rucksack seems to contain a somewhat romanticizing attitude to the nomad. For Herzog, though, it is a matter not of hostility or romanticism, but of making a point about wandering, the nomadic alternative, that corresponds to his *cinema of the And*. The nomad thinks not in terms of fixed points and identities, but in terms of movement, carefree paths instead of fixed owner status. This is the lifestyle of the *And*.

In *Minima Moralia*, Theodor Adorno insists that art can introduce chaos into order. In the same work, he discusses the nomadic as a kind of disorder in contrast to sedentary thought, that is, thought patterns typical of the truth of accountants. He cites Friedrich Nietzsche, who writes in *The Gay Science*: 'It is even part of my good fortune not to be a house owner.'[7] Herzog's alien in *The Wild Blue Yonder* takes after Adorno and Nietzsche; the criticism is directed not at houses or at living in the same place one's whole life, but at living and thinking under the roof of fixed identities. This is analogous to settling down with a form of thought and life that operates with clearly bounded identities – European, Christian, German – in an exclusionary relationship to non-European, non-Christian, non-German. The alien's critique does not express hatred towards concrete ownership or concrete identities, but is an oblique challenge to embrace the nomadic, which, just like art, foments disorder.

Any-identity-whatever

'Nomads have no points, paths or land,' write Deleuze and Guattari.[8] For them, nomadic disorder means nomadic thinking (*pensée nomade*), a principle of thought that equates to thinking rhizomatically, existing in the spaces in-between in a state of constant becoming, like Herzog's new images, joyfully hovering as potential. In Herzog's and Chatwin's respective Australian works, *Where the Green Ants Dream* and *The Songlines*, the Aboriginal mythology of wandering is staged as a horizontal rhizomatic form in which landscape, community and individual weave in and out of each other in lines and thus constitute an alternative to settled society (the tree structure). The songlines have the potential to grow wild like couch grass, because each new encounter is a new line created in a song-meeting between landscape, community and individual, always in a state of becoming.

The nomadic as a principle of thought therefore also becomes a principle of resistance to the truth of accountants. This can already be seen in *Signs of Life*, in the person of the friendly, open-minded

'Remember that the Internet is not a cloud of information. It is not little particles in a mist. It is servers in enormous chilled silos, which can easily be controlled and which can also very easily be knocked out of action with a couple of hand grenades. Give me a bazooka and I'll do it,' said Herzog at the Sundance Film Festival when *Lo and Behold – Reveries of the Connected World* (2016) had its premiere. The film is an essay about the greatest paradigm shift in recent times, the Internet, which – like almost everything else in our time – came, for good or ill, from California. 'This is where questions of civil rights and gay rights and gender equality and technological progress have all originated since the 1960s. As well as all the stupidity with New Age philosophy and the like,' says Herzog. In connection with *Wheel of Time* he spoke with the Dalai Lama; they were in agreement that not all cultures can simply be lifted from one place and inserted into another. But in *Lo and Behold* we see monks tweeting instead of meditating. As Herzog commented at Sundance: 'I've never seen a single tweet that was truly interesting. 100,000 tweets are just 100,000 times 140 characters of stupidity.'

gypsy king in his encounter with the German occupiers, and very clearly in the plane-crash films about Dieter Dengler and Juliane Koepcke, in which walking becomes an expression of creativity, the ability to act and the will to live. Instead of sitting still and accepting the worldview of the truth of accountants, the nomad is always finding new images in the spaces in-between, and possible new paths in life. As Deleuze might say, the nomad uproots the tree in his head and plants grass.

Nomadic disorder is thus not about moving physically, but about holding thought open. In *The Minnesota Declaration* Herzog writes: 'Tourism is sin, and travel on foot virtue.' The tourist, as Herzog claims, is an adequate name for a *cinéma vérité* director, wandering to the ends of the Earth without ever creating nomadic disorder. The tourist photo is always just a record of a visit, a gaze from the outside and from the perspective of the truth of accountants, before the tourist goes home again. If one always travels with a specific goal and comes home with a snapshot, one is too concerned with this process of mastery and risks scaring away new becomings and trampling the fragile shoots underfoot.

Despite all his many journeys and shifts in identity, Herzog has frequently pointed out that he *is* a man, *is* from Germany, *is* from Sachrang in Bavaria, and although in *Wheel of Time* he converses with the Dalai Lama, he *is* still a part of Christian European culture (a view Herzog also makes clear in 'Meeting Gorbachev' (2018)). Herzog and the Dalai Lama actually agree that it makes no sense to deny one's cultural context completely. That would just be 'religious tourism'.

When I ask Herzog directly if he, with his love for the nomad and his scepticism about the development of civilization (including his recent critique of the Internet in *Lo and Behold*, 2016, in which funnily enough we see monks tweeting instead of meditating), thinks we should wander back in time, back to the cave – the hunters' grotto in Chauvet, which he filmed in *Cave of Forgotten Dreams* – he shakes his head forcefully.

Our glimpse into that cave shows that the germ of the modern human was already present. There was a well-developed sense of art and of stories and a longing for answers, 32,000 years ago. But we can't go back. It's not possible, and it's not desirable. The poet must not avert his eyes from reality, but look at what there is. But in the shift from nomadic to settled lies the origin not just of all the great gains of civilization, the pyramids, space travel and the internet, but the origin of problems and self-destructiveness too.

Leaving our pig husbandry behind and setting out on the road like nomads is thus not about running away from our background or geographical origin, or turning back time in the belief that it was all better in the old days. It's about thinking *as if* we were nomads. A nomad seeks out the spaces inbetween in order to find new paths, new thoughts, and embodies the principles of less limited forms of life, less exclusive communities.

Just as Herzog's images in the pure optical situations create any-spaces-whatever, in which the potential of the image emerges as a singular event, nomadic wandering is an extremely physical any-space-whatever. Just as Herzog's images break with known truths, the nomad breaks with known identities and emerges as a singular event, bursting forth from the homogeneous story, an any-identity-whatever analogous to the film's any-space-whatever.

In his travel novel *Vom gehen im Eis. München – Paris 23.11 bis 14.12 1974* (*Of Walking in Ice*, 1978), it becomes clear that Herzog also sees in the nomadic principle the possibility of a community in which everyone holds their thinking open and thinks consistently in terms of potentials and meetings of equals, without settling down under the roof of the truth of accountants.

Walking for a frail freedom

Of Walking in Ice is written in the form of a diary, and recounts the possibly true story of Herzog's journey on foot from Munich to the deathbed of the film historian Lotte Eisner in late 1974. He walks through the wintry landscape to Paris, but more important than making it to the French capital is the fact that Eisner is on the verge of dying.

Herzog is unhappy, and fears that Eisner is going to die, but there's nothing he can do about her illness; he is *useless*. But from this ground zero, he simply starts to live. His walk to Paris makes no sense in the light of the truth of accountants. If he wanted to reach Eisner's sickbed in time, he could travel by plane or train or car, but he chooses to travel on foot. There is not much about Eisner in the diary. She and her illness feature along with the geographical coordinates in the first few pages of the book, but she is mentioned in passing only twice before Herzog gets to Paris. The facts, the truths of accountants, are abandoned in favour of a real intimacy in the in-between space of walking, which emerges in the form of stories that have something to do with Herzog's friendship with Eisner. The walk develops into a poetic act and a conquest of the useless: a walk for life in defiance of the greatest obstacle imaginable – death.

Herzog writes at the start of the book: 'My steps are firm. And now the earth trembles. When I move, a buffalo moves. When I rest, a mountain reposes.' He sets his foot down with his whole weight, and writes the poetry of walking in the white winter landscape; he reasserts his useless existence with every step.

The steps become stories, songlines of friendship in a sense, whereby his feelings for Eisner – whom he refers to as 'Eisnerinden' – flow into a zone of inseparability between her, Herzog and the landscape though which he wanders. He walks through storms and lets himself be blown around by them. He meets lonely ravens.

Lovely fields, dead landscapes, unbearable cold and rain. Every night he breaks into a hut or a caravan to sleep, and overcomes the urge to stay. 'No movement, no thoughts,' as he writes. When one is walking, 'the brain rages'.[9]

Along the way, the mind rampages to wild places. Thought leaves its domicile (the concrete, down-to-earth descriptions of the walk and the places where he spends the night) and opens up to wild fantasies and the telling of good stories to himself: like the story about the grandfather who refused to rise from his chair for half a lifetime. Once a week, his wife brought his shoes to encourage him to stand up, but in vain, until one day the old shoes disappeared and the wife bought a new pair, and the man got up out of sheer curiosity to try them on. He lived for another two-and-a-half years in full vigour, whereupon his weak heart gave out under the pressure of his love of life.

The concrete descriptions of Herzog's exterior world of walking and the fantastical stories of his inner life conquer the narrative along the way, and when he after several weeks finally reaches Paris (Saturday, 14 December 1974), it is as though the destination and goal of the trip have disappeared in the face of something porous and intimate. He has left behind the familiar identities and finds himself in a space in-between as an any-identity-whatever, and his language tags along. Whereas he describes himself as a bison in the first pages of the book, and makes the Earth tremble like Aguirre, he is now, like Walter Steiner, transformed into a bird, and he steps vulnerably over the threshold:

> I went to Madame Eisner, she was still tired and marked by her illness. Someone must have told her on the phone that I had come on foot, I didn't want to mention it. I was embarrassed and placed my smarting legs up on a second armchair, which she pushed over to me. In the embarrassment a thought passed through my head, and since the situation was strange anyway, I told it to her. Together, I said, *we shall*

boil fire and stop fish. Then she looked at me and smiled very delicately, and since she knew that I was someone on foot and therefore unprotected, she understood me. For one splendid, fleeting moment something mellow flowed through my deadly tired body. I said to her, open the window, *from these last days onward I can fly.*[10]

The poetic act of the walk has created an any-space-whatever, a consciousness of the gap between words and things, an ecstatic truth about the contingency of identities. Herzog arrives useless(ly), and Eisner cherishes his useless gesture. And in these spaces inbetween, in this identity-less intimacy, there is perhaps a glimpse of the possibility of a community that may be rather small, but is not based on the identities of the truth of accountants and its settled relations of ownership (Christian, European, German . . .). It is based on something in-between footsteps, a travelling on foot that again and again opens up encounters and paths *as if* we were nomads. Eisner sees Herzog's fragility and friendship, and in the mutual intimacy arises a frail kind of freedom. It is mysterious and ungraspable and can be achieved only through poetry, but it is the only kind of freedom to be found in Herzog's work.

An ecstatic onlooker; a Herzogian penguin

My investigation of Werner Herzog's new images could end here. But there is one last oddment . . . an oddment of useless love that's making its presence felt. At the Rogue Film School I was asked which Herzog film was my favourite – and then, to rank the best ones. I felt this was difficult, maybe even a kind of sacrilege, but not for one moment am I in doubt about the single scene from Herzog's oeuvre that I will always return to. It is a scene that inspires me as a filmmaker, and makes me smile as a fan, and lends itself to academic analysis – and yet, and this is a good thing, it's a scene that sticks out as one of a kind.

When I'm sitting talking to Herzog one-on-one, I tell him about it. It's the scene with the lonely penguin in *Encounters at the End of the World*. He laughs heartily. Just nods.

Encounters at the End of the World is Herzog's report on, and homage to, the Antarctic. There's an old saying that anyone not lashed securely to a ship will eventually tumble overboard and end up at the edge of the world, and it feels like a poetic inevitability that Herzog should end up filming there, among dreamers, researchers, lovable eccentrics and travellers of every stripe.

After *Grizzly Man*, Herzog was awarded a research stipend, and in 2006 he obtained permission to live for six weeks in this unfathomable place. Six weeks to paint a portrait of a whole continent. Six weeks on a 5,000 km (3,000 mi.) expanse of ice, people and animals. It was an almost impossible task. Herzog's solution was Virgil.

Virgil's classic *Georgics* is a poetic description of the life of a country peasant in Italy. What Virgil writes is essentially a psalm, says Herzog; he recites the details of the land – the clouds, the fields, the bees – as if it were a litany of the saints. And this is how Herzog wanted to present the Antarctic: to present what it is and who lives there, animals, ice formations, volcanos and people in an *and* followed by an *and* followed by an *and* . . .

At the Rogue Film School, Herzog inveighs against the ability of the digital camera to film indefinitely, obviating the need to make choices on the ground: 'We are not garbage collectors – we are filmmakers!' he shouts at the room. Nonetheless, in those six weeks he shot 60 hours of footage (when I ask him what you do if you end up with 60 hours despite your better judgement, he says: 'Watch it all the way through with someone you trust. Quickly. Insert an exclamation mark when you see something in a shot that works, insert two exclamation marks when you see something good, insert three exclamation marks when you know that this is something your film can't live without, no matter what'). Those 60 hours were cut down to the length of a

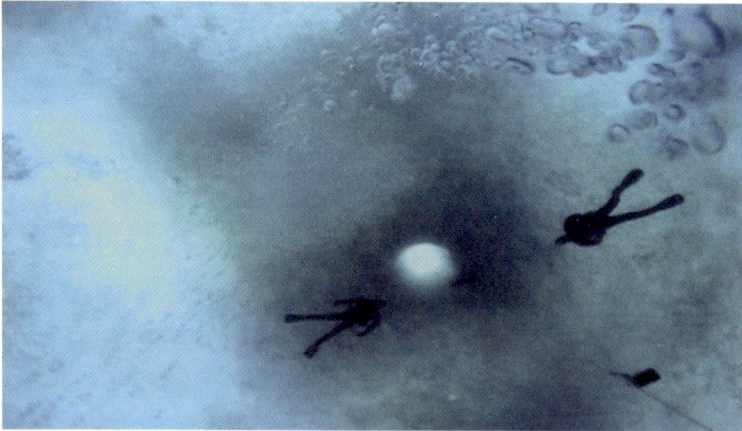

Images of divers under the ice are used in both *The Wild Blue Yonder* and *Encounters at the End of the World*. Herzog describes them as ecstatic dives down into a world full of curious species. At the Rogue Film School, Virgil's *Georgics* is on the reading list. Virgil's descriptive tributes to the landscape have been an important inspiration for Herzog – in his encounters both with nature and with people.

Herzog in *Encounters at the End of the World*: at the volcano Erebus, and with train tractor and on foot in the Antarctic.

The penguin specialist Dr David Ainley in *Encounters at the End of the World*, with the world's most southerly penguin colony.

feature film, Herzog's poetic litany of each and every encounter at the end of the world.

But for me, one of those encounters stands out from the rest. An encounter with a penguin.

Herzog had sworn blind that he wouldn't film a single penguin. 'That was around the time they gave an Oscar to a film with cute little anthropomorphic animals,' he recalls, referring to the French documentary *La Marche de l'empereur* (*March of the Penguins,*

2005). 'I love using animals in my films, staging them. But not in that vanilla, Disneyfied way. And I made it clear to all the finance guys that I was not coming home with a film about cute penguins. But then this lonely penguin suddenly came wandering past – at least 70 kilometres [45 mi.] from where it ought to be.'

His voiceover in *Encounters at the End of the World* betrays his reluctance, but he gets in touch with a penguin researcher anyway, Dr David Ainley.

Ainley had spent the previous twenty years studying the penguin colony at Cape Royd, the world's southernmost colony of Adélie penguins, and he had lost his instinct for dealing with humans. He has a whiff of J. A. Baker about him, the author of *The Peregrine* (1967), which Herzog mentions at every possible opportunity; at the Rogue Film School he read almost the whole thing aloud in pure excitement. *The Peregrine* is a poetic-descriptive text amalgamating Baker's long-term studies of falcons with his dejection about the human race and civilized society. It is, according to Herzog, the book every filmmaker should read, if they only ever read one book. 'It is a text that is in ecstasy,' he says, 'in the most radical sense of the word. There are moments when Baker ceases to be a person and becomes a falcon, when the narrative I slides imperceptibly over into a we. And this is what I do when I make a film: I step outside of myself into an *ekstasis*; in Greek, to step outside of your own body.'[11]

In that respect, Herzog and Baker both have an affinity with Timothy Treadwell in *Grizzly Man* and Walter Steiner in *The Great Ecstasy of Woodcarver Steiner*, who seek to become bear and bird respectively. And they all have something in common with Ainley in *Encounters at the End of the World*, who has become one with the penguin colony. Herzog tries to get him to talk; he succeeds when the questions start to get a bit weird, in the way that only Herzog can pose them: is there strange sexual behaviour in the colony? Is there insanity? 'I try to avoid the definition of insanity or derangement. I don't mean that a penguin might believe he or

235

she is Lenin or Napoleon Bonaparte, but could they just go crazy because they've had enough of their colony?' And this is where the penguin becomes Herzogian, for Ainley understands him and answers that penguins sometimes become so disorientated that 'they end up in places they shouldn't be.'

In the community, the penguin has two paths to choose from. They can either be in the colony or hunt for food. But sometimes a penguin chooses a third way. And that's the penguin Herzog captures on film. At first it is part of a group. The group is moving to the right – towards the water. But two of them stop. One moves to the left, back towards the colony, but our penguin stands still – and then he starts waddling over the ice, towards the mountains in the distance.

Ainley explains that even if he himself caught the penguin and brought it back to the colony, it would immediately, as soon as it had the opportunity, head for the mountains again. 'But why?' asks Herzog – not asking Ainley this time, but registering his bafflement on the voiceover, without giving or expecting an answer. 'With 5,000 kilometres ahead of him, he's heading towards certain death.'

Herzog moves on. There's nothing to see in the image, except something incomprehensible and yet recognizable. A tiny shape disappearing into the distance? A mad penguin? A revolutionary dwarf? An insane conquistador? An elusive ski jumper? A suicidal Stroszek? A visionary opera lover, dreaming of another world? A soldier of cinema, travelling on foot into the infinite whiteness?

REFERENCES

Translator's note on the title:

The title of this book is a direct translation of the original title in Danish. Readers who are familiar with Herzog's own published writings may wonder why we settled on the subtitle *Ecstatic Truth and Other Useless Conquests*. Why did we not adopt *conquest of the useless*, a concept often used by Herzog and immortalized in the English title of his diary from the production of *Fitzcarraldo*? The answer is that the aim of this book is to establish a set of concepts that blend Herzog's own thinking with the critical philosophy discussed here, including Adorno, Deleuze and the nomadic theory of aesthetics. This book's title, then, gestures to Herzog's language, rather than adopting it wholesale. To do otherwise would be to reduce the *conquest of the useless* to just another *truth of accountants*.

Author's note:

Unless otherwise indicated, quotations are from my time at the Rogue Film School, and from my own interviews with and articles on Werner Herzog. Any book on Werner Herzog owes a debt of gratitude to Paul Cronin for his interview book *Herzog on Herzog* (revised and expanded as *Werner Herzog: A Guide for the Perplexed*), and to Eric Ames for his edited collection *Werner Herzog: Interviews*.

Translator's note:

Many of the quotations listed in these notes were translated into Danish from other languages by the author of this book. Where possible I have replaced these with quotations from the published English translations, as indicated below. Where no published English translation exists, I have translated from Kristoffer Hegnsvad's Danish rendering. Similarly, where sections of film dialogue and voiceover are quoted, I have transcribed from the relevant films as closely as possible and cross-referenced with online and published screenplays.

ONE NEW IMAGES: AN INTRODUCTION TO WERNER HERZOG

1 Werner Herzog, *Of Walking in Ice*, trans. Marje Herzog and Alan Greenberg (e-book; London, 2014), section 32. Originally published as *Vom Gehen im Eis* (Munich, 1978).

2 Werner Herzog and Mark Kermode are quoted roughly from the BBC2 interview. Most of the clip can be found on YouTube, and Kermode's own account of the incident can be found in his memoir: *It's Only a Movie* (London, 2010).

3 Bruce Chatwin, 'Werner Herzog in Ghana', in *What Am I Doing Here?* (London and New York, 1989), p. 138.

4 Roger Ebert, *Awake in the Dark: The Best of Roger Ebert* (Chicago, IL, 2006), p. xxv.

5 David Schwartz, 'A Pinewood Dialogue with Werner Herzog and Jonathan Demme', Museum of the Moving Image, 5 June 2008, www.movingimagesource.us.

6 Until just a few years ago, the academic material on Herzog's *oeuvre* was limited. Older publications worthy of note include the French study *Werner Herzog* by Emmanuel Carrère (Paris, 1982) and Brad Prager's *The Cinema of Werner Herzog: Aesthetic Ecstasy and Truth* (London, 2007). Then there are various anthologies, the best-known of which is Timothy Corrigan's edited volume *The Films of Werner Herzog: Between Mirage and History* (London, 1986). Recently, many more publications have appeared. In particular I would highlight the German study by Chris Wahl, *Lektionen in Herzog* (Munich, 2011); *Segni di vita: Werner Herzog e il cinema* (Milan, 2008), by the Venezuelan-Italian Grazia

Pagnelli; Eric Ames's *Ferocious Reality: Documentary According to Werner Herzog* (Minneapolis, MN, 2012); and, in French, Hervé Aubron and Emmanuel Burdeau's *Manuel de survie* (Paris, 2013). Then there are the two interview books, *Werner Herzog: Interviews*, edited by Eric Ames (Jackson, MS, 2014), and Paul Cronin's major anthology *Herzog on Herzog*, which was recently revised and reissued with the title *A Guide for the Perplexed* (London, 2002, 2014).

There are two tendencies in the academic literature on Herzog. In France, there has been an emphasis on philosophical approaches to his fiction film, and analyses based on the poststructuralist philosophers have dominated, with an emphasis on Gilles Deleuze. The Americans have been particularly good at teasing out the red threads of Herzog's documentary work and at producing overviews of his career and biographical or historical studies. Most recently Blackwell has published *A Companion to Werner Herzog*, edited by Brad Prager (Oxford, 2012), offering a range of perspectives on his work. A biographical study is provided by Moritz Holfelder's unauthorized *Werner Herzog: Die Biografie* (Stuttgart, 2012), but a more exciting biographical account is Alan Greenberg's memoir *Every Night the Trees Disappear* (Boston, MA, 2012) – from the time Greenberg and Herzog worked together.

7 Quoted from the Oberhausen Manifesto. English translation at https://nickvdk.tumblr.com (accessed 26 April 2020).

8 Quoted in Cronin, *Herzog on Herzog*, p. 8.

9 Quoted ibid., p. 218.

10 Quoted ibid., p. 2.

11 Quoted ibid., p. 34.

12 Quoted ibid., p. 151.

13 Ibid., p. 228.

14 Quoted in Greenberg, *Every Night the Trees Disappear*, p. 9.

15 See www.roguefilmschool.com (accessed 26 April 2020).

TWO LESSONS OF DARKNESS: AN INTRODUCTION TO HERZOG'S CONCEPTS

1 Quoted in Alan Greenberg, *Every Night the Trees Disappear* (Boston, MA, 2012), p. 39.

2 Werner Herzog, *Of Walking in Ice*, trans. Marje Herzog and Alan Greenberg (London, 2014), section 32.

3 Werner Herzog, *Conquest of the Useless*, trans. Krishna Winston (e-book; London, 2010), p. 58.

4 Ibid., p. 146.

5 Quoted in Paul Cronin, *Herzog on Herzog* (London, 2002), pp. 238–9.

6 Quoted in Steve Rose, 'Werner Herzog on Death, Danger and the End of the World', *The Guardian*, 14 April 2012, www.theguardian.com.

7 Quoted in Cronin, *Herzog on Herzog*, p. 240.

8 Ibid., p. 214.

9 Walter Benjamin, 'Theses on the Philosophy of History', in *Illuminations*, ed. Hannah Arendt, trans. Harry Zorn (Boston, MA, 2019), p. 208.

10 Ibid., p. 200.

11 Translator's note: in Danish, the word for 'history' and 'story' is the same: *en historie*. Here and elsewhere, Hegnsvad plays with this ambiguity, as well as the notion of the 'storyteller' that runs through Benjamin's work. I have tried to indicate this where appropriate and possible in English.

12 Benjamin, 'Theses on the Philosophy of History', p. 200.

13 Ibid., p. 205.

14 Ibid., p. 207.

15 Ibid., p. 198.

16 Quoted in Eric Ames, *Ferocious Reality* (Minneapolis, MN, 2012), p. 1.

17 Werner Herzog, 'Werner Herzog Reads His Minnesota Declaration: Truth and Fact in Documentary Cinema', Walker Art Center, 30 April 1999, www.walkerart.org.

18 Werner Herzog, 'Werner Herzog Makes Trump-era Addition to his Minnesota Declaration', Walker Art Center, 19 June 2017, www.walkerart.org.

19 Quoted in Julie Miller, 'Werner Herzog on his Technology Nemesis and the Aspect of the Internet Too Disturbing for his New Film', *Vanity Fair*, 22 January 2016, www.vanityfair.com.

20 Benjamin, 'Theses on the Philosophy of History', p. 198.

21 William Van Vert, 'Last Words: Observations on a New Language', in *The Films of Werner Herzog: Between Mirage and History*, ed. Timothy Corrigan [1986] (London, 2014), p. 55.

THREE THE TRUTH OF ACCOUNTANTS

1 For an overview of Rancière's concepts in English see, for example, the anthology of his work *Dissensus: Politics and Aesthetics*, ed. and trans. Steven Corcoran (London, 2010).

2 See Werner Herzog, *Conquest of the Useless*, trans. Krishna Winston (e-book; London, 2010). It is interesting to note that in the dialogue in *Fitzcarraldo*, the rubber baron calls Fitzcarraldo a 'conquistador of the useless'.

3 A bilingual German–English edition of *Lenz* is available: Georg Büchner, *Lenz*, trans. Richard Sieburth (New York, 2004).

4 My analysis here draws on Brad Prager's *The Cinema of Werner Herzog* (London, 2007), pp. 65–6. David Overbey's comment can be found in the article 'Every Man for Himself', *Sight and Sound*, XLV/2 (Spring 1975), pp. 73–7.

5 Jacques Rancière, *The Ignorant Schoolmaster: Five Lessons in Intellectual Emancipation*, trans. and introduction by Kristin Ross (Stanford, CA, 1991), p. 114. More generally, Rancière's philosophy has been very valuable in my analyses in this chapter. Much of his writing is available in English.

6 Quoted in Paul Cronin, *Herzog on Herzog* (London, 2002), p. 112.

7 Quoted ibid., p. 202.

8 Ibid., p. 2.

9 Emmanuel Carrère, *Werner Herzog* (Paris, 1982), p. 84 (emphasis added). Carrère's monograph is, probably because it dates from 1982, more focused on the Romantic tendencies than this book is. More recently the Romantic connection has notably been taken up by Laurie Ruth Johnson in *Forgotten Dreams: Revisiting Romanticism in the Cinema of Werner Herzog* (London, 2016), and by Brad Prager in *A Companion to Werner Herzog* (Oxford, 2012).

FOUR THE IMPOSSIBILITY OF DIRECT REVOLT

1 Lars-Olav Beier, 'Werner Herzog's German Comeback: Cinema Legend Heads Berlinale Jury', *Spiegel International*, 11 February 2010, www.spiegel.de.

2 The English translation adopts the recognized form 'dwarfs' for the actors and characters who have dwarfism; here the term 'dwarves' refers to the mythological creature.

3 See Nielsen's foreword to his Danish translation of Georg Büchner's *Lenz & Woyzeck* (Copenhagen, 2014). [Translator's note: Nielsen is a Danish conceptual artist who goes by one name only, thus in itself a kind of performance of the point about Woyzeck or 'X' being made here.]

4 Michel Foucault, *History of Sexuality*, vol I: *The Will to Knowledge*, trans. Robert Hurley (New York, 1978), pp. 139–40, 144 (emphasis added). The example of the panopticon discussed in this chapter is to be found in Foucault's *Discipline and Punish: The Birth of the Prison* (New York, 1977).

5 Quoted in Hervé Aubron and Emmanuel Burdeau, *Manuel de survie* (Paris, 2008), pp. 91–2 (emphasis added). [Translator's note: my English translation is based on both Hegnsvad's Danish translation of the French and the French original.]

6 Quoted ibid., p. 91.

7 Giorgio Agamben, *The Coming Community*, trans. Richard Hardt (Minneapolis, MN, 1993), pp. 85–6.

8 'Werner Herzog on Chickens', www.youtube.com (accessed 28 April 2020).

9 Gilles Deleuze, *Foucault*, trans. Seán Hand (Minneapolis, MN, 1988), pp. 92–3.

FIVE ECSTATIC TRUTH: A COOKBOOK FOR THE REVOLUTIONARY FILMMAKER

1 The recipe for 'Chaussures Confit' was reconstructed by the chef Alice Waters, who back in the day helped Herzog to cook his shoes. It can be found in Jeffrey Kastner's article 'Ingestion: More Shoes! More Boots! More Garlic!', *Cabinet Magazine*, 28 July 2008, www.cabinetmagazine.org.

2 See Les Blank's film *Werner Herzog Eats His Shoe* and read Herzog's description of the 'happening' in Paul Cronin's *Herzog on Herzog* (London, 2002), pp. 166–7.

3 Cronin, *Herzog on Herzog*, p. 66.

4 Quoted ibid., pp. 166–7.

5 Ibid., p. 167.

6 Theodor W. Adorno, *Minima Moralia: Reflections on a Damaged Life*, trans. E.F.N. Jephcott (London, 2005), p. 222.

7 Theodor W. Adorno, *Aesthetic Theory* (London, 2013), p. 7.

8 Ibid., p. 2.

9 Ibid., p. 315.

10 Werner Herzog, *Conquest of the Useless*, trans. Krishna Winston (e-book; London, 2010), pp. 18–19.

11 'Was wäre Hoffnung ohne Ferne?' in the original German. Theodor W. Adorno, 'Anfang', in *Gesammelte Schriften Band 4: Minima Moralia. Reflexionen aus dem beschädigten Leben* (Frankfurt am Main, 1980), p. 290. The aphorism in which the quotation is to be found, 'Les Adieux', seems not to have been included in the published English translations of *Minima Moralia*.

12 Quoted in Steve Rose, 'Werner Herzog on Death, Danger and the End of the World', *The Guardian*, 14 April 2012, www.theguardian.com.

13 Herzog in conversation with Errol Morris, originally published as the transcript of a conversation moderated by Alice Arshalooys Kelikian: 'Werner Herzog in Conversation with Errol Morris', *The Believer*, 1 March 2008, www.believermag.com. I first wrote about the visit to Kemper in an article in the Danish newspaper *Politiken* in 2010, on the basis of the article in *The Believer*. Many thanks to Errol Morris and Werner Herzog for clarifying details that were essential to my reconstruction of the visit.

14 Livia Bloom, *Errol Morris: Interviews* (Jackson, MS, 2010), p. 220. [Translator's note: the English is back-translated from the Danish, rather than a direct quotation from the source, which was not accessible.]

15 Quoted ibid., p. 227.

16 Robert Walser, 'Helblings Geschichte' (Frankfurt am Main, 1915). The quotations in English are taken from 'Helbling's Story', in *The Walk*, trans. Christopher Middleton et al. (London, 2013), p. 34.

17 Ibid., pp. 39–40.

18 Ibid., p. 38.

19 Adorno, *Minima Moralia*, trans. Jephcott, p. 157.

SIX A NEW GRAMMAR OF IMAGES

1 Herzog riffs on this theme in his conversation with Paul Holdengräber: 'Was the Twentieth Century a Mistake?', *Brick*, 82 (22 August 2016), www.brickmag.com.

2 Gilles Deleuze and Félix Guattari, *A Thousand Plateaus: Capitalism and*

Schizophrenia, trans. Brian Massumi (Minneapolis, MN, 2005), p. 15. In this chapter I draw mainly on Deleuze and Guattari's *Mille Plateaux*, but large parts of Chapter Six (and the section 'Form under pressure' in Chapter Five) have been heavily influenced by Deleuze's books on film: *Cinéma 1 – L'image-movement* and *Cinéma 2 – L'image-temps* (see translated editions below).

3 Quoted in Paul Cronin, *Herzog on Herzog* (London, 2002), p. 48.
4 Quoted ibid., p. 46.
5 Quoted ibid., p. 83.
6 Gilles Deleuze, *Cinema 2: The Time-image*, trans. Brian Massumi (London, 2005), p. 20.
7 Quoted in Cronin, *Herzog on Herzog*, p. 104.
8 Deleuze and Guattari, *A Thousand Plateaus*, p. 25.

SEVEN THE NOMADIC ALTERNATIVE

1 Quoted in Paul Cronin, *Herzog on Herzog* (London, 2002), p. 283. An account of the meeting can also be found in Nicholas Shakespeare's biography: *Bruce Chatwin* (London, 1999), pp. 530–31.
2 Quoted ibid.
3 Bruce Chatwin, *What Am I Doing Here?* (e-book; New York, 2014), n.p.
4 Translator's note: Herzog comments in his conversation with Paul Holdengräber ('Was the Twentieth Century a Mistake?', *Brick*, 82 (22 August 2016), www.brickmag.com), 'I would be careful to call it walking . . . there is no real expression in English' for what he prefers to call 'travelling on foot'. In the Danish, Hegnsvad tends to use the word *vandring*, which has connotations of 'wandering'. Thus the kind of activity being discussed here is more epic than the workaday term 'walking' in English, and it was not always possible to incorporate this explicitly into the English translation.
5 Bruce Chatwin, *In Patagonia* (London, 1998), p. 43.
6 Such ideas are expanded in Chatwin's unpublished magnum opus *The Nomadic Alternative*, excerpts of which can be found in the anthology of his writings *Anatomy of Restlessness: Selected Writings, 1969–1989* (London, 1997).
7 Theodor W. Adorno, '18: Refuge for the Homeless', in *Minima Moralia*, trans. E.F.N. Jephcott (e-book; London, 2005).
8 Gilles Deleuze and Félix Guattari, *A Thousand Plateaus: Capitalism and*

Schizophrenia, trans. Brian Massumi (Minneapolis, MN, 2005), p. 381.

9 Werner Herzog, *Of Walking in Ice*, trans. Marje Herzog and Alan Greenberg (e-book; London, 2014), sections 32, 277.

10 Ibid., section 848 (emphasis added).

11 Quoted in Robert McFarlane, 'Violent Spring: The Nature Book that Predicted the Future', *The Guardian*, 15 April 2017, www.theguardian.com.

FILMOGRAPHY
WITH SYNOPSES

This filmography would not be so extensive and detailed without the painstaking work of Chris Wahl (*Lektionen in Herzog*), Paul Cronin (*Herzog on Herzog: A Guide for the Perplexed*), Grazia Paganelli (*Segni di Vita*), Timothy Corrigan (*Between Mirage and History*), Rubén Higueras Flores (*Werner Herzog*) and Beat Presser (*Werner Herzog*), all of whom have contributed to the details collected here. And not least Hans Henrik Rasmussen, whose wide knowledge and sense of detail have been invaluable during the preparation of the book and filmography. I owe them all a huge vote of thanks.

The film titles used in this filmography (and in the book as a whole) are the original titles in German, supplemented with English titles. German titles dominate in the earlier period of Herzog's career, and English titles latterly. Where films have original titles both in German and in English, which is primarily the case with films from the 1980s, I have selected a primary title on the basis of the film's origins and focus. For example, in the case of *Where the Green Ants Dream*, which was shot and co-produced in Australia, I use the English title as the primary title. (In this translation of the book as a whole, the German original titles are given first as appropriate, and then the English titles tend to be used.)

Information on format and length has been sourced from www.wernerherzog.com, IMDB and the Spanish academic anthology *Werner Herzog* (ed. Rubén Higueras Flores); where doubts arose, information was sourced directly from Werner Herzog Filmproduktion. The category 'Music' in most cases indicates the primary composer of the films' original scores, but in some places other music is also included. The category 'Production' covers the relevant producer(s), sometimes including production manager, executive producer, and so on, since these roles are not always clearly or formally differentiated in Herzog's productions.

HERAKLES

Short film. West Germany 1962
Length: 10 min. *Format:* 35 mm, 1.37:1, b/w
Direction: Werner Herzog. *Screenplay:* Werner Herzog. *Cinematography:* Jaime Pacheco. *Editing:* Werner Herzog. *Music:* Uwe Brandner. *Sound:* Werner Herzog. *Production:* Werner Herzog, Walter Krüttner. *Production company:* Werner Herzog Filmproduktion, Cineropa Film. *Featuring:* Reinhard Lichtenberg (Mr Germany 1962).
Synopsis: Herakles is a montage of clashing images. It was edited together from original footage of bodybuilders, among them Mr Germany, and from archival images of a terrible car crash in a motor race, of ruined cities hit by earthquakes and avalanches, and of a rubbish dump. Herzog later pronounced the film to be extremely bad.

SPIEL IM SAND

(Game in the Sand)
Short film. West Germany 1964
Length: 14 min. *Format:* 35 mm, 1.37:1, b/w
Direction: Werner Herzog. *Screenplay:* Werner Herzog. *Cinematography:* Jamie Pacheco. *Editing:* Werner Herzog. *Music:* Uwe Brandner. *Sound:* Werner Herzog. *Production:* Werner Herzog. *Production company:* Werner Herzog Filmproduktion.
Synopsis: The film was never distributed, allegedly because it contains such gruesome images (such as children torturing a hen) that its release would be ethically indefensible. This film has developed into a myth in Herzog circles, and is often alluded to, although no one has seen it or even knows for sure that it exists.

DIE BEISPIELLOSE VERTEIDIGUNG DER FESTUNG DEUTSCHKREUZ

(The Unprecedented Defence of the Fortress Deutschkreuz)
Short film. West Germany 1966–7 (premiere 1967 at Kurzfilmtage Oberhausen)
Length: 15 min. *Format:* 35 mm, 1.33:1, b/w
Direction: Werner Herzog. *Screenplay:* Werner Herzog. *Cinematography:* Jaime

Pacheco. *Editing:* Werner Herzog. *Sound:* Uwe Brandner. *Production:* Werner Herzog, Bruno Zöckler. *Production company:* Werner Herzog Filmproduktion, Arpa Film. *Location:* Schloss Deutschkreuz (Austria). *Featuring:* Peter Brumm, Georg Eska, Karl-Heinz Steffel, Wolfgang von Ungern-Sternberg.

Synopsis: A satire of war and of the terrible things that war drives people to do, which are presented as senseless, even uninteresting, to the outside world. Concerns four young people who enter a deserted fort, where they find military uniforms and start to stage a strange war game. Their violent acts during this game seem increasingly senseless in relation to the society around them, in which workers go about their quiet, everyday lives in the countryside.

LETZTE WORTE

(Last Words)

Short film. Germany 1968

Length: 13 min. *Format:* 35 mm, 1.33:1, b/w

Direction: Werner Herzog. *Screenplay:* Werner Herzog. *Cinematography:* Thomas Mauch. *Editing:* Beate Mainka-Jellinghaus. *Sound:* Herbert Prasch. *Production:* Werner Herzog. *Production company:* Werner Herzog Filmproduktion. *Location:* Crete, Kos (Greece). *Featuring:* Lefteris Daskalakis, Antonis Papadakis.

Synopsis: A short film shot in two days during the production of *Lebenszeichen* (see below). The inhabitants of a Greek island take turns to tell the story of an old man who was taken away from the island of Spinalonga. On the island lived a colony of people with cerebral palsy, and this man was suddenly removed and brought back to civilization. The man refuses to speak and will only go out in the evening to play his lyre. He keeps himself to himself, but everyone else talks about him a lot, which seems absurd since he does not seem to wish to participate in society. Herzog illustrates the absurdity by showing that the inhabitants repeat the same words until they no longer make sense. This is a linguistic version of the circularity that Herzog explores in many other films.

LEBENSZEICHEN

(Signs of Life)

Feature film. West Germany 1968

Length: 87 min. *Format:* 35 mm, 1.37:1, b/w

Direction: Werner Herzog. *Screenplay:* Werner Herzog. *Cinematography:* Thomas Mauch. *Editing:* Beate Mainka-Jellinghaus, Maximiliane Mainka. *Music:* Stavros Xarchakos. *Sound:* Herbert Prasch. *Production:* Werner Herzog.

Production company: Werner Herzog Filmproduktion. Location: Crete, Kos (Greece). Featuring: Peter Brogle, Jannis Frasakis, Wolfgang Reichmann, Athina Zacharopoulous, Achmed Hafiz, Henry van Lyck, Julio M. Pinheiro, Florian Fricke, Wolfgang von Ungern-Sternberg.

Synopsis: The wounded parachute jumper Stroszek is sent with his wife, Nora, and two soldiers to a fort on a secluded island, which functions as an ammunition store. The two soldiers are very different characters: Meinhard is a violent type, whereas Becker is an intellectual and fascinated by ancient Greek culture. They live in close quarters, and this is not without its tension. Stroszek becomes very affected by his living conditions. One day he wanders into a valley and encounters 10,000 spinning windmills. Overwhelmed by the sight, he goes completely mad and barricades himself into the fort. From there, he runs amok and opens fire over the town in an apparently senseless protest.

MASSNAHMEN GEGEN FANATIKER

(Precautions Against Fanatics)
Short film. West Germany 1969
Length: 12 min. Format: 35 mm, 1.33:1, Eastmancolor
Direction: Werner Herzog. Screenplay: Werner Herzog. Cinematography:
Dieter Lohmann, Jörg Schmidt-Reitwein. Editing: Beate Mainka-Jellinghaus.
Sound: Werner Herzog. Production: Werner Herzog. Production company:
Werner Herzog Filmproduktion. Location: Munich (Germany). Featuring:
Petar Radenković, Mario Adorf, Herbert Hisel, Hans Tiedemann.

Synopsis: Herzog stages life on a horse-racing track, where the horse owners claim they have to protect the horses against fanatics. Through a number of interviews the horse owners tell of a man who comes to feed and pet the horses. They don't understand the friendly man's motivations, and accuse him of being the kind of fanatic they must protect the horses from. Stylistically, the film is reminiscent of television reportage, in which the interviewees look directly into the camera.

DIE FLIEGENDEN ÄRZTE VON OSTAFRIKA

(The Flying Doctors of East Africa)
Documentary film. West Germany 1969
Length: 44 min. Format: 35 mm, 1.33:1, Eastmancolor
Direction: Werner Herzog. Screenplay: Werner Herzog. Cinematography:
Thomas Mauch. Editing: Beate Mainka-Jellinghaus. Sound: Werner Herzog.
Production: Werner Herzog, Eleonora Semler. Production company: Werner

Herzog Filmproduktion, African Medical & Research Foundation. *Location:* Kenya, Uganda, Tanzania. *Featuring:* James Kabale, Dr Michael Wood, Dr Ann Spoery, Dr Rottcher. *Voiceover:* Wilfried Klaus.

Synopsis: A traditional documentary about a group of volunteer doctors who practise in isolated areas in East Africa, to which they fly in small planes. The film was commissioned, and has a traditional structure with footage from daily life in the hospitals, which Herzog uses to try to attract attention to the work of the doctors.

FATA MORGANA

Feature film. West Germany 1969–71 (premiere at Cannes Film Festival 1971)
Length: 79 min. *Format:* 35 mm, 1.37:1, Eastmancolor
Direction: Werner Herzog. *Screenplay:* Werner Herzog. *Cinematography:* Jörg Schmidt-Reitwein. *Editing:* Beate Mainka-Jellinghaus. *Music:* Wolfgang Amadeus Mozart, Blind Faith, François Couperin, Third Ear Band, Leonard Cohen. *Sound:* Hans von Mallinckrodt. *Production:* Werner Herzog. *Production company:* Werner Herzog Filmproduktion. *Location:* Kenya, Tanzania, Algerian Sahara, Nigeria, Upper Volta (Burkina Faso), Mali, Ivory Coast, Lanzarote (Canary Islands). *Featuring:* Wolfgang von Ungern-Sternberg, Eugen Des Montagnes, James William Gledhill. *Voiceover:* Lotte Eisner.

Synopsis: Fata Morgana is divided into three chapters: Creation, Paradise and the Golden Age. In the first chapter we see a peaceful universe. There exist only clouds and wide blue sea. Then we see a desert landscape with sand dunes and mountains, peppered sparsely with signs of civilization. The German film historian Lotte Eisner quotes passages from the Quiché, or K'iche', people's creation story. In the chapter Paradise, different people appear, and the camera starts to focus on them. The narrator describes life in paradise, which has a surreal and hypnotizing effect. In the last chapter, the Golden Age, we see a state of absolute decline in which nature no longer exists. The film is famous for its images of mirages and strange stories: no representations are solidly anchored, and they all gesture to something else. No story can be told as it actually was. Herzog describes the film as an experimental one, which he initially did not dare to show in public, but Eisner and Amos Vogel arranged for it to be screened at Cannes in 1971.

AUCH ZWERGE HABEN KLEIN ANGEFANGEN

(Even Dwarfs Started Small)

Feature film. West Germany 1970

Length: 96 min. *Format:* 35 mm, 1.37:1, b/w

Direction: Werner Herzog. *Screenplay:* Werner Herzog. *Cinematography:*
Thomas Mauch, Jörg Schmidt-Reitwein. *Editing:* Beate Mainka-Jellinghaus,
Maximiliane Mainka. *Music:* Florian Fricke (Popol Vuh), Felisa Arrocha
Marin, Werner Herzog. *Sound:* Herbert Prasch. *Production:* Werner Herzog.
Production company: Werner Herzog Filmproduktion. *Location:* Lanzarote
(Canary Islands). *Featuring:* Helmut Döring, Gerd Gickel, Paul Glauer,
Alfredo Piccini, Gertraud Piccini, Gisela Hertwig, Hertel Minkner, Lajos
Zsarnoczay.

Synopsis: An almost experimental film about a revolt at an institution for
dwarfs on Lanzarote. The film comprises scene after scene of crazy acts of
apparently senseless rebellion, and the institution head's equally meaningless
attempts to keep order. All the actors in the film are dwarfs. The film was a
great source of inspiration for Harmony Korine and David Lynch, but when
released it attracted intense criticism from the political left and right wings
alike. Herzog was attacked on the street, and in the wake of this film he was
frequently referred to as 'the fascistoid filmmaker Werner Herzog'.

BEHINDERTE ZUKUNFT

(Handicapped Future)

Documentary film. West Germany 1971

Length: 43 min. *Format:* 16 mm, 1.33:1, Eastmancolor

Direction: Werner Herzog. *Screenplay:* Werner Herzog, Hans-Peter Meier
(idea). *Cinematography:* Jörg Schmidt-Reitwein. *Editing:* Beate Mainka-
Jellinghaus. *Music:* Johann Sebastian Bach, Antonio Vivaldi. *Sound:* Werner
Herzog. *Production:* Werner Herzog. *Production company:* Werner Herzog
Filmproduktion, North Rhine-Westphalia. *Location:* Hanover, Munich
(Germany), Los Angeles (USA). *Featuring:* Adolf Ratzka. *Voiceover:* Rolf Illig.

Synopsis: Documentary film about disabled children in post-war Germany.
Herzog interviews children and their parents. The disabled people talk about
how they can develop themselves and participate in society, but also about
how their disabilities inspire disgust in the society around them. The documentary concludes in Los Angeles, where a polio survivor struggles with his
illness, but with the help and understanding of those around him manages to
become a university researcher. Herzog says this was a commissioned film.

LAND DES SCHWEIGENS UND DER DUNKELHEIT

(Land of Silence and Darkness)

Documentary film. Germany 1971

Length: 85 min. *Format:* 16 mm, 1.33:1, Eastmancolor

Direction: Werner Herzog. *Screenplay:* Werner Herzog. *Cinematography:* Jörg Schmidt-Reitwein. *Editing:* Beate Mainka-Jellinghaus. *Sound:* Werner Herzog. *Production:* Werner Herzog. *Production company:* Werner Herzog Filmproduktion, North Rhine-Westphalia. *Location:* Hanover, Munich, Bavaria (Germany). *Featuring:* Fini Straubinger, M. Baaske, Heinrich Fleischmann, Elsa Fehrer. *Voiceover:* Rolf Illig.

Synopsis: The main character, a blind and deaf-mute woman called Fini Straubinger, opens up a lonely, painful world to us. She has been deaf-mute since she was very young, and now spends all her time visiting others with the same condition. Herzog wrote much of Fini's dialogue in the film, including a dream of hers that everyone should be allowed to feel a joyful sense of hovering, such as that felt by ski jumpers in the air. Herzog had to learn Fini's tactile hand-language, whereby touch on specific areas of the hand creates meaning.

AGUIRRE, DER ZORN GOTTES

(Aguirre, the Wrath of God)

Feature film. Germany 1972

Length: 93 min. *Format:* 35 mm, 1.33:1, Eastmancolor

Direction: Werner Herzog. *Screenplay:* Werner Herzog. *Cinematography:* Thomas Mauch. *Editing:* Beate Mainka-Jellinghaus. *Music:* Florian Fricke (Popol Vuh). *Sound:* Herbert Prasch. *Production:* Werner Herzog, Hans Prescher. *Production company:* Werner Herzog Filmproduktion, Hessischer Rundfunk. *Location:* Urubamba Valley, Huallaga and Nanay rivers, Cuzco, the Andes (Peru). *Featuring:* Klaus Kinski, Ruy Guerra, Edward Roland, Peter Berling, Cecilia Rivera, Helena Rojo, Julio Martinez, Del Negro, Alejandro Repullés.

Synopsis: When the Spanish adventurer Gonzalo Pizarro hears of a golden city, he leads an expedition into the Peruvian rainforest in 1560–61 to find El Dorado. But he meets great obstacles on the journey and is forced to halt. To investigate the terrain he sends a boat downstream, led by Don Lope de Aguirre (Klaus Kinski) and Don Pedro de Ursua. They soon encounter problems in this inaccessible region. Don Pedro chooses to return to camp, but Aguirre is drunk on power and decides to continue, appointing himself the leader of the entire expedition. He also rebels against Philip II of Castile and, finally, against God. Aguirre proves to be an oppressive leader and shows no mercy to those he suspects of disloyalty. On their journey, the company is attacked by the local tribespeople and weakened by hunger. Aguirre's resources run out, and the self-declared Wrath of God dies in 1561. A tragic end to an absurd mission.

DIE GROSSE EKSTASE DES BILDSCHNITZERS STEINER
(The Great Ecstasy of Woodcarver Steiner)
Documentary film. West Germany 1974
Length: 47 min. *Format:* 16 mm, 1.33:1, Eastmancolor
Direction: Werner Herzog. *Screenplay:* Werner Herzog. *Cinematography:* Jörg Schmidt-Reitwein, Francisco Joán, Frederik Hettich, Alfred Chrosziel, Gideon Meron. *Music:* Florian Fricke (Popol Vuh). *Editing:* Beate Mainka-Jellinghaus. *Sound:* Benedikt Kuby. *Production:* Werner Herzog, Jorschi Arpa, Walter Saxer. *Production company:* Werner Herzog Filmproduktion, Süddeutscher Rundfunk. *Location:* Garmisch-Partenkirchen, Oberstdorf (Germany), Wildhaus (Switzerland), Planica (Slovenia). *Featuring:* Walter Steiner, Werner Herzog. *Voiceover:* Werner Herzog.
Synopsis: Herzog follows the ski jumper Walter Steiner for a whole season in the run-up to a competition in March 1974 in Planica, Slovenia. It is not the World Championship that interests Herzog, but Steiner's day-to-day life, where he works as a woodcarver. While he is doing carpentry, Steiner tells us about how extremely dangerous ski jumping is, and why he does it. Herzog films him at his most nerve-wracking moments. At Oberstdorf, Steiner jumps 179 m (587 ft) and breaks the world record. At Planica he breaks the world record again during training, but is slightly injured. At the final competition he achieves the most perfect jump in the history of ski jumping. But at the end of the film, Herzog focuses on the private Steiner, who tells us of his friendship with a crow that was bullied by other crows because it could no longer fly. Another theme in the film is Steiner's evasive manoeuvre: he refuses to jump as demanded by the competition authorities and the public. They try to pressure him into attempting records, but he reacts by jumping from lower starting points. For him it is about feeling free in the air, and, with quotations from Robert Walser's 'Helbling's Story', Steiner's dream is revealed to be that he wants to be naked, alone in the world and free of external pressure. This equates to the joyful hovering that Fini Straubinger describes in *Land of Silence and Darkness,* and the two films share some footage. This is also the first film in which Herzog explicitly appears as the narrator.

JEDER FÜR SICH UND GOTT GEGEN ALLE

(The Enigma of Kaspar Hauser: Every Man for Himself and God Against All)
Feature film. West Germany 1974
Length: 109 min. *Format:* 35 mm, 1.66:1, Eastmancolor
Direction: Werner Herzog. *Screenplay:* Werner Herzog. *Cinematography:*
Jörg Schmidt-Reitwein, Klaus Wyborny. *Editing:* Beate Mainka-Jellinghaus,
Martha Lederer. *Scenography:* Henning von Gierke. *Music:* Florian
Fricke (Popol Vuh). *Sound:* Haymo Henry Heyder. *Production:* Werner
Herzog, Jorschi Arpa, Walter Saxer. *Production company:* Werner Herzog
Filmproduktion, ZDF, Filmverlag der Autoren. *Location:* Dinkelsbühl
(Germany), Ireland, Spanish Sahara. *Featuring:* Bruno S., Walter Steiner,
Clemens Scheitz, Florian Fricke, Walter Ladengast, Herbert Achternbusch.
Synopsis: Kaspar Hauser has been imprisoned in a cave all his life. The only
things he knows are to eat, sleep and play with a little wooden toy. One day,
a man appears who removes him from his prison, dresses him and leaves
him in the town square in N., with a letter for the authorities in his hand.
It is a request that they take care of him. Professor Daumer takes Kaspar in
and teaches him to read, speak and write, and about logic, ethics and music.
Daumer and the townspeople around Kaspar are excited about his ability to
learn, but Kaspar becomes more and more depressed by how the world works,
and longs to be back in the cave. In the end he is attacked twice, and the
second assault proves fatal.

MIT MIR WILL KEINER SPIELEN

(No One Will Play with Me)
Short film. West Germany 1976
Length: 14 min. *Format:* 16 mm, 1.33:1, Kodak Ektachrome colour
Direction: Werner Herzog. *Screenplay:* Werner Herzog (based on a story by
Walter Steiner). *Cinematography:* Jörg Schmidt-Reitwein. *Editing:* Beate
Mainka-Jellinghaus. *Sound:* Haymo Henry Heyder. *Production:* Werner
Herzog. *Production company:* Werner Herzog Filmproduktion, Institut für
Film und Bild in Wissenschaft und Unterricht. *Location:* Munich (Germany).
Synopsis: Herzog portrays children between the ages of four and six in a
nursery. He focuses especially on Martin, a little boy who does not seem to be
able to interact with the other children. One day, Martin makes friends with
a girl called Nicole; he is so happy that he introduces her to the crow, his best
friend. The story is inspired by Walter Steiner's narrative in *The Great Ecstasy
of Woodcarver Steiner.*

HERZ AUS GLAS
(Heart of Glass)
Feature film. West Germany 1976
Length: 97 min. *Format:* 35 mm, 1.66:1, Eastmancolor
Direction: Werner Herzog. *Screenplay:* Werner Herzog, Herbert Achternbusch.
Cinematography: Jörg Schmidt-Reitwein, Klaus Wyborny. *Editing:* Beate
Mainka-Jellinghaus. *Music:* Florian Fricke (Popol Vuh). *Sound:* Haymo Henry
Heyder, Peter van Anft. *Production:* Werner Herzog, Jorschi Arpa, Walter
Saxer. *Production company:* Werner Herzog Filmproduktion, ZDF. *Location:*
Frauenau, Schloss Walchsing (Germany), Pischelsdorf (Austria), Via Mala
(Graubünden, Switzerland), Skellig Rocks (County Kerry, Ireland), Alaska,
Monument Valley, Yellowstone National Park, Niagara Falls (USA). *Featuring:*
Josef Bierbichler, Herbert Achternbusch, Claude Chiarini, Stefan Güttler,
Clemens Scheitz, Sonja Skiba, Janos Fischer, Stepp Müller.
Synopsis: The prophet Hias can foresee the future. He predicts a catastrophe
in a town in Bavaria that starts with a fire in the town's glass factory, where
most of the townspeople work. The inventor of ruby-red glass, Mühlbeck, is
dead and has taken the formula with him to the grave. The townspeople are
desperate to find the formula, because the future of the factory depends on it.
This desperation leads to absurd events; the townspeople suspect each other
and even kill each other. The factory owner is convinced that human blood
is the secret ingredient and kills his servant Ludmilla, but when that doesn't
work either he sets the factory on fire, and the whole town is consumed.
The factory owner is thrown into jail, where the prophet is already being
held, having been convicted of predicting the future. All the residents of the
town were hypnotized before the shoot, which produces a strangely detached
feeling. Many of the scenes are shot in stop-motion, whereby the individual
image breaks with cinema's normal flowing motion over to the next image.
Heart of Glass is widely considered an experimental film.

HOW MUCH WOOD WOULD A WOODCHUCK CHUCK . . .
Documentary film. West Germany 1976
Length: 45 min. *Format:* 16 mm, 1.33:1, Eastmancolor
Direction: Werner Herzog. *Screenplay:* Werner Herzog. *Cinematography:*
Thomas Mauch, Francisco Joán, Edward Lachmann. *Editing:* Beate
Mainka-Jellinghaus. *Music:* Shorty Eager and the Eager Beavers. *Sound:*
Walter Saxer. *Production:* Walter Saxer. *Production company:* Werner
Herzog Filmproduktion, Süddeutscher Rundfunk. *Location:* New Holland

(Pennsylvania, USA). *Featuring:* Ralph Wade, Alan Ball, Abe Diffenbach, Steve Liptay.

Synopsis: At the World Livestock Auctioneer Championships in New Holland, Pennsylvania, Herzog records how the auctioneers compete among each other with their verbal skills and high-speed delivery. The film's title refers to a tongue exercise the auctioneers use. Apart from this competition and an interview with the winner, Herzog also encounters the Amish people who live in the local area. Ralph Wade later appears as the auctioneer in *Stroszek* (see below).

STROSZEK

Feature film. West Germany 1977
Length: 108 min. *Format:* 35 mm, 1.66:1, Eastmancolor
Direction: Werner Herzog. *Screenplay:* Werner Herzog. *Cinematography:* Thomas Mauch, Edward Lachmann. *Editing:* Beate Mainka-Jellinghaus. *Music:* Chet Atkins, Ludwig van Beethoven, Tom Paxton, Michael Gahr. *Sound:* Harald Maury. *Production:* Werner Herzog, Willi Segler. *Production company:* Werner Herzog Filmproduktion, Skellig Edition, ZDF. *Location:* Berlin, Munich Neo-natal Department (Germany), New York, Plainfield (Wisconsin), Cherokee (North Carolina). *Featuring:* Bruno S., Eva Mattes, Clemens Scheitz, Ralph Wade.

Synopsis: Bruno Stroszek has just been released from jail and heads off to find his old apartment and his buddy Scheitz. One evening in a bar, Stroszek meets a sex worker, Eva. He wants to save her from her nasty pimps and asks her to move in with him. But the pimps won't let her go, and beat them both up. Stroszek and Eva run away, with help from Scheitz, and head for the United States. There they get some peace, until Eva starts working as a prostitute again to pay the ever-increasing bills. Their house is put up for auction; Eva leaves for Canada and Stroszek carries out a grotesque and tragic raid on a barber's shop with Scheitz. Scheitz is immediately arrested, whereas Stroszek continues his eternal flight from a society in which he can't seem to function. In the end he kills himself, while we watch images of burning cars, animals in cages and a chairlift moving in circles.

LA SOUFRIÈRE – WARTEN AUF EINE UNAUSWEICHLICHE KATASTROPHE

(La Soufrière – Waiting for an Inevitable Disaster)
Documentary film. West Germany 1977
Length: 31 min. *Format:* 16 mm, 1.33:1, Eastmancolor
Direction: Werner Herzog. *Screenplay:* Werner Herzog. *Cinematography:* Jörg

Schmidt-Reitwein, Edward Lachmann. *Editing:* Beate Mainka-Jellinghaus. *Music:* Felix Mendelssohn, Johannes Brahms, Sergei Rachmaninov, Richard Wagner. *Sound:* Werner Herzog. *Production:* Werner Herzog. *Production company:* Werner Herzog Filmproduktion. *Location:* Guadeloupe. *Voiceover:* Werner Herzog.

Synopsis: In 1976 scientists observed that there was abnormal activity in the volcano La Soufrière on Guadeloupe. The consensus was that the volcano would soon erupt and cause a significant catastrophe. Residents of the southern part of the island were evacuated, except for two men who refused to leave. In a situation where almost everyone was fleeing, Herzog was fascinated by the extreme conditions. He travelled to Guadeloupe with two cameramen to witness the eruption, which was predicted to have the strength of five or six atomic bombs. But the volcano never blew. On the other hand, Herzog noticed that the Black residents of the island were not evacuated, and did not think there was any reason to save their own lives. The film is sometimes screened with the subtitle 'Waiting for an Inevitable Disaster', which can be seen as an early example of Herzog's mockery of the documentary approach of waiting out a situation like a fly on the wall until the drama unfolds.

NOSFERATU – PHANTOM DER NACHT
(Nosferatu: The Vampyre)
Feature film. West Germany/France 1979
Length: 103 min. *Format:* 35 mm, 1.85:1, Eastmancolor
Direction: Werner Herzog. *Screenplay:* Werner Herzog (based on F. W. Murnau's *Nosferatu, eine Symphonie des Grauens,* 1922). *Cinematography:* Jörg Schmidt-Reitwein, Michael Gast. *Editing:* Beate Mainka-Jellinghaus. *Scenography:* Henning von Gierke, Peter Holz. *Music:* Florian Fricke (Popol Vuh). *Sound:* Harald Maury. *Production:* Werner Herzog, Walter Saxer. *Production company:* Werner Herzog Filmproduktion, ZDF, Gaumont. *Location:* Czechoslovakia, the Netherlands, Mexico. *Featuring:* Klaus Kinski, Isabelle Adjani, Bruno Ganz, Roland Topor, Walter Ladengast.

Synopsis: Jonathan Harker is sent to Transylvania to persuade Count Dracula to sell part of his property. Despite his wife's frightened misgivings, Jonathan leaves the Netherlands and travels to the Count's gloomy and forbidding castle. When he arrives, he sees Dracula loading a coffin onto a cart and disappearing, whereupon Jonathan is completely alone in the castle. In the meantime, a ship arrives in Wismar, full of rats, which stream out onto the streets and spread plague. Jonathan succeeds in escaping and returning to the town, but he is ill and unable to explain what happened. His wife, Lucy, can sense the truth, and after reading a book about vampires she resolves to sacrifice herself by keeping Dracula occupied until sunrise. Nosferatu's bite into Lucy's neck was, until *Bad Lieutenant*, the closest Herzog got to a classic erotic shot. The film is based on F. W. Murnau's *Nosferatu, eine Symphonie des Grauens*, and is one part of Herzog's project of re-legitimizing German culture, the other part being his film *Woyzeck* (see below). The two films were shot back to back in 1978.

WOYZECK

Feature film. West Germany 1979
Length: 81 min. *Format:* 35 mm, 1.66:1, Eastmancolor
Direction: Werner Herzog. *Screenplay:* Werner Herzog (based on the play by Georg Büchner). *Cinematography:* Jörg Schmidt-Reitwein and Michael Gast. *Editing:* Beate Mainka-Jellinghaus. *Scenography:* Henning von Gierke. *Music:* Antonio Vivaldi, Benedetto Marcello. *Sound:* Harald Maury. *Production:* Werner Herzog, Walter Saxer. *Production company:* Werner Herzog Filmproduktion, ZDF. *Location:* Telč (Czechoslovakia). *Featuring:* Klaus Kinski, Eva Mattes, Wolfgang Reichmann.
Synopsis: In a small town in Germany in the mid-nineteenth century lives a soldier by the name of Franz Woyzeck. He is a nice, naive and poor man, who loves his partner, Marie, dearly, and they have a son. To support his family he supplements his modest soldier's wage with different part-time jobs. For example, he participates in a medical experiment that takes a serious toll on his health. Eventually his friends melt away and his wife is unfaithful to him with an army major. Woyzeck starts to feel humiliated and worn down by his circumstances. He challenges the major, but that only results in further humiliation. In response, he invites Marie down to the lake and kills her on the bank. *Woyzeck* is an adaptation of Georg Büchner's unfinished drama. It and *Nosferatu* constitute Herzog's project of re-legitimizing German culture. The two films were shot back to back in 1978.

GLAUBE UND WÄHRUNG. DR GENE SCOTT, FERNSEHPREDIGER
(God's Angry Man)
Documentary film. West Germany 1981
Length: 44 min. *Format:* 16 mm, 1.33:1, colour
Direction: Werner Herzog. *Screenplay:* Werner Herzog. *Cinematography:* Thomas Mauch. *Editing:* Beate Mainka-Jellinghaus. *Sound:* Walter Saxer. *Production:* Werner Herzog. *Production company:* Werner Herzog Filmproduktion, SDR, Sudfunk Stuttgart. *Location:* Glendale (California). *Featuring:* Dr Gene Scott.

Synopsis: Herzog investigates Gene Scott, a famous television preacher in California. The preacher has a very aggressive temperament that finds expression in the extreme language of his evangelical broadcasts, in which he encourages viewers to transfer money into his bank account. Herzog persuades the preacher to talk about himself and his private life.

HUIE'S PREDIGT

(Huie's Sermon)
Documentary film. West Germany 1981
Length: 43 min. *Format:* 16 mm, 1.33:1, colour
Direction: Werner Herzog. *Screenplay:* Werner Herzog. *Cinematography:* Thomas Mauch, Edward Lachmann. *Editing:* Beate Mainka-Jellinghaus. *Sound:* Walter Saxer. *Production:* Werner Herzog. *Production company:* Werner Herzog Filmproduktion, SDR. *Location:* Brooklyn, New York City (USA). *Featuring:* Huie L. Rogers.
Synopsis: A documentary about a Black community in Brooklyn, New York. Huie is a minister in this small congregation; he sings and encourages his enthusiastic flock in the crowded church. He crafts a unique sermon that intensifies little by little through the rhythm of his language.

FITZCARRALDO

Feature film. West Germany/Peru 1982
Length: 137 min. *Format:* 35 mm, 1.85:1, Eastmancolor
Direction: Werner Herzog. *Screenplay:* Werner Herzog. *Cinematography:* Thomas Mauch, Rainer Klausmann, Beat Presser. *Editing:* Beate Mainka-Jellinghaus, Carola Mai, Linda Kuusisto. *Scenography:* Ulrich Bergfelder, Henning van Gierke. *Music:* Florian Fricke (Popol Vuh). *Sound:* Dagoberto Juarez, Zezé d'Alice. *Production:* Werner Herzog, Lucki Stipetić, Willi Segler, Renzo Rossellini, Walter Saxer. *Production company:* Werner Herzog Filmproduktion, ZDF, Filmverlag der Autoren, Wildlife Films S.A. *Location:* Lima, Pucallpa, Iquitos and surrounding region, Camisea and Urubamba rivers (Peru), Manaus, Amazon and Rio Negro rivers (Brazil), Rome (Italy). *Featuring:* Klaus Kinski, Claudia Cardinale, José Lewgoy, Huerequeque Enrique Bohórquez, Miguel Ángel Fuentes, Ruy Polanah.
Synopsis: Brian Sweeney Fitzgerald, also known as Fitzcarraldo, has a dream: he will build the world's greatest opera house in the middle of the Amazon, and have it opened by the world-renowned tenor Enrico Caruso. To finance his dream he has to exploit the rubber trees that are to be found deep in the Amazon jungle, where no ship has ever penetrated because of the

unpredictable currents. But Fitzcarraldo has a plan to sail down an as yet unexplored river which runs parallel with the un-navigable river that leads to the rubber trees. To reach this point and avoid the dangerous currents, they must drag the steamship *Molly Aida* over a mountain. Fitzcarraldo manages to persuade a tribe of indigenous people to sail with him and move the ship over the mountain, but the dream of the opera house is never realized, as the tribe sacrifices the ship to the river. The ship and its crew float back to their starting point, but they behave as if it were a victory. Instead of building his opera house, Fitzcarraldo organizes one single concert, the greatest concert the Amazon has ever witnessed, in which the musicians and singers perform while sailing down the river on board the *Molly Aida*. Herzog himself has referred to *Fitzcarraldo* as both an opera and his best ever documentary.

BALLADE VOM KLEINEN SOLDATEN

(Ballad of the Little Soldier)

Documentary film. West Germany 1984

Length: 45 min. *Format:* 16mm, 1.33:1, colour

Direction: Werner Herzog. *Screenplay:* Werner Herzog, Denis Reichle. *Cinematography:* Jorge Vignati, Michael Edols. *Editing:* Maximiliane Mainka. *Sound:* Christine Ebenberger. *Production:* Werner Herzog. *Production company:* Werner Herzog Filmproduktion, SDR. *Location:* Nicaragua, Honduras. *Featuring:* Werner Herzog, Denis Reichle. *Voiceover:* Werner Herzog.

Synopsis: Herzog met the journalist Denis Reichle in Nicaragua to find out how things were going for the Misquito people, who live on the banks of the Rio Coco. They are engaged in a violent and bloody war with the Sandinistas. Instead of depicting the war as such, Herzog focuses on how children as young as nine years old are being trained as soldiers and sent into battle. He was vociferously criticized for this film, which the German left wing interpreted as sympathetic to the United States instead of the Sandinistas. Herzog insisted he did not sympathize with anyone other than the children being forced to go to war.

GASHERBRUM – DER LEUCHTENDE BERG

(The Dark Glow of the Mountains)

Documentary film. West Germany 1984

Length: 45 min. *Format:* Super 8 mm/16mm, 1.33:1, Eastmancolor

Direction: Werner Herzog. *Screenplay:* Werner Herzog. *Cinematography:* Rainer Klausmann, Jorge Vignati, Reinhold Messner. *Editing:* Maximiliane Mainka. *Music:* Florian Fricke (Popol Vuh). *Sound:* Christine Ebenberger.

Production: Werner Herzog, Manfred Nägele. *Production company:* Werner Herzog Filmproduktion, Sudfunk Stuttgart, Süddeutscher Rundfunk. *Location:* Karakoam Mountains, Gasherbrum I, Gasherbrum II (China, Pakistan). *Featuring:* Werner Herzog, Hans Kammerlander, Reinhold Messner.

Synopsis: Herzog visits the Himalayas with one of history's greatest mountaineers, Reinhold Messner. Messner wants to climb Gasherbrum I and Gasherbrum II with Hans Kammerlander. It will be the first time that the two 8,000-m-high (26,000 ft) summits have been conquered one after the other. The men don't just intend to climb the mighty peaks; they plan to intensify the challenge by not bringing oxygen or setting up base camp. All they have is their little rucksacks. Before Messner sets off, Herzog talks to him about his many expeditions, which have left Messner's own brother and many others dead. The film includes Messner's own footage from the climb, which documents the extreme risks of the expedition.

WHERE THE GREEN ANTS DREAM

(Wo die grünen Ameisen Träumen)
Feature film. Australia/West Germany 1984
Length: 100 min. *Format:* 35 mm, 1.85:1, Eastmancolor
Direction: Werner Herzog. *Screenplay:* Werner Herzog, Bob Ellis.
Cinematography: Jörg Schmidt-Reitwein, Michael Edols. *Editing:* Beate Mainka-Jellinghaus. *Scenography:* Ulrich Bergfelder, Trevor Orford. *Music:* Richard Wagner, Wandjuk Marika (didgeridoo). *Sound:* Claus Langer, Peter Rappel. *Production:* Werner Herzog, Samantha Krishna Naidu, Willi Segler, Lucki Stipetić. *Production company:* Werner Herzog Filmproduktion, ZDF, Filmverlag der Autoren. *Location:* Coober Pedy, Melbourne (Australia). *Featuring:* Bruce Spence, Roy Marika, Norman Kaye, Wandjuk Marika, Roy Marika, Bob Ellis.

Synopsis: The mining company Ayers is scoping for uranium on Aboriginal territory. The Aborigines cannot accept this, because the many explosions involved are imperilling a sacred territory: the place where the green ants dream about the creation of the world. If this place is destroyed, humankind will not have a future. The company tries to persuade the locals to allow their incursion, even offering them an aircraft, but they do not give in. The case goes to court, and the verdict goes in favour of the company, allowing them to continue their search for uranium. But the young geologist who is leading the expedition suddenly understands how meaningful the terrain is for the proud Aborigines, and leaves his job to go walkabout in the desert. At the same time as Herzog was working on this film, his friend and kindred spirit Bruce Chatwin was writing his book *The Songlines* (1986), about the Aboriginal songlines.

WERNER HERZOG – FILMEMACHER

(Portrait Werner Herzog)
Documentary film. West Germany 1986
Length: 30 min. *Format:* 16 mm, 1.33:1, colour
Direction: Werner Herzog. *Screenplay:* Werner Herzog. *Cinematography:* Jörg Schmidt-Reitwein. *Editing:* Maximiliane Mainka. *Sound:* Christine Ebenberger. *Production:* Werner Herzog. *Production company:* Werner Herzog Filmproduktion, Transtel. *Location:* Munich, Sachrang (Germany). *Featuring:* Werner Herzog, Lotte Eisner, Reinhold Messner.
Synopsis: A self-portrait. Werner Herzog discusses his films and his film theory.

COBRA VERDE

Feature film. West Germany 1987
Length: 110 min. *Format:* 35 mm, 1.85:1, Agfacolor/Eastmancolor
Direction: Werner Herzog. *Screenplay:* Werner Herzog (based on Bruce Chatwin's novel *The Viceroy of Ouidah*, 1980). *Cinematography:* Viktor Ružička, Thomas Mauch, Jorge Ruiz, William Sefa, Hermann Fahr. *Editing:* Maximiliane Mainka, Rainer Standke. *Music:* Florian Fricke (Popol Vuh). *Sound:* Haymo Henry Heyder. *Production:* Lucki Stipetić, Francis Anna, Salvatore Basile, Kofi Bryan, Walter Saxer, George Smith, Kofi Yerenkyi. *Production company:* Werner Herzog Filmproduktion, zDF, Ghana Film Industry Corporation. *Location:* Dahomey (Benin), Elmira, Tamale (Ghana), Cali, Cartagena, Villa de Leyva, La Guajira (Colombia), Juazeiro do Norte, Bahia, Serra Pelada (Brazil). *Featuring:* Klaus Kinski, King Ampaw, José Lewgoy, Peter Berling.
Synopsis: The Brazilian Francisco Manoel da Silva kills a mine owner for refusing to pay his workers' wages. Thereafter he roams around like a bandit under the name Cobra Verde, and is feared by all. The plantation owner Don Octavio hires him to supervise his slaves, but regrets it the moment he realizes that all three of his daughters are pregnant by the uncontrollable Cobra Verde. Fearing a direct confrontation, Octavio sends Cobra Verde to Africa to trade slaves. The aim of the plan is to ensure Cobra Verde's death, since the expedition is to a particularly dangerous area. Cobra Verde manages to subdue the territory, however, and achieves great success until he becomes involved in a civil war. *Cobra Verde* is a film adaptation of Bruce Chatwin's novel *The Viceroy*

of Ouidah (1980), and Chatwin wrote about the shooting of the film in *What Am I Doing Here?* (1988).

LES GAULOIS

Documentary film. France 1988
Length: 12 min. (part of the series *Les Français vus par . . .* (The French Viewed By . . .)). *Format:* 16 mm, 1.33:1, colour
Direction: Werner Herzog. *Screenplay:* Werner Herzog. *Cinematography:* Jörg Schmidt-Reitwein. *Editing:* Rainer Standke. *Sound:* Bernard Aubouy. *Production:* Daniel Toscan du Plantier, Danielle Foatelli. *Production company:* Erato Film, Le Figaro, Antenne 2. *Location:* Toulouse (France), Frankfurt (Germany). *Featuring:* Jean Clemente, Claude Josse, Robyn Sumners, the Toulouse rugby team.
Synopsis: The newspaper *Le Figaro* took the initiative for a miniseries in which foreign filmmakers investigate what makes France special. In Herzog's episode, he focuses on two things that he thinks should be the pride and joy of the French: rugby and wine tasting. In the first part, he films two sommeliers at a special wine tasting, and in the second part he focuses on rugby players getting ready for a match. The other short films in this series were directed by Jean-Luc Godard, David Lynch, Luigi Comencini and Andrzej Wajda.

WODAABE – DIE HIRTEN DER SONNE

(Wodaabe: Herdsmen of the Sun)
Documentary film. Germany/France 1989
Length: 52 min. *Format:* 16 mm, 1.33:1, Eastmancolor
Direction: Werner Herzog. *Screenplay:* Werner Herzog. *Cinematography:* Jörg Schmidt-Reitwein. *Editing:* Maximiliane Mainka. *Music:* George Frideric Handel, Wolfgang Amadeus Mozart, Giuseppe Verdi. *Sound:* Walter Saxer. *Production:* Werner Herzog, Patrick Sandrin, Catherine Jacques, Jörg Dattler. *Production company:* Werner Herzog Filmproduktion, Les Film Ariane, Antenne 2, Canal+, Arion Productions. *Location:* Southern Sahara (Western Nigeria). *Voiceover:* Werner Herzog.
Synopsis: Herzog has travelled to Africa to document the lives of a nomadic tribe of the Sahel region, the Wodaabe people. The tribe claims to consist of the most beautiful people on Earth, and expresses this in its celebration of beauty and love. This festival is defined by some quite particular rituals: the men beautify themselves with decorative costumes and special make-up. Each man strives to be the most attractive in order to win the heart of the best woman. Then the men dance and sing for the women, and each woman

chooses a man. Because of a terrible drought in the Sahel in 1984, the most beautiful tribe in the world has been forced to relocate to an enormous slum on the Algerian border. There they feel like prisoners and can see no way out, but they still feel beautiful.

ECHOS AUS EINEM DÜSTEREN REICH
(Echoes from a Sombre Empire)
Documentary film. Germany/France 1990
Length: 87 min. *Format:* 16 mm, 1:33.1, colour
Direction: Werner Herzog. *Screenplay:* Werner Herzog. *Cinematography:* Jörg Schmidt-Reitwein, Martin Manz. *Editing:* Rainer Standke, Thomas Balkenhol. *Music:* Johann Sebastian Bach, Béla Bartók, Sergei Prokofiev, Franz Schubert. *Sound:* Harald Maury. *Production:* Werner Herzog, Galesha Moravioff, Walter Saxer. *Production company:* Werner Herzog Filmproduktion, SERA Filmproduktionens GmbH, Films sans Frontières.
Location: Central African Republic, France, Venice (Italy). *Featuring:* Michael Goldsmith, Werner Herzog, Augustine Assemat.
Synopsis: A documentary about the dictator Jean-Bédel Bokassa. In 1977 the South African journalist Michael Goldsmith reported from the coronation as emperor of the Central African Republic of the dictator Jean-Bédel Bokassa. Goldsmith was accused of espionage and imprisoned. In this film, Goldsmith returns to the Central African Republic, accompanied by Herzog. They revisit the prison where he was incarcerated and almost beaten to death, as well as the dictator's villa and the zoo. Goldsmith also talks to Bokassa's last wife, Augustine Assemat, his lovers, his numerous children and his cousin, David Dacko, who was president before and after Bokassa. The film is famous for its symbolic stagings of barbarism, not least a caged cigarette-smoking chimpanzee.

JAG MANDIR. DAS EXZENTRISCHE PRIVATTHEATER DES MAHARADJAH VON UDAIPUR
(Jag Mandir: The Eccentric Private Theater of the Maharaja of Udaipur)
Documentary film. Austria 1991
Length: 83 min. *Format:* 16 mm, 1.33:1, colour
Direction: Werner Herzog. *Screenplay:* Werner Herzog. *Cinematography:* Rainer Klausmann, Wolfgang Dickmann, Anton Peschke, Claudius Kelterborn, Daniel Koppelmann, Bernard Watzek. *Editing:* Michou Hutter, Ursula Darrer. *Sound:* Rainer Wiehr, Alois Unger. *Production:* Wolfgang Rest. *Production company:* Neue Studio Film GmbH, ZDF, ORF. *Location:* Udaipur

(India). *Featuring:* André Heller. *Voiceover:* Werner Herzog.
Synopsis: Herzog films a project run by the Austrian theatre director André Heller that aims to preserve the culture of the Maharajahs. It consists of a 24-hour stage play with dancers, fakirs, musicians and artists from all over India.

SCREAM OF STONE
(Cerro Torre: Schrei aus Stein)
Feature film. Canada/Germany/France 1991
Length: 105 min. *Format:* 35 mm, 1.85:1, Fujicolor
Direction: Werner Herzog. *Screenplay:* Hans-Ulrich Klenner, Walter Saxer, Robert Geoffrion, Reinhold Messner (idea). *Cinematography:* Rainer Klausmann, Herbert Raditschnig, Claudius Kelterborn, Fulvio Mariani, Gerhard Baur, Jorge Vignati. *Editing:* Suzanne Baron, Anne Wagner. *Music:* Sarah Hopkins, Alan Lamb, Ingram Marshall, Atahualpa Yupanqui. *Sound:* Christopher Price. *Production:* Walter Saxer. *Production company:* SERA Filmproduktionens GmbH, Molecule, Les Films Stock International, ZDF, Canal+, Films A2, Téléfilm Canada, Lucky Red, Radiot, Rai 2. *Location:* Munich, Frankfurt am Main region (Germany), Cerro Torre, Patagonia (Argentina, Chile). *Featuring:* Vittorio Mezzogiorno, Mathilda May, Stefan Glowacz.
Synopsis: After an indoor climbing competition won by Martin Edelmeier, the world's most successful alpine-style climber, Roccia Innerkopfler claims that a competition climber would never be able to manage a real mountain. To test out their premise, Martin and Roccia travel to the impregnable Cerro Torre, which 'is more a scream of stone than a mountain'. The weather is not immediately suitable for climbing and they have to wait, but one day Martin recklessly sets off from their camp with his friend Hans Adler, while Roccia has gone to get supplies. Adler dies on the mission, but Martin returns, claiming that he has climbed the mountain. Meanwhile, Roccia has met a climber and passionate Mae West fan who modestly claims he lost four fingers at the summit of Cerro Torre. The man is called Fingerless, because after his climb he can no longer remember his name. The media doubt that Martin really made it to the top, so he climbs the mountain again with Roccia. Martin dies during the climb, but when Roccia reaches the summit he finds an ice axe with a photo of Mae West. Fingerless had been there first.

FILM STUNDE

(Film Lessons 1–4)

Television series. Austria 1991

Length: Four parts, respectively 60, 62, 60 and 58 min. *Format:* Betacam Sp, 1.33:1, colour

Direction: Werner Herzog. *Screenplay:* Werner Herzog. *Cinematography:* Karl Kofler, Michael Ferk. *Editing:* Albert Skalak. *Sound:* Gerhard Sandler. *Production:* Gerda Weissenberger. *Production company:* ORF. *Location:* Viennale, 1991, Vienna (Austria). *Featuring:* Werner Herzog, Ryszard Kapuscinski, Michael Kreihsl, Philippe Petit, Kamal Saiful Islam, Volker Schlöndorff, Jeff Sheridan, Peter Turrini.

Synopsis: A documentary series based on a range of encounters with directors and inspiring people that Werner Herzog set up during the 1990–91 Viennale Film Festival. This is a meeting of magicians, mathematicians and line dancers in the hope of reaching an understanding of what aesthetics is, and what it can do. This 'circus tent' of cinema is a forerunner of what became the Rogue Film School.

LEKTIONEN IN FINSTERNIS

(Lessons of Darkness)

Documentary film. Germany/France/UK 1992

Length: 52 min. *Format:* Super 16 mm, 1.78:1, colour

Direction: Werner Herzog. *Screenplay:* Werner Herzog. *Cinematography:* Paul Beriff, Simon Werry, Rainer Klausmann. *Editing:* Rainer Standke. *Music:* Edward Grieg, Gustav Mahler, Arvo Pärt, Sergei Prokofiev, Franz Schubert, Giuseppe Verdi, Richard Wagner. *Sound:* John G. Pearson. *Production:* Werner Herzog, Paul Berriff, Lucki Stipetić. *Production company:* Werner Herzog Filmproduktion, Canal+, Première. *Location:* Kuwait. *Voiceover:* Werner Herzog.

Synopsis: After the Gulf War of 1991, Herzog travelled to Kuwait with a small film crew. He wanted to depict the 'scream' of the war. But this is not a classic documentary, for he views the dramatic images of burning oilfields as if he were an alien investigating humankind. The documentary consists of thirteen titled sequences. A voiceover relates the noise of civilization and the stillness of the desert and describes what we are seeing, but not always truthfully. We see some of the victims of the war, such as a woman and a child who have lost the power of speech because of war trauma. The documentary was harshly criticized in Germany. This criticism would later move Herzog to write his *Minnesota Declaration*.

GLOCKEN AUS DER TIEFE
(Bells from the Deep)
Documentary film. Germany/USA 1993
Length: 60 min. *Format:* Super 16 mm, 1.37:1, Eastmancolor
Direction: Werner Herzog. *Screenplay:* Werner Herzog. *Cinematography:* Jörg
Schmidt-Reitwein, Martin Manz. *Editing:* Rainer Standke. *Sound:* Vyacheslav
Belozerou. *Production:* Lucki Stipetić, Mark Slater, Ira Barmak. *Production
company:* Werner Herzog Filmproduktion. *Location:* Russia. *Featuring:* Anna
Hitch, Sergey Anatolyevitch Torop. *Voiceover:* Werner Herzog.
Synopsis: Herzog goes to Siberia to investigate myths and legends. In so-called
modern Russia, superstitions and faiths are thriving side by side. There are
various shamans, New Age preachers and healers who use holy water. Herzog
follows in particular a young man who claims to be Jesus. His story fades out,
however, and the film's final focus is an invisible city on the lake bed, Kitezh.
The legend goes that if you put your ear to the ice on the lake and your heart
is pure, you can hear the church bells of the sunken city ringing.

DIE VERWANDLUNG DER WELT IN MUSIK
(The Transformation of the World into Music)
Documentary film. Germany 1994.
Length: 92 min. *Format:* Super 16 mm, 1.33:1, colour.
Direction: Werner Herzog. *Screenplay:* Werner Herzog. *Cinematography:* Jörg
Schmidt-Reitwein. *Editing:* Rainer Standke. *Sound:* Ekkehard Baumung.
Production: Jenny Erpenbeck, Evelyn Paulmann, Lucki Stipetić. *Production
company:* Werner Herzog Filmproduktion, ZDF, Arte. *Location:* Bayreuth
and Schloss Linderhof (Germany). *Featuring:* Norbert Balatsch, Daniel
Barenboim, Plácido Domingo.
Synopsis: Scenes from the famous Bayreuth Festival, where the world's
best-known opera singers perform Richard Wagner. Herzog documents
the work of staging Wagner's operas.

GESUALDO – TOD FÜR FÜNF STIMMEN
(Gesualdo: Death for Five Voices)
Documentary film. Germany 1995
Length: 60 min. *Format:* Super 16 mm, 1.33:1, colour.
Direction: Werner Herzog. *Screenplay:* Werner Herzog. *Cinematography:*
Peter Zeitlinger, Thomas Prodinger. *Editing:* Rainer Standke. *Music:* Carlo
Gesualdo. *Sound:* Ekkehard Baumung, Klaus Handstein. *Production:* Jenny
Erpenbeck, Evelyn Paulmann, Lucki Stipetić. *Production company:* Werner

Herzog Filmproduktion, ZDF. *Location:* Naples, Ferrara, Castel Gesualdo, Arezzo, Venosa (Italy). *Featuring:* Pasquale D'Onofrio, Salvatore Catorano, Angelo Carrabs. *Voiceover:* Werner Herzog.

Synopsis: Herzog goes to Italy to make a film portrait of the eccentric sixteenth-century composer and alchemist Carlo Gesualdo, Prince of Venosa. Gesualdo's interests were alchemy and music, and experts have said that his music was ahead of its time. Legend has it that Gesualdo's ghost still haunts the town, so Herzog asks the townspeople of Venosa about him. Gesualdo killed his wife and her lover in a rather brutal way when he discovered their affair. He then mummified them both and exhibited them where they were discovered.

LITTLE DIETER NEEDS TO FLY

(Flucht aus Laos)

Documentary film. Germany/France/UK 1997

Length: 80 min. (Television version: Flucht aus Laos, 52 min.) *Format:* Super 16 mm, 1.85:1, colour.

Direction: Werner Herzog. *Screenplay:* Werner Herzog. *Cinematography:* Peter Zeitlinger, Les Blank, Erik Söllner. *Editing:* Rainder Standke, Joe Bini, Glen Scantlebury. *Music:* Richard Wagner, Béla Bartók, Tuva Singers. *Sound:* Ekkehart Baumung. *Production:* André Singer, Lucki Stipetić. *Production company:* Werner Herzog Filmproduktion, ZDF, BBC, Arte. *Location:* Wildberg and district (Germany), San Diego, San Francisco, Tucson (USA), Laos, Thailand. *Featuring:* Dieter Dengler. *Voiceover:* Werner Herzog.

Synopsis: A reconstruction of the extraordinary story of Dieter Dengler, who was shot down over Laos during a Vietnam war mission with the U.S. Air Force. Miraculously he survived, but he was soon captured and imprisoned with other Americans. Dengler succeeded in escaping the prison camp and headed out into the jungle, eventually reaching safety just as he was ready to collapse. The film also exists as a shorter television version, and Herzog later based the feature film *Rescue Dawn* on the same story (see below).

JULIANES STURZ IN DEN DSCHUNGEL

(Wings of Hope)

Documentary film. Germany/UK 1999

Length: 70 min. (Television version from 2000: 42 min.) *Format:* Super 16mm, 1.33:1, colour

Direction: Werner Herzog. *Screenplay:* Werner Herzog. *Cinematography:* Peter Zeitlinger, Erik Söllner. *Editing:* Joe Bini, Maya Hawke. *Music:* Richard

Wagner, Igor Stravinsky. *Sound:* Eric Spitzer. *Production:* Lucki Stipetić.
Production company: Werner Herzog Filmproduktion, ZDF, BBC.
Location: Lima, Peruvian jungle. *Featuring:* Werner Herzog, Juliane
Koepcke, Juan Zaplana Ramirez. *Voiceover:* Werner Herzog.
Synopsis: The film tells the incredible story of Juliane Koepcke, the only
survivor of a plane crash in the Amazon. The young woman managed
to trek out of the enormous, labyrinthine jungle by herself, despite minor
injuries. Herzog and some of his *Aguirre* film cast and crew should have
been on precisely that same flight, but could not board because of
overbooking.

MEIN LIEBSTER FEIND – KLAUS KINSKI
(My Best Fiend)
Documentary film. Germany/Finland/UK/USA 1999
Length: 95 min. *Format:* Super 16 mm, 1.66:1, b/w and colour
Direction: Werner Herzog. *Screenplay:* Werner Herzog. *Cinematography:* Peter
Zeitlinger, Les Blank, Erik Söllner. *Editing:* Joe Bini, Thomas Staunton, Thad
Povey, Renate Hähner. *Sound:* Eric Spitzer, Chris Simon. *Production:* Lucki
Stipetić, Christine Ruppert, André Singer, James Mitchell, Sabine Rollberg.
Production company: Werner Herzog Filmproduktion, ZDF, BBC, IFC, Outpost,
Cafe Productions, Arte, Bayerischer Rundfunk, Westdeutscher Rundfunk.
Location: Munich (Germany), Lima, Iquitos and Urubama Valley (Peru),
district of San Francisco (USA), Telč (Czech Republic), Delft (the
Netherlands), Paris (France). *Featuring:* Klaus Kinski, Eva Mattes,
Claudia Cardinale, Werner Herzog. *Voiceover:* Werner Herzog.
Synopsis: In the 1950s, when both Werner Herzog and Klaus Kinski were very
young, they shared an apartment. The egocentric, crazy Kinski smashed up
their home in a blind rage over two days. Out of this chaos grew not just
a long working relationship, but an enduring love-hate friendship. This is
a personal documentary that focuses on the many ups and downs that laid
the foundations of the relationship that produced five feature films: *Aguirre,
Nosferatu, Woyzeck, Fitzcarraldo* and *Cobra Verde.*

GOTT UND DIE BELADENEN
(Christ and Demons in New Spain).
Documentary film. Germany 1999
Length: 43 min. *Format:* DV-cam, 1.33:1, colour
Direction: Werner Herzog. *Screenplay:* Werner Herzog, Günther Klein.
Cinematography: Jorge Vignati, Edward Lachman, Gonzalo Tapia. *Editing:* Joe

Bini, Thomas Staunton. *Music:* Charles Gounod, Orlando di Lasso. *Sound:* Francisco Adrianzén. *Production:* Lucki Stipetić. *Production company:* Tellux Film. *Location:* Antigua, San Andrés Itzapá (Guatemala), Paris (France). *Featuring:* Donald Arthur. *Voiceover:* Werner Herzog.
Synopsis: A film about the Catholic Church's conquest of Latin America. Herzog analyses different forms of worship, but the red thread in the film is the consequences that religious colonialism has for the native population. This was episode 9 of the television series *2000 Jahre Christentum* (2000 Years of Christendom).

INVINCIBLE

Feature film. Germany/UK 2001
Length: 130 min. *Format:* 35 mm, 1.85:1, colour
Direction: Werner Herzog. *Screenplay:* Werner Herzog. *Cinematography:* Peter Zeitlinger. *Editing:* Joe Bini. *Scenography:* Ulrich Bergfelder. *Music:* Hans Zimmer, Klaus Badelt. *Sound:* Simon Willis. *Production:* Werner Herzog, Gary Bart, Christine Ruppert, Michael André, James Mitchell, Simone Stewens, Paul Webster, Robertas Urbonas, Lucki Stipetić. *Production company:* Werner Herzog Filmproduktion, TatFilm Produktion. *Location:* Bad Honnef, Berlin, Düsseldorf, Cologne (Germany), Warsaw (Poland), Riga (Latvia), Lithuania, Netherlands, Christmas Island (Australia), Monterey Bay Aquarium (USA), Black Island Studios (London, UK). *Featuring:* Tim Roth, Udo Kier, Herb Golder, Jouko Ahola.
Synopsis: The Polish-Jewish locksmith Zishe is a sensitive but physically strong young man. He attracts the attention of an entrepreneur, who persuades him to travel to Berlin to become the world's strongest man. Zishe exercises in preparation for his performance every night in the house of the Danish hypnotist Hanussen. But Zishe starts to harbour doubts about what God has planned for his life, and leads a revolt with Hanussen, who is a follower of Hitler and anti-Semitism.

PILGRIMAGE

Documentary film. Germany/UK 2001
Length: 18 min. *Format:* Super 16 mm, 1.66:1, colour
Direction: Werner Herzog. *Screenplay:* Werner Herzog. *Cinematography:* Jorge Pacheco, Jörg Schmidt-Reitwein, Erik Söllner. *Editing:* Joe Bini. *Music:* John Tavener. *Sound:* Neil Pemberton. *Production:* Lucki Stipetić. *Production company:* Werner Herzog Filmproduktion, BBC, Pipeline Films. *Location:* Mexico, Siberia (Russia).

Synopsis: This documentary was part of the BBC series *Sound and Film.* Herzog collaborates with the contemporary composer John Tavener on a documentary about religion. Apart from an epigraph (which is fake) there are no words in the film – only music.

TEN THOUSAND YEARS OLDER

Documentary film. Germany/UK 2002
Length: 10 min. (part of Ten Minutes Older: The Trumpet). *Format:* DigiBeta/ Super 16, 1.37:1, colour
Direction: Werner Herzog. *Screenplay:* Werner Herzog. *Cinematography:* Vicente Ríos. *Editing:* Joe Bini. *Music:* Paul Englishby/Hugh Masekela. *Sound:* Walter Saxer. *Production:* Lucki Stipetić. *Production company:* Werner Herzog Filmproduktion, Ten Minutes Older Ltd. *Location:* Brazil. *Featuring:* Tarí, Wapo.
Synopsis: In 1981 a nomadic tribe was identified in the most remote region of the Brazilian rainforest, and the hitherto undiscovered tribe came into contact with civilization for the first time. They quickly died of the common cold, since they had no immunity. Today, the few living survivors and descendants speak Portuguese only and are ashamed of their roots, as they discuss in this documentary. This short film was part of the series *Ten Minutes Older: The Trumpet*; other films in the series were directed by Aki Kaurismäki, Víctor Erice, Jim Jarmusch, Wim Wenders, Spike Lee and Chen Kaige.

RAD DER ZEIT

(Wheel of Time)
Documentary film. Germany/Austria/Italy 2003
Length: 80 min. *Format:* Super 16, 1.85:1, colour
Direction: Werner Herzog. *Screenplay:* Werner Herzog. *Cinematography:* Peter Zeitlinger, Erik Söllner, Werner Herzog. *Editing:* Joe Bini, Maya Hawke. *Music:* Florian Fricke (Popol Vuh). *Sound:* Eric Spitzer. *Production:* Lucki Stipetić. *Production company:* Werner Herzog Filmproduktion, West Park Pictures, Café Productions, Dario de Luca Tipota Movie Company. *Location:* Graz (Austria), Bodhgaya (India), Kailash Mountain (Tibet, China). *Featuring:* Madhurita Negi Anand, Vaidya Bihaya, Dalai Lama. *Voiceover:* Werner Herzog.
Synopsis: In 2002 the Tibetan Buddhists held a great ritual in India in the presence of the Dalai Lama. Over six weeks hundreds of thousands of Buddhists take part in the ritual, giving themselves over completely to prayer and meditation, all of which is represented in the mandala wheel, which

disappears in the wind when the ritual is finished. After long-term discussions with the Dalai Lama, Herzog attends the ritual to observe the pilgrimage. He also records the second iteration of the ritual in Graz, Austria.

THE WHITE DIAMOND

(White Diamond – Im Luftschiff über den Dshungel)
Documentary film. Germany 2004
Length: 87 min. *Format:* HD-cam/35mm, 1.78:1, colour
Direction: Werner Herzog. *Screenplay:* Werner Herzog, Rudolph Herzog, Annette Scheurich, Rainer Bergomaz, Marion Pöllmann. *Cinematography:* Henning Brümmer, Klaus Scheurich, Rainer Bergomaz, Bernd Curschmann, Marcus Pfeiffer. *Editing:* Joe Bini. *Music:* Ernst Reijseger, Eric Spitzer. *Sound:* Eric Spitzer, Simon Normanton. *Production:* Werner Herzog, Rudolph Herzog, Walter Saxer, Annette Scheurich, Lucki Stipetić. *Production company:* Marco Polo Film, NDR Naturfilm, NHK, BBC. *Location:* Bedford (UK), Guyana. *Featuring:* Werner Herzog, Graham Dorrington, Red Man, The Rooster, Dieter Plage. *Voiceover:* Werner Herzog.
Synopsis: The engineer Graham Dorrington heads out on a journey in a gigantic white air balloon towards the Kaieteur waterfall in Guyana, hoping that the airship will carry him over the treetops. The adventure is not without risk. Twelve years earlier a friend of his went on a similar expedition over the rainforest, and it ended in tragedy. Herzog joins Dorrington's expedition and investigates the untouched rainforest region. The film jumps from character to character, constantly following new paths.

GRIZZLY MAN

Documentary film. USA 2005
Length: 103 min. *Format:* 35 mm/HD, 1.85:1, colour
Direction: Werner Herzog. *Screenplay:* Werner Herzog. *Cinematography:* Peter Zeitlinger, Timothy Treadwell, Erik Söllner. *Editing:* Joe Bini, Maya Hawke. *Music:* Richard Thompson. *Sound:* Ken King, Spencer Palermo. *Production:* Erik Nelson, Kevin L. Beggs, Alana Berry. *Production company:* Discovery Docs, Lion Gate Films, Real Big Production. *Location:* Katmai National Park, Alaska (USA). *Featuring:* Timothy Treadwell, Werner Herzog, Jewel Palovak, David Letterman. *Voiceover:* Werner Herzog.
Synopsis: Timothy Treadwell chose to live in Alaska, in close contact with grey bears, for many years. He filmed his stays in extreme wilderness together with the bears. In October 2003 the sorry remains of Treadwell were found; he had been eaten by the bears. Herzog explores both wild nature and human nature

by collating Treadwell's recordings into a documentary, in which he also involves Treadwell's friends and family.

THE WILD BLUE YONDER

Feature film. Germany/UK/France 2005
Length: 81 min. *Format:* Super16/HD/35mm, 1.85:1, b/w and colour
Direction: Werner Herzog. *Screenplay:* Werner Herzog. *Cinematography:* Henry Kaiser, Tanja Koop, Klaus Scheurich, Jorge Vignati, the astronauts of STS-34. *Editing:* Joe Bini, Christophe Nadeau. *Music:* Ernst Reijsiger. *Sound:* Joe Crabb, Eric Spitzer. *Production:* André Singer, Jill Coulon, Norm Hill, Christine Le Goff, Pedro G. Ortega, Lucki Stipetić. *Production company:* Werner Herzog Filmproduktion, West Park Pictures Production, Tétra Media, France 2, BBC, CNC. *Location:* Niland (California, USA), images from McMurdo Sound (Antarctic) and NASA Mission STS-34 (*Galileo* spacecraft). *Featuring:* Brad Dourif, Donald Williams, Dr Ellen Baker.
Synopsis: The Wild Blue Yonder is simultaneously a feature film and a documentary, and thus an amalgam of the two genres. An alien tells the sad story of how it has become impossible for them to stay on Earth because it is so polluted and destroyed. It has also become impossible for people, and so some astronauts set out to find another planet that is inhabitable by the human race. Herzog uses original NASA footage and Henry Kaiser's documentary recordings from the depths of the Atlantic.

RESCUE DAWN

Feature film. USA 2006
Length: 126 min. *Format:* 35 mm, 1.85:1, colour
Direction: Werner Herzog. *Screenplay:* Werner Herzog. *Cinematography:* Peter Zeitlinger, Erik Söllner. *Editing:* Joe Bini. *Scenography:* Arin Pinjivarak. *Music:* Klaus Badelt. *Sound:* Paul Paragon, Tammy Douglas. *Production:* Elton Brand, Harry Knapp, Steve Marlton. *Production company:* Top Gun Productions, Gibraltar Films, MGM, Thema, Bruin Grip Services. *Location:* Thailand. *Featuring:* Christian Bale, Steve Zahn, Jeremy Davies.
Synopsis: Rescue Dawn grew out of the documentary *Little Dieter Needs to Fly* (see above), in which Herzog reconstructs the story of the pilot Dieter Dengler. This time, Herzog makes a feature film about Dieter's dream of becoming a pilot, and his mission in Vietnam. To realize his dream, Dieter travels to the United States to join the army. Shortly before the outbreak of the Vietnam War, he is sent on a mission on the Vietnam–Laos border. The plane goes down in the jungle, and Dieter is taken prisoner by anti-American

guerrilla soldiers, but he manages to escape. The escape is a very dangerous journey during which he has to take extreme measures to avoid being imprisoned again.

ENCOUNTERS AT THE END OF THE WORLD

Documentary film. USA 2007
Length: 99 min. *Format:* HD-cam, 1.85:1, colour
Direction: Werner Herzog. *Screenplay:* Werner Herzog. *Cinematography:* Peter Zeitlinger. *Editing:* Joe Bini. *Sound:* Werner Herzog. *Production:* Henry Kaiser. *Production company:* Discovery Films, Creative Differences Productions, Discovery Channel. *Location:* Antarctica. *Featuring:* Werner Herzog, Scott Rowland, Stefan Pashov, Libor Zicha. *Voiceover:* Werner Herzog.
Synopsis: At the end of the world hides a whole society. Around 1,000 people live in the Antarctic, putting their lives on the line for science every day. This is a small community consisting of philosophers, linguists and other scientists, who, for the first time, feel they belong. Together with just one cameraman, Herzog observes this little group and tries to break through the ice to the lonely nature and lonely people of the Antarctic, who have found community here.

BAD LIEUTENANT: PORT OF CALL NEW ORLEANS

Feature film. USA 2009
Length: 121 min. *Format:* 35mm, 1.85:1, colour
Direction: Werner Herzog. *Screenplay:* William M. Finkelstein (inspired by Abel Ferrara's *Bad Lieutenant*, 1992). *Cinematography:* Peter Zeitlinger. *Editing:* Joe Bini. *Music:* Mark Isham. *Sound:* Jay Meagher. *Production:* Stephen Belafonte, Randall Emmett, Alan Polsku, Gabe Polsky, Edward R. Pressman, John Thompson. *Production company:* Lieutenant Productions, Nu Image Films, Osiris, Polsky, Saturn Films, Edward R. Pressman Film. *Location:* New Orleans (Louisiana, USA). *Featuring:* Nicolas Cage, Eva Mendes, Val Kilmer, Michael Shannon, Brad Dourif.
Synopsis: This is a film directed by Herzog from William M. Finkelstein's screenplay, which was inspired by Abel Ferrara's dark masterpiece *Bad Lieutenant* (1992) ('It's not a remake, I haven't seen Ferrara's film,' says Herzog). Terence McDonagh, a criminal commissioner in New Orleans, is promoted after saving a convict from drowning in the aftermath of Hurricane Katrina. During the rescue his back was badly injured, and one year on he is addicted to drugs that dull his pain. We follow McDonagh's work to find the

drug dealer Big Fate, who has killed an entire family of Senegalese immigrants, while watching McDonagh fight his own demons and his dependence on sex and cocaine. The film is a cornucopia of elements from other Herzog films, and thus a kind of reunion with a range of stylistic signatures, all gathered in one film, among them the manic mouth organ and bizarre animals.

LA BOHÈME

Short film. UK 2009
Length: 4 min. *Format:* HD-cam, 1.78:1, colour
Direction: Werner Herzog. *Screenplay:* Giuseppe Giacosa (libretto), Luigi Illica (libretto). *Cinematography:* Richard Blanchard. *Editing:* Joe Bini. *Music:* Giacomo Puccini. *Production company:* Sky Arts, English National Opera. *Location:* Ethiopia. *Featuring:* Peter Auty, Mary Plazas. *Voiceover:* Werner Herzog.
Synopsis: A short film about the well-known opera by Puccini. There is a moving interpretation of the duet 'A soave fanciulla' among the Mursi people of southwestern Ethiopia. This is an original attempt to create an amalgam of opera and film.

MY SON, MY SON, WHAT HAVE YE DONE

Feature film. USA/Germany 2009
Length: 93 min. *Format:* HD-cam, 1.85:1, colour
Direction: Werner Herzog. *Screenplay:* Werner Herzog, Herb Golder. *Cinematography:* Peter Zeitlinger. *Editing:* Joe Bini, Omar Daher. *Sound:* Ronald Eng. *Production:* Eric Basset, Jack Sojka, David Lynch. *Production company:* Industrial Entertainment, DeFilm, Paper Street Films. *Location:* Los Angeles, San Diego (USA), Calgary (Canada), Kashgar (China), Tijuana (Mexico), Cuzco, Urubamba river (Peru). *Featuring:* Michael Shannon, Grace Zabriskie, Udo Kier, Braden Lynch, Brad Dourif, Willem Dafoe, Chloë Sevigny.
Synopsis: The wannabe actor Brad is to play a role in Sophocles' Greek tragedy *Electra*, and he carries out the same act in reality as he does in the play: he kills his mother. The film opens with the discovery of the mother in a pool of blood, and Brad has barricaded himself in a house and seems to have taken hostages. Thereafter we see, through flashbacks, why he has been driven to such psychological extremes, and discover that he has experienced terrible events in his life. The film was produced in collaboration with David Lynch.

HAPPY PEOPLE: A YEAR IN THE TAIGA

Documentary film. Germany 2010

Length: 90 min. *Format:* DV-cam, 1.85:1, colour

Direction: Dmitry Vasyukov, Werner Herzog. *Screenplay:* Rudolf Herzog, Werner Herzog, Dmitry Vasyukov. *Cinematography:* Alexy Matveev, Gleb Stepanov, Arthur Sibirski, Michael Tarkovsky. *Editing:* Joe Bini, Maxim Perepelkin, Dmitry Vasyukov, Alexey Stanevich. *Music:* Klaus Badelt. *Sound:* Robert Getty. *Production:* Christoph Fisser, Vladimir Prepelkin, Nick Raslan, Charlie Woebcken, Werner Herzog. *Production company:* Studio Babelsberg. *Location:* Siberia (Russia). *Featuring:* Nikolay Nikiforovitch Siniaev, Gennday Soloviev, Anatoly Tarkovsky. *Voiceover:* Werner Herzog.

Synopsis: Just like *Grizzly Man* (see above), this film is largely based on found footage – an annexing and re-editing of, and commentary on, other people's recordings. This time, the source material is Dmitry Vasyukov's almost four-hour-long documentary series *Schastlivyye lyudi* (Happy People, 2007–), about life as a hunter in Siberia. The film departs in many ways from Herzog's oeuvre as a whole, and should perhaps be seen more as an elegant re-editing by Joe Bini, but there is a thematic affinity (the unshakable urge to survive and the good dogs) that makes Herzog's adoption of the project understandable. It is not always included in Herzog's filmography.

CAVE OF FORGOTTEN DREAMS

Documentary film. USA/Germany/France 2010

Length: 91 min. *Format:* Stereoscopic 3D, 1.85:1, colour

Direction: Werner Herzog. *Screenplay:* Werner Herzog. *Cinematography:* Peter Zeitlinger, Erik Söllner. *Editing:* Joe Bini, Maya Hawke. *Music:* Ernst Reijseger. *Sound:* Eric Spitzer. *Production:* Adrienne Ciuffo, Erik Nelson. *Production company:* Werner Herzog Filmproduktion, Arte France, More4, Creative Differences. *Location:* Chauvet-Pont-d'Arc cave, Ardèche (France). *Featuring:* Werner Herzog, Jean Clottes, Gilles Tosello, Julien Monney. *Voiceover:* Werner Herzog.

Synopsis: Werner Herzog was the only filmmaker given permission to shoot in the Chauvet cave, where *Homo sapiens* produced cave paintings 32,000 years ago. Permission was granted by the French Ministry of Culture, which employed Herzog on a symbolic salary of 1 euro. Herzog filmed in the cave in 3D, but he is just as interested in the people who dedicate their lives to studying the cave and who project their dreams onto it. In a fantastical epilogue, he tells the story of the albino crocodiles who supposedly live in greenhouses not far from the cave.

ODE TO THE DAWN OF MAN
Documentary film. USA 2011
Length: 39 min: *Format:* DV-cam, 1.77:1, colour
Direction: Werner Herzog. *Screenplay:* Werner Herzog. *Cinematography:*
Werner Herzog. *Editing:* Maya Hawke. *Music:* Ernst Reijseger. *Sound:* Werner
Herzog. *Production:* Werner Herzog. *Production company:* Werner Herzog
Filmproduktion. *Location:* the Netherlands. *Featuring:* Ernst Reijseger, Sean
Bergin, Harmen Fraanje.
Synopsis: This film does tend to be included in Herzog's filmography, but
should be regarded primarily as extra material from *Cave of Forgotten Dreams*
(see above). It gives insight into the composer Ernst Reijseger's work on the
music for *Cave of Forgotten Dreams*.

INTO THE ABYSS – A TALE OF DEATH, A TALE OF LIFE
Documentary film. USA/UK/Germany 2011
Length: 105 min. *Format:* HD-cam, 1.85:1, colour.
Direction: Werner Herzog. *Screenplay:* Werner Herzog. *Cinematography:*
Peter Zeitlinger. *Editing:* Joe Bini. *Music:* Mark Degli Antoni. *Sound:* Steve
Osmon, Eric Spitzer. *Production:* Werner Herzog, Erik Nelson, Lucki Stipetić.
Production company: Sundance Selects, Creative Differences, Investigation
Discovery, More4, Spring Films, Werner Herzog Filmproduktion. *Location:*
Huntsville, Livingston, Conroe (Texas, USA). *Featuring:* Jason Burkett, Fred
Thompson, Michael Perry. *Voiceover:* Werner Herzog.
Synopsis: In 2001 Michael Perry and Jason Burkett killed three people in
a car robbery. Herzog talks with them in prison, in Perry's case just eight
days before he is to be executed. He also speaks to Burkett's father and to
the woman who married Burkett even though he had been sentenced to life
imprisonment. Herzog is an opponent of the death penalty but addresses
the issue dispassionately, both as an objective observer of the crimes and
as a curious interviewer of people who are facing death. The prison chaplain,
the executioner and relatives of the victims also feature.

ON DEATH ROW (PARTS 1 AND 2)
Documentary television series. USA/UK/Austria 2012–13
Length: Two seasons with eight episodes in total, 52 minutes each.
Format: HD-cam, 1.85:1, colour *Direction:* Werner Herzog. *Screenplay:* Werner
Herzog. *Cinematography:* Peter Zeitlinger (season 1), Dave Roberson
(season 2). *Editing:* Joe Bini (season 1), Marco Capalbo (season 2). *Music:*
Mark Degli Antoni. *Sound:* Eric Spitzer, Steve Osmon. *Production:* Nathaniel

O. Calloway (season 1), Erik Nelson (season 2). *Production company:* Werner Herzog Filmproduktion, Skellig Rock, Spring Films, Creative Differences, Investigation Discovery. *Location:* Texas (USA). *Featuring:* Hank Skinner, James Barnes, Linda Carty. *Voiceover:* Werner Herzog.

Synopsis: Herzog interviewed a number of prisoners on death row in Texas. As well as the film *Into the Abyss* (see above), the material resulted in this television series based on the interviews. Each episode presents a different prisoner's story.

THE KILLERS: UNSTAGED

Documentary short. USA 2012

Length: 7 min. *Format:* HD-cam, 1.77:1, colour

Direction: Werner Herzog. *Cinematography:* Henning Brümmer. *Editing:* Marco Capalbo. *Production:* Nick Barrios, Andrew Kelly, Amelia Sutton. *Production company:* American Express. *Location:* USA.

Synopsis: A video featuring the band The Killers as part of a series of music videos sponsored by Amex. Other contributors to the series include David Lynch and Gary Oldman. The video functioned as a trailer for the live streaming of a concert (which also sometimes sneaks into Herzog's filmography as a 95-minute documentary), but it has an unmistakably Herzogian look.

FROM ONE SECOND TO THE NEXT

Documentary film. USA 2013

Length: 34 min. *Format:* HD-cam, 1.77:1, colour

Direction: Werner Herzog. *Screenplay:* Werner Herzog. *Cinematography:* Peter Zeitlinger. *Editing:* Joe Bini. *Music:* Mark Degli Antoni. *Sound:* Steve Osmon. *Production:* George Sholley. *Production company:* AT&T, Verizon Communications, Sprint Mobile TV, Werner Herzog Filmproduktion. *Location:* Milwaukee (USA).

Synopsis: A public-information film on texting in traffic, featuring interviews with victims of car accidents caused by drivers sending SMS messages. The film was distributed on YouTube and, according to Herzog, is his most widely viewed film.

QUEEN OF THE DESERT

Feature film. USA 2015

Length: 128 min. *Format:* Red Epic/Red Epic Dragon/Red Scarlet, 2.35:1, b/w and colour

Direction: Werner Herzog. *Screenplay:* Werner Herzog. *Cinematography:* Peter Zeitlinger. *Editing:* Joe Bini. *Scenography:* Ulrich Bergfelder. *Music:* Klaus Badelt. *Sound:* Laurent Kossayan. *Production:* Michael Benaroya, Cassian Elwes, Nick Raslan. *Production company:* Werner Herzog Filmproduktion, H. Films, Raslan Company of America, Benaroya Pictures. *Location:* Morocco, Jordan, England. *Featuring:* Nicole Kidman, James Franco, Damian Lewis, Robert Pattinson.

Synopsis: One of the rare films by Herzog with a woman protagonist. It tells the tale of the 'other' Lawrence of Arabia: the adventurer Gertrude Bell (Nicole Kidman), who refused to be bound by the norms of the Western world and travelled to the desert in search of the Bedouin peoples, to find the freedom she could not find elsewhere. The film reuses familiar Herzogian motifs and themes such as the free nomad, the gaze of the outsider and the desert as a space of longing.

LO AND BEHOLD – REVERIES OF THE CONNECTED WORLD

Documentary film. USA 2016

Length: 98 min. *Format:* HD-cam, 1.78:1, colour

Direction: Werner Herzog. *Screenplay:* Werner Herzog. *Cinematography:* Peter Zeitlinger. *Editing:* Marco Capalbo. *Music:* David Byrne, Mark Degli Antoni, Lisa Germano, Colin Stevens. *Sound:* Werner Herzog. *Production:* Werner Herzog, Rupert Maconick. *Production company:* Werner Herzog Filmproduktion. *Location:* California (USA). *Featuring:* Elon Musk, Kevin Mitnick, Lawrence Krauss. *Voiceover:* Werner Herzog.

Synopsis: With the same legendary essayistic voiceover he uses in *Encounters at the End of the World* (see above), Herzog explores the genealogy of the greatest revolution of recent times: the digital turn. He starts with the birth of the Internet (at UCLA, California, in 1969) and traces its development to the present day via questions regarding robot engineers, Internet pioneers, Internet addicts, Wi-Fi allergies and digital cosmologists. It is a self-consciously incomplete journey, an essay on the emerging ways in which humankind is connected (when even Tibetan monks are on Twitter), and the implications for the human condition.

INTO THE INFERNO

Documentary film. USA 2016

Length: 104 min. *Format:* Red, 1.85:1, colour

Direction: Werner Herzog. *Screenplay:* Werner Herzog (based on Clive Oppenheimer's *Eruptions that Shook the World*, 2011). *Cinematography:* Peter

Zeitlinger. *Editing:* Joe Bini. *Music:* Ernst Reijseger. *Sound:* Laurent Kossayan. *Production:* André Singer, Lucki Stipetić. *Production company:* Werner Herzog Filmproduktion, Netflix, Dogwoof, Matter of Fact Media. *Location:* Antarctica, Iceland, Vanuatu, Philippines, Indonesia, North Korea, Ethiopia. *Featuring:* Clive Oppenheimer, Werner Herzog, Maurice Krafft. *Voiceover:* Werner Herzog.

Synopsis: Into the Inferno grows out of *Encounters at the End of the World* (see above), where Herzog meets the volcano specialist Clive Oppenheimer at the Erebus volcano in Antarctica. The footage from that meeting is included in *Into the Inferno* and used as a starting point for the two men's tour of the world's volcanos. Herzog investigates volcanos and the cultures that surround them. He interviews scientists and nature lovers about what humankind is, but all the while with his essayistic voiceover as a corrective: volcanos could not care less about what we're doing here. 'This boiling mass is just monumentally uninterested in scuttling cockroaches, retarded reptiles and boring old humans alike.' It is a film full of references to Herzog's earlier works, with clips from *La Soufrière* (see above), Herzog's first volcano film.

SALT AND FIRE

Feature film. USA 2016
Length: 93 min. *Format:* Red 2.35:1, colour
Direction: Werner Herzog. *Screenplay:* Werner Herzog (based on Tom Bissell's story 'Aral'). *Cinematography:* Peter Zeitlinger. *Editing:* Joe Bini. *Scenography:* Ulrich Bergfelder. *Music:* Klaus Badelt. *Sound:* Laurent Kossayan. *Production:* Nina Maag, Werner Herzog, Michael Benaroya, Pablo Cruz. *Production company*: Arte, Benaroya Pictures. *Location:* Bolivia. *Featuring:* Michael Shannon, Veronica Ferres, Gael García Bernal, Lawrence Krauss.

Synopsis: A delegation of scientists, sent by the United Nations, arrive in Bolivia to investigate an environmental catastrophe in Sala de Uyuni. Because of a failed redirection of the river systems, a salt desert has emerged near the supervolcano Uturunku. When the scientists arrive, however, they are kidnapped by the CEO of the consortium that is responsible for the catastrophe. He (Michael Shannon) proves to be not completely evil, but plagued with guilt and his fear of the volcano, which is showing signs of activity. The kidnapped leader of the UN delegation, Laura (Veronica Ferres), is left in the salt desert with two partially sighted children, and enough water for a week. That way, the CEO hopes Laura will come to understand the extent of the catastrophe on a deeper level than measurements and statistics can show. The story is based on Tom Bissell's novella 'Aral', which is set in the dried-out Aral Sea, Central Asia.

MEETING GORBACHEV

Documentary. Great Britain 2018

Length: 90 min. *Format:* ZEISS CP.3, 1.77:1, colour

Direction: Werner Herzog, André Singer. *Screenplay:* Werner Herzog.
Cinematography: Yuri Burak. *Editing:* Michael Ellis. *Music:* Nicholas Singer.
Sound: Vasily Amochkin, Andy Coles, Vladimir Rizun. Production: Richard
Melman, Svetlana Palmer, Lucki Stipetić. *Production company:* Werner Herzog
Filmproduktion, Spring Films. *Location:* Russia. *Featuring:* Werner Herzog,
Mikhail Gorbachev

Synopsis: André Singer brought Werner Herzog in on this project – that is,
primarily three interviews between Herzog and Mikhail Gorbachev, the
eighth and last leader of the Soviet Union. The interviews were conducted
over the span of six months while Gorbachev was very ill. The film ends
with Gorbachev reciting the poem 'I Go Out on the Road Alone' by
Mikhail Lermontov.

NOMAD: IN THE FOOTSTEPS OF BRUCE CHATWIN

Documentary. Great Britain 2019

Length: 85 min. *Format:* Digital, 1.77:1, colour

Direction: Werner Herzog. *Screenplay:* Werner Herzog. *Cinematography:*
Louis Caulfild, Mike Paterson *Editing:* Marco Capalbo. *Music:* Ernst
Reijseger. *Sound:* Marco Capalbo, Juan Defis, Joseph Ditaillis, Martin
Evanson, Alan Hill. *Production:* Richard Bright, Steve O'Hagan, Lucki
Stipetić. *Production company:* Werner Herzog Filmproduktion, Sideways
Films, BBC. *Location:* Patagonia (Argentina), England, Australia. *Featuring:*
Werner Herzog, Bruce Chatwin (archive footage), Karin Eberhard, Nicholas
Shakespeare, Elizabeth Chatwin.

Synopsis: Bruce Chatwin and Werner Herzog met and became friends in
Australia, while they were both working on *The Songlines* and *Where The
Green Ants Dream.* They shared a view of the world, a passion for nomadic
tribes and for walking. When Chatwin died of AIDS he gave his rucksack to
Herzog. Many years later Herzog made this documentary about his friend
and kindred spirit.

FAMILY ROMANCE, LLC

Feature film. Germany/USA/Japan 2019

Length: 85 min. *Format:* Digital, Canon x400 and 4K, 1.77:1, colour

Direction: Werner Herzog. *Screenplay:* Werner Herzog. *Cinematography:*

Werner Herzog. *Editing:* Sean Scanell. *Music:* Ernst Reijseger. *Sound:* Simon Herzog, Mark A. Mangini *Production:* Roc Morin *Production company:* Werner Herzog Filmproduktion. *Location:* Japan. *Featuring:* Ishii Yuichi, Mahiro Tanimoto, Miki Fujimaki

Synopsis: A feature film about a real man, the owner of Family Romance, LLC, which provides the service of private company. If you want someone to play your friend, or a father to your child, Mr. Ishii Yuichi can provide that service. This is a fictionalized account of a real company and real practice, where the product is fake intimacy. It is a true Herzogian theme. It revisits themes and locations similar to Wim Wenders's *Tokyo-Ga* and deals with what truth, true intimacy and love are in our modern world. The idea for the film came from Rogue Film School student Roc Morin, who produced the film. It was shot on location in Japan without permits and financed by Herzog with the money he made from playing the villain in *The Mandalorian*. It premiered in Cannes.

FIREBALL: VISITORS FROM DARKER WORLDS

Documentary. USA 2020

Length: 97 min. *Format:* Digital, 1.77:1, colour

Direction: Werner Herzog, Clive Oppenheimer. *Screenplay:* Werner Herzog, Clive Oppenheimer. *Cinematography:* Richard Blanshard. *Editing:* Marco Capalbo. *Music:* Ernst Reijseger. *Sound:* Simon Herzog, Mark A. Mangini. *Production:* Greg Bousted, Oli Harbottle, Jessica Harrop, Richard Melman, André Singer, Lucki Stipetić. *Production company:* Werner Herzog Filmproduktion, Spring Films, Sandbox Films. *Location:* Mexico, India, Saudi Arabia, Norway, France, Vatican, Italy. *Featuring:* Werner Herzog, Clive Oppenheimer.

Synopsis: The third collaboration between Herzog and Oppenheimer. After looking at volcanos in *Encounters at the End of the World* and *Into the Inferno*, they now turn their investigative gaze towards meteors and comets, looking at their influence on ancient religions, and other cultural and physical impacts they have had on Earth.

OTHER WORKS

This section lists films and television programmes where Werner Herzog plays himself, or appears in an acting role or voiceover, and so on

Werner Herzog appears in minor cameos in several of his films (including *Salt and Fire, Heart of Glass, Signs of Life, Nosferatu, Invincible* and *Scream of*

Stone), but he also has an extensive resumé as an actor in minor roles, voice parts or cameos in other directors' films and television series.

Geschichte vom Kubelkind by Edgar Reitz and Ula Stöckl, 1970 (Germany)
Anderthalb Tage Fußweg by György Polnauer 1974 (Germany)
Was ich bin, sind meine Filme by Christian Weisenborn and Erwin Keusch, 1978 (Germany)
Werner Herzog Eats His Shoe by Les Blank, 1980 (USA/Germany)
Burden of Dreams by Les Blank, 1982 (USA)
Chambre 666. N'importe quand . . . by Wim Wenders, 1982 (Germany)
Man of Flowers by Paul Cox, 1983 (USA)
Tokyo-Ga by Wim Wenders, 1985 (USA)
Es ist nicht leicht ein Gott zu sein by Peter Fleischmann, 1989 (Germany)
Gekauftes Glück by Urs Odermatt, 1989 (Germany)
Brennendes Herz by Peter Patzak, 1995 (Germany)
Julien Donkey-Boy by Harmony Korine, 1999 (USA/France)
Der Ball ist ein Sauhund by Christian Weisenborn and Rudolph Herzog, 2000 (Germany/USA)
Der Boxprinz by Gerd Kroske, 2002 (Germany)
Incident at Loch Ness by Zak Penn, 2004 (USA)
Walking to Werner by Linas Phillips, 2006 (USA)
Mister Lonely by Harmony Korine, 2007 (USA)
The Grand by Zak Penn, 2007 (USA)
Plastic Bag by Ramin Bahrani, 2009 (USA)
The Boondocks (season 3, episode 1, 'It's a Black President, Huey Freeman') by Sung-hoon Kim, 2010 (USA)
Ebert Presents: At the Movies (season 1, episode 1) by Scott Dummler and Don DuPree, 2011 (USA)
The Simpsons (season 22, episode 15, 'The Scorpion's Tale') by Matthew Schofield, 2011 (USA)
Metalocalypse (season 4) by Tommy Blacha and Brendon Small, 2012 (USA)
Jack Reacher by Christopher McQuarrie, 2012 (USA)
Dinotasia by Erik Nelson and David Krentz, 2012 (USA)
Die andere Heimat – Chronik einer Sehnsucht by Edgar Reitz, 2013 (Germany)
The Wind Rises (Kaze tachinu) by Hayao Miyazaki, 2013 (Japan)
Lemonade War by Rahmin Bahrani, 2013 (USA)
Penguins of Madagascar by Eric Darnell and Simon J. Smith, 2014 (USA)
Parks and Recreation (season 7, episode 1) by Greg Daniels and Michael Schur, 2015 (USA)

Rick and Morty (season 2, episode 8) by Dan Harmon and Justin Roiland, 2015 (USA)
Freaks of Nature by Robin Pickering, 2015 (USA)
The Mandalorian (season 1, episode 1,3,7) by Jon Favreau 2019 (USA)
Dear Werner by Pablo Maqueda, 2020 (Spain)

STAGINGS OF OPERA

Since *Fitzcarraldo*, Werner Herzog has been invited to direct several operas.

Doktor Faust by Ferruccio Busoni, Teatro Comunale, Bologna, 1985
Lohengrin by Richard Wagner, Richard-Wagner-Festspielhaus, Bayreuth, Bavaria, 1987
Giovanna d'Arco by Giuseppe Verdi, Teatro Comunale, Bologna, 1989
Die Zauberflöte by Wolfgang Amadeus Mozart, Teatro Bellini, Catania, 1991
La donna del lago by Gioachino Rossini, Teatro La Scala, Milan, 1992
Der fliegende Holländer by Richard Wagner, Opera Bastille, Paris, 1993
Il Guarany by Antônio Carlos Gomes, Bonn Opera, 1994
Norma by Vincenzo Bellini, Arena di Verona, 1994
Il Guarany by Antônio Carlos Gomes, Washington Opera, 1996
Chusingura by Shigeaki Saegusa, Opera Tokyo, 1997
Tannhäuser by Richard Wagner, Teatro de la Maestranza, Seville, 1997
Tannhäuser by Richard Wagner, Opera Royal de Wallonie, Lüttich, 1997
Tannhäuser by Richard Wagner, Teatro di San Carlo, Naples, 1998
Tannhäuser by Richard Wagner, Teatro Massimo, Palermo, 1998
Tannhäuser by Richard Wagner, Teatro Real, Madrid, 1999
Die Zauberflöte by Wolfgang Amadeus Mozart, Teatro Bellini, Catania, 1999
Fidelio by Ludwig van Beethoven, Teatro La Scala, Milan, 1999
Tannhäuser by Richard Wagner, Baltimore Opera Company, 2000
Giovanna d'Arco by Giuseppe Verdi, Teatro Carlo Felice, Genoa, 2001
Tannhäuser by Richard Wagner, Teatro Municipal, Rio de Janeiro, 2001
Tannhäuser by Richard Wagner, Grand Opera, Houston, 2001
Die Zauberflöte by Wolfgang Amadeus Mozart, Baltimore Opera Company, 2001
Der fliegende Holländer by Richard Wagner, Domstufen Festspiele, Erfurt, 2002
Parsifal by Richard Wagner, Palau de les Arts, Valencia, 2008

OTHER STAGE PRODUCTIONS

Variété by Mauricio Kagel, Hebbel Theater, Berlin, 1992
A Midsummer Night's Dream by William Shakespeare, Teatro João Caetano, Rio de Janeiro, 1992
Specialitaeten, Etablissement Ronacher, Vienna, 1993

NOVELS AND SELECTIONS OF POEMS AND ESSAYS BY WERNER HERZOG

Mit den Wölfen heulen, Filmkritik 1968
Vom Gehen im Eis. München – Paris 23.11 bis 14.12 1974, Carl Hanser Verlag 1978 (in English as *Of Walking in Ice*, trans. Marje Herzog and Alan Greenberg, Tanum Press 1980 and Vintage 2014, including e-book)
Eroberung des Nutzlosen, Carl Hanser Verlag 2004 (in English as *Conquest of the Useless*, trans. Krishna Winston, HarperCollins 2009)
'Warum ist überhaupt Seiendens und nicht vielmehr Nichts?' *Kino* 2, 1974 (in English as 'Why Is There Being at All, Rather than Nothing?', *Framework* 24–7, 1976)
'On the Absolute, the Sublime and the Ecstatic Truth', in *Segni di vita*, ed. Grazia Paganelli, Il Castoro 2008
The Minnesota Declaration, Walker Art Center (www.walkerart.org), 1999
'Thinking about Germany', in Paul Cronin, *A Guide for the Perplexed*, Faber & Faber 2014
'Ten Poems', in Paul Cronin, *A Guide for the Perplexed*, Faber & Faber 2014
'Schwangen gehen mit ganzen Provinsen', in *Werner Herzog: An den Grenzen*, ed. Kristina Jaspers and Rüdiger Zill, Bertz & Fischer 2015
'Hörensagen der seele', in *Werner Herzog: An den Grenzen*, ed. Kristina Jaspers and Rüdiger Zill, Bertz & Fischer 2015

WERNER HERZOG AS EXECUTIVE PRODUCER

Incident at Loch Ness by Zak Penn, 2004
The Act of Killing by Joshua Oppenheimer, 2012
The Look of Silence by Joshua Oppenheimer, 2014
Red Army by Gabe Polsky, 2014
A Grey State by Erik Nelson, 2017

PHOTO ACKNOWLEDGEMENTS

The author and publishers wish to express their thanks to the below sources of illustrative material and/or permission to reproduce it:

© Beat Presser: pp. 170, 171, 215; Greg Boustead, courtesy of Sandbox Films: p. 95; © Danish Film Institute and Werner Herzog: pp. 20–21, 83, 85 (*top*), 114 (*top*), 181, 214; © Danish Film Institute and Zak Penn: p. 29; © Danish Film Institute, The Discovery Channel and Werner Herzog: p. 11 (*top*); © Deutsche Kinemathek – Werner Herzog Film and Werner Herzog: pp. 11 (*bottom*), 12, 22, 32, 36–7, 38, 39, 55, 58, 69, 73, 79, 80, 84, 92, 100–101, 103, 105 (*top*), 110, 114 (*bottom left*), 117, 124, 125, 126, 141, 161, 173, 177, 180 (*top*), 192, 200, 201 (*top*), 205 (*top*), 212–13, 217, 220, 232 (*top*); © The Discovery Channel and Werner Herzog: pp. 17, 105 (*bottom*), 138, 149 (*middle, bottom*), 152, 203, 232 (*bottom*), 233, 234, 236, 237 (*bottom*); © Anthony Dod Mantle and Harmony Korine: p. 61; © Maureen Gosling and Les Blank Film: pp. 26, 130, 135; © Werner Herzog: pp. 85 (*middle, bottom*), 114 (*bottom right*), 149 (*top*), 168, 169, 180 (*bottom*), 188, 189, 193, 201 (*bottom*), 205 (*bottom*), 208, 222, 225; © Werner Herzog and Astrid Friis Reitzel: p. 237 (*top*); courtesy © Lucasfilm Ltd/Disney: pp. 64–5; © Netflix/Lead Agency and Werner Herzog: pp. 89, 102 (*bottom*); © Sideways Film and Werner Herzog: p. 210; © Werner Herzog Filmproduktion and Werner Herzog: pp. 44, 45, 65 (*bottom*), 68, 78, 102 (*top*), 144; © Wim Wenders Stiftung 2014: p. 165; Peter Zeitlinger, courtesy of Sandbox Films: pp. 96–7.